HANDBOOK OF INVENTORY MANAGEMENT

Robert L. Janson, CPIM

Illustrated by
John J. Plut
and
Fred C. Parrott

Prentice-Hall, Inc.
Englewood Cliffs, NJ

Prentice-Hall International, Inc., *London*
Prentice-Hall of Australia, Pty. Ltd., *Sydney*
Prentice-Hall Canada, Inc., *Toronto*
Prentice-Hall of India Private Ltd., *New Delhi*
Prentice-Hall of Japan, Inc., *Tokyo*
Prentice-Hall of Southeast Asia Pte. Ltd., *Singapore*
Editora Prentice-Hall do Brasil Ltda., *Rio de Janeiro*
Prentice-Hall Hispanoamericana, S.A., *Mexico*

© 1987 by

PRENTICE-HALL, INC.

Englewood Cliffs, N.J.

Third Printing . . . . . April 1988

Other books by the author

Purchasing Agent's Desk Book, Prentice-Hall
Production Control Desk Book, Prentice-Hall

Library of Congress Cataloging-in-Publication Data

Janson, Robert L.
    Handbook of inventory management.

    Includes index.
1. Inventory control. I. Title.
HD40.J36 1987   658.7'87   86-21254
ISBN 0-13-378720-6

About the Author

ROBERT L. JANSON, CPIM, is a senior manager of Management Consulting Services in the Cleveland Office of Ernst & Whinney. Formerly, he was a plant manager for Otis Elevator. Mr. Janson began his business career as a purchasing agent with Clevite Imperial, and subsequently was a production control manager, manufacturing supervisor, and new products manager.

He is a member of the American Production and Inventory Control Society (APICS), having served as general chairman of its National Conference, was a past president of the Cleveland chapter and earned the Certified Production and Inventory Management designation. He is also active in the National Association of Purchasing Management (NAPM) and is a Certified Purchasing Manager (CPM). Mr. Janson is a trustee of the Cleveland Engineering Society and belongs to the American Society for Hospital Materials Management, who awarded him their "Fellow" designation.

This is Mr. Janson's third book published by Prentice-Hall; his first was the *Production Control Desk Book* and the second, *Purchasing Agent's Desk Book*. He contributed to sections in the *Purchasing Handbook* and the *Production and Inventory Control Handbook* (McGraw-Hill).

He has a Bachelor of Science degree from Purdue University, is a frequent speaker before professional societies and conferences, and has contributed over 50 articles to business magazines, including his concept of Productivity Measurement, "Graphic Indicators of Operations," in the *Harvard Business Review*.

How This Book Will HelpYou Dramatically Improve Your Inventory Control and Accounting System

Whether you manage a million-dollar corporation or a small, private firm, your greatest asset is your inventory. This book will help you develop—or improve upon—your management and accounting approach for *all* types of inventories.

You'll find detailed steps on how to set up an inventory program that best suits your company's objectives, as well as suggestions on how to improve your present inventory management to be more aggressive and cost efficient.

There are tips on why you should use a computer to help manage your inventory investment more efficiently, with emphasis on implementing an advanced, computerized on-line real time, inventory system. Computer input forms and output forms are illustrated to show the many ways in which the EDP device can serve as your "electronic memory."

There are numerous examples of manually produced reports, Cathode Ray Tube (CRT) and EDP output reports, many based on the fictitious but typical R.G. CEPT Company.

You'll find this book to be a practical and timely handbook for better controlling and managing your inventory system. You will find that it

- Presents seven important perspectives to assist in understanding the inventory environment (Chapter 1).
- Explains the nine steps to establish an effective inventory management system (Chapter 1).
- Discusses the five major inventory control organizational schemes: Central, Decentral, Combination, Materials Management, and Logistics (Chapter 1).
- Presents the components of an inventory policy statement based on the company's strategic marketing plan (Chapter 1).
- Details the ingredients of a company's Inventory Improvement Action Program (Chapter 1).
- Discusses the inventory item master file and the ways to establish accurate specifications (Chapter 2).
- Explains the importance of understanding lead times (Chapter 2).

- Compares the relationship between forecast error and safety stock, then illustrates the carrying costs at various stock service levels (Chapter 2).

- Lists the six different requisition types showing when to use each kind (Chapter 2).

- Illustrates a method to calculate the carrying costs for your company; and its relationship to the EOQ (Chapter 2).

- Defines in nonaccounting terminology the major accounting methods: FIFO, LIFO, and Average Cost (Chapter 3).

- Presents a 20-point checklist to appraise the company's computerized inventory system (Chapter 4).

- Illustrates the nine-step inventory control operations appraisal including a method to summarize the results (Chapter 4).

- Lists the two major computer inventory systems (Reorder Point and Material Requirements Planning), then details the numerous variations of each (Chapter 5).

- Explains Material Requirements Planning (MRP), using a clear step-by-step example (Chapter 5).

- Compares Reorder Point and MRP inventory systems stressing the accuracy differentials (Chapter 5).

- Clarifies the need for a good forecast as the key ingredient to planning future requirements for successful inventory control (Chapter 6).

- Discusses the pros and cons of the commonly used computerized forecasting techniques (Chapter 6).

- Provides 31 methods to improve the efficiency of the annual physical inventory (Chapter 7).

- Shows how to plan the counting procedures, including the transaction error analysis report (Chapter 7).

- Compares the advantages and disadvantages of cycle counting versus the annual physical inventory (Chapter 7).

- Lists the ten major sections of the physical inventory instructions, showing the various subtopics (Chapter 7).

- Explains the importance of determining the absolute or total error as the primary measure of record accuracy (Chapter 8).

- Provides a technique to ascertain vendor packing slip accuracy (Chapter 8).

- Presents a method to utilize bar coding as an inventory control technique (Chapter 8).

- Illustrates the basic inventory positions along with the job duty lists of the major position, the inventory controller (Chapter 9).

- Illustrates a step-by-step CRT transaction input and output procedure for inventory personnel (Chapter 9).

- Presents a four-phase inventory training program with sections for overview, procedures, techniques, and specialized seminars (Chapter 9).

- Describes methods to calculate the proper inventory investment target by five groups for part number, commodity group, product line, and the entire company (Chapter 10).

- Illustrates procedures to simulate possible future increases and/or decreases in inventory requirements (Chapter 10).

- Provides the procedure to first define and then calculate existing and potential excess and obsolete inventory (Chapter 10).

- Illustrates a plan (for immediate three-month and longer range twelve-month results) to reduce inventory investment yet maintain or even improve customer service levels (Chapter 10).

- Lists 81 ways to reduce inventory investment (Chapter 10).

- Explains practical methods to utilize just-in-time vendor delivery methods to reduce work-in-process inventory (Chapter 11).

- Shows the method to project the forecast into an inventory Vendor Requirements Planning program to improve deliveries and lessen inventory investment (Chapter 11).

- Shows how to use the item number as a fixed storage location (Chapter 12).

- Presents a baker's dozen of ideas to increase storeroom employee efficiency (Chapter 12).

- Explains the effective flow of inventory into the "high bay" warehouse and for distribution to ultimate customers (Chapter 12).

- Explains the various inventory control methods for hospitals, service industries, government and retail (Chapter 13).

- Shows how to use the Supply Catalog for service industries (Chapter 13).

- Explains a unique inventory control method for retail stores that groups items by type and by price classes (Chapter 13).

- Describes nine categories of inventory reports (Chapter 14).

- Depicts a nine-element statistical Key Indicator Report that is provided monthly to the company chief executive to use in monitoring inventory investment effectiveness utilization (Chapter 14).

- Details a special purchasing budget that permits control of inventory levels by close monitoring of order commitments (Chapter 14).

- Describes the procedure to build on computer power to account for inventory as the business grows by use of a four-phase program (Chapter 15).

- Tells how to design and then implement a computerized inventory system in 19 steps, making the transition from manual procedures to computer batch processing, and finally, to a real-time CRT operation (Chapter 15).
- Lists all significant inventory management documents, indicating which are mandatory, nice to have, or optional (Appendix A).
- Provides a ready-to-use physical inventory instruction procedure (Appendix B).

About the R.G. CEPT Company

**Gratia Autem
Dei Sum Id Quod Sum**

Company Symbol

CEPTmobile Product

One of the problems a consultant has is using a company case history to make a point. Everyone wonders which client was used as the example!

The R.G. CEPT Company was created in 1975 as a typical company for just this purpose. Using imagination, we created our first product—the CEPTmobile—to be used by senior citizens as a method of transportation. Since then the company has grown to three operating units: the original CEPTmobile Division controlled by Material Requirements Planning techniques, the Plastatron Division under Reorder Point inventory control, and the CEPTstores Distribution Center to warehouse and ship the finished products. This last division, of course, is controlled using the Distribution Requirements Planning technique.

The company name was derived from the first initials of the six members of our family, Robert and Gloria plus our four children—Christopher, Elizabeth, Patrick, and Timothy.

In Appreciation

Dozens of people work diligently to produce a book; only one of them is fortunate enough to put his name on the cover. Therefore, my heart-felt thanks to:

- Denise M. Jaras for all her most patient manuscript typing with numerous revisions.
- Sandra L. Hocevar, Sandra R. Moore, Cynthia L. Santa, and Virginia B. Libertine, who provided so much secretarial assistance.
- John J. Plut and Fred C. Parrott for the fine artwork.
- Timothy R. Corman for his tactful critiques and numerous ideas.
- Terrence R. Ozan for being such a supportive partner.
- The many consultants at Ernst & Whinney, especially Daniel E. Baumgartner, Richard L. Davis, David M. Fouts, Allen M. Friedman, Roger M. Koeberle, Andrew W. Moock, John P. Negrelli, Jeffrey D. Schad, Gerhard T. Schmidt, and Harvey N. Shycon, who made numerous suggestions.
- The unheralded Print Shop employees: Edward Hrebek, Roman D. Ochrin, and Douglas S. Brown, directed by Edwin R. Schnupp, who prepared manuscript copies.
- Mary Lou Buckley and Shannon M. Madigan for their thorough proofreading, and assisted by Keith A. Boland, James A. Chippi, Sandy M. Ertter, Marie E. Garofalo, Alan V. Jannzzi, and Richard H. Myers.
- Ernst & Whinney for permission to utilize computer printouts from their LOGISTEK III, PLANNER and Plastic Advisor Software Packages.
- So many company employees who, by asking thought-provoking questions, stimulated topical research and subsequent copy.

Contents

7. TAKING THE COUNT: HOW TO OBTAIN MORE EFFICIENT RECORDS THROUGH THE CYCLICAL AND ANNUAL PHYSICAL INVENTORY 137

8. HOW TO ACHIEVE DOCUMENT ACCURACY: GUIDELINES FOR MEASURING TOLERANCE LEVELS AND MONITORING TRANSACTIONS 159

Inventory Management: Guidelines for Developing a More Aggressive and Cost-Efficient Program

1

CHAPTER HIGHLIGHTS

Successful inventory control requires aggressive management. Inventory should be looked upon as converted money—an investment that must earn a fair return for your company. This chapter shows how you can develop an inventory management program that will be managed in a manner consistent with your company business plan and strategic market plan.

It begins with a look at the changing climate of inventory control, sparked primarily by fluctuating prime interest rates, new inventory management systems, and foreign competition.

An overview of how to assess your present inventory environment is also included, which contains information on how to determine inventory value in terms of months' supply, the costly impact of inaccurate inventory balances, and carrying costs versus inflation.

The last section gives nine detailed steps on how to dramatically improve the way in which you manage your inventory levels.

THE CHANGING CLIMATE OF INVENTORY CONTROL

The world of inventory control has dramatically changed in recent years. This change was due to the peaking of the interest rates at the all-time high of 20.5 percent. Many of us have forgotten that the prime interest rate was only 3 percent in 1954, rose gradually for several years, jumped to the all-time high, and has since dropped below 10 percent. However, few people expect the rate to go below 8 percent in the foreseeable future. Figure 1–1 presents a display of the prime bank interest rates during a 30-year period.[1]

Inventory control has changed for two other reasons: the introduction of material requirements planning inventory systems and foreign competition, especially from the Japanese, who have aptly demonstrated that their products can be manufactured effectively and sold using low levels of inventory.

REASSESSING YOUR COMPANY'S INVENTORY ENVIRONMENT: SIX FACTORS TO CONSIDER

Before we delve into the characteristics of a coordinated, more aggressive method of managing inventory, the following six perspectives will assist us in understanding the inventory environment:

1. The size of the company investment in the asset called inventory.
2. The composition of the inventory in terms of months' supply of inventory on hand.
3. The effect of inaccurate inventory records on reordering decisions.
4. The effect of various customer service levels on gross profit margins.
5. The impact of inflation, in terms of various carrying costs, on profits.
6. The turnover of United States inventories compared to Japanese companies—as well as American competition.

Inventory Investment: Your Company's Largest Asset

The inventory investment usually comprises the largest single asset for a manufacturing company. A survey[2] of manufacturing companies showed that inventories averaged 27.3% of their total assets—a point illustrated by Figure 1–2. For the R.G. CEPT Company (our fictitious but typical manufacturing company that will be utilized throughout this book), the 27% of inventory assets represents $2,591,000 of the total company assets of $9,595,000.

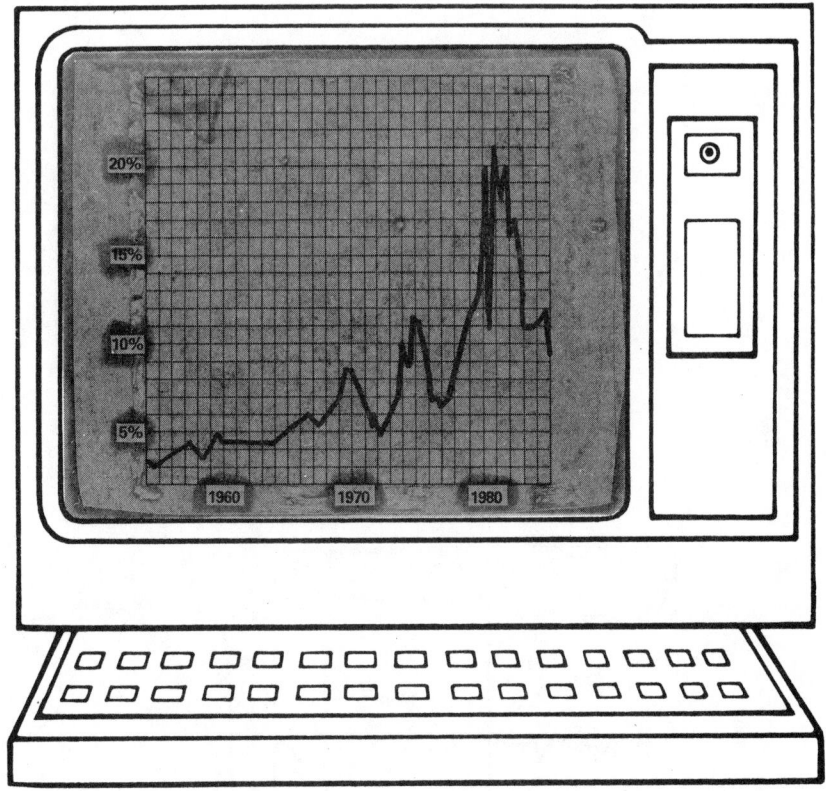

FIGURE 1–1: 30 Years of Prime Interest Rates

On Hand or Out of Hand?
Determining Inventory Value
in Terms of Months' Supply

You might be surprised if you analyzed your inventory on hand in terms of the months' supply it represents, based on the last 12 months' usage. For many companies, the dollarized inventory value in terms of months' supply on hand looks like the following:

	Parts in Inventory (%)
No inventory on hand	12
From one day to six months' supply	36
From six to twelve months' supply	24
More than twelve months' supply	28
Total	100

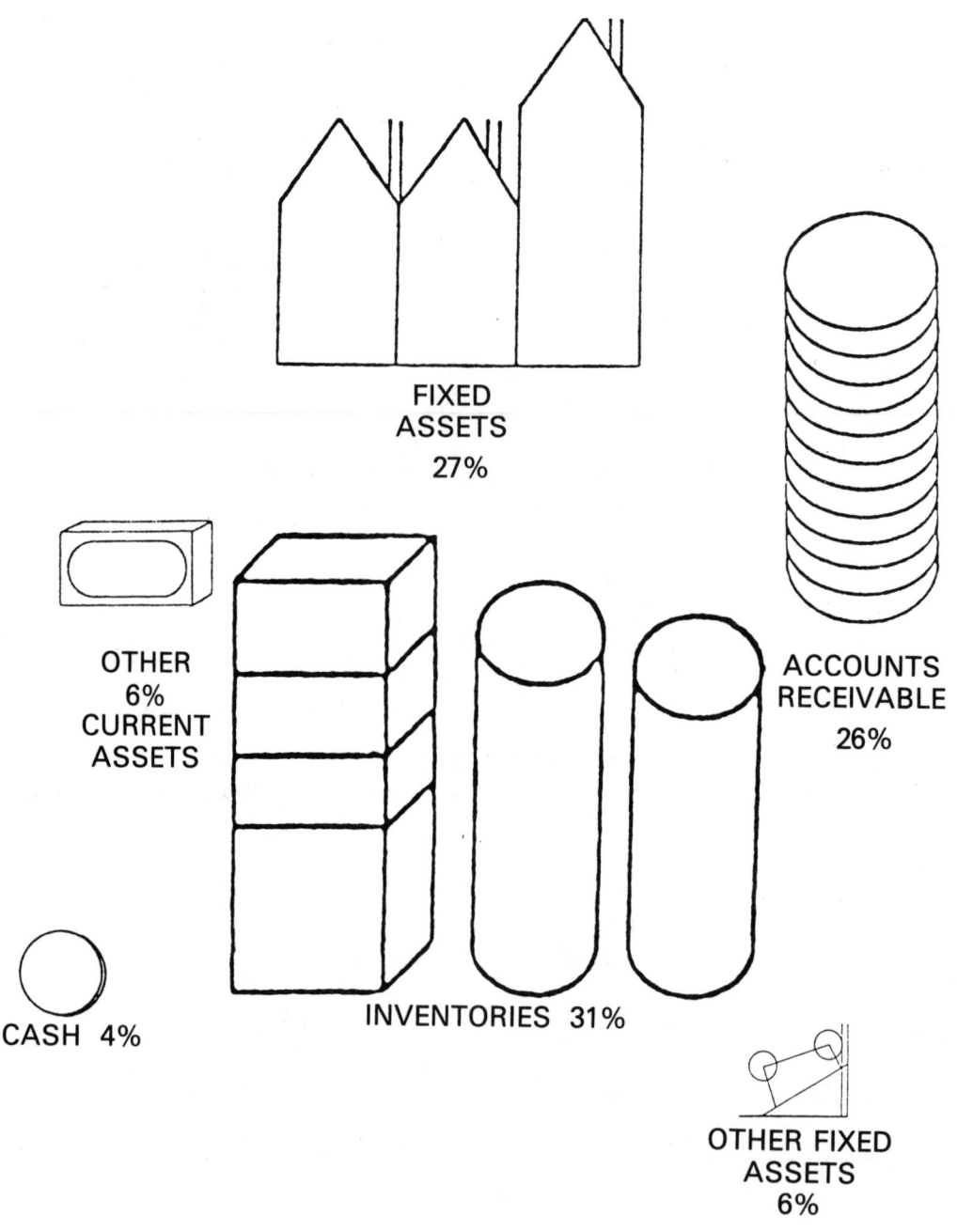

FIXED
ASSETS
27%

OTHER
6%
CURRENT
ASSETS

ACCOUNTS
RECEIVABLE
26%

CASH 4%

INVENTORIES 31%

OTHER FIXED
ASSETS
6%

FIGURE 1–2: Assets of Manufacturing Companies

In looking at these typical statistics, the 12 percent represents too many stock-outs, since many "ideal" inventory systems should have about 5 percent out-of-stock items at any point in time. And 52 percent of its dollarized inventory representing six or more months' supply on hand is excessive. This inventory and many others are out of balance; too many stock-outs for some items, yet too much inventory for other parts. Only the "one day to six months' supply" (36 percent) is the proper level.

Inaccurate Inventory Balances:
The Costly Impact of Reordering
Decisions

Numerous reordering decisions, based on inaccurate inventory balances on hand, can be devastating. Such decisions cause Manufacturing and Purchasing to order and bring in thousands of dollars worth of material too soon. Even worse is to not order material *now* when it actually is required—and then pay higher prices plus premium transportation for rush delivery of the goods when the unexpected stockouts occur. All this creates additional unnecessary expense.

The R.G. CEPT Company with a raw material inventory investment of $791,960 (on FIFO basis) helps illustrate inventory inaccuracy and the effect of its purchasing actions. The active inventory records (refer to Figure 1–3) were studied to determine the accuracy of the decision necessary regarding reordering items. The original decision—as is normal—was made on the basis of comparing the perpetual record on hand to certain preestablished reorder points. These reordering decisions were then recalculated, second-guessing the original decision using the actual (counted) inventory on hand balance in the raw material storeroom.

On that review date, 19 percent of the inventory requisitioning and 40 percent of the purchasing order decisions were incorrect. While the dollar purchases would be about the same if the correct data were used, the company would be obtaining more usable inventory and thus maximizing the effectiveness of its on-hand inventory. In this example, the 22 percent of the items not requisitioned with adequate lead time would eventually be ordered on a rush basis and one or more of the above extra costs would have to be paid.

Maintaining High Service Levels
to Satisfy Customer Requirements

Another important management consideration when looking at inventory investment is the service level. Service level is defined as that percent of the time inventory will be on the shelf (in stock) to meet a customer's requirements. To have a high service level at least 90 percent of the time (and conceivably as high as 99.999 percent of the time) requires a very different amount of

	INVENTORY DECISIONS PERCENT	PURCHASING DECISIONS PERCENT
A. <u>CORRECT RECORDS AND DECISIONS</u>		
1. No requisition necessary	59%	—
2. Requisitioned	22%	60%
Subtotal	81%	60%
B. <u>WRONG RECORDS AND DECISIONS</u>		
1. Requisitioned but not needed	9%	18%
2. Did not requisition but needed	10%	22%
Subtotal	19%	40%
Grand Total	100%	100%

FIGURE 1–3: Correct Versus Wrong Reordering Decisions

inventory. The various service levels can range from 50 percent to a high of 99.999 percent, but there is a wide range of costs associated with each level. For example, calculated with 24 percent carrying costs:

Service Level (%)	Stock-Out Frequency (%)	Additional Inventory Investment (%)
50	50	—
84	16	14
93	7	21
97	3	28
99.9	0.1	43
99.999	0.001	57

Carrying Costs Versus Inflation

The gradual but steady increase in the prime interest rates can easily erode company profits. Consider Figure 1–4, which shows simulated inventory car-

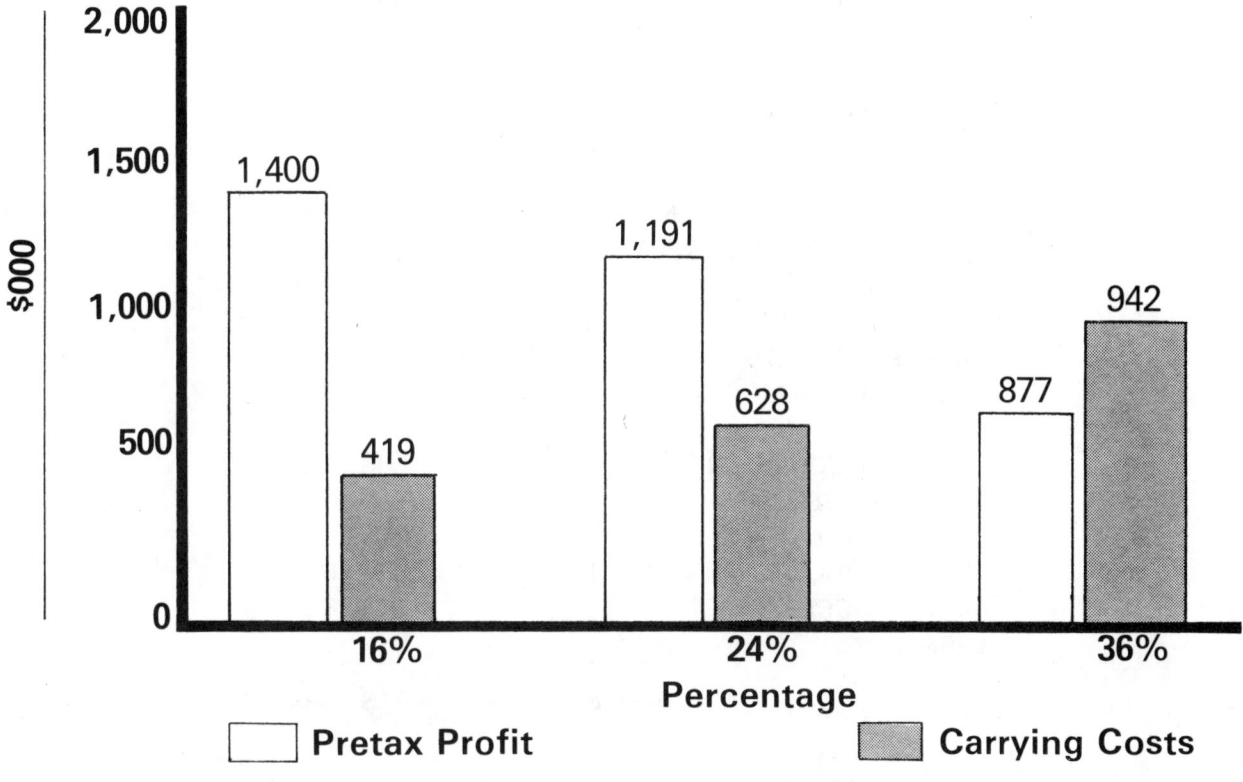

FIGURE 1–4: Effects of Carrying Costs on Profits

rying costs impact of 16 percent, 24 percent, and 36 percent upon company pretax profits. This example assumes the same inventory investment, but the $1,400,412 profit at 16 percent carrying costs decreases to $877,212 profit at 36 percent carrying costs. Unfortunately, this loss can occur quickly if management is not attuned to controlling its costs adequately or pricing its product correctly.

Inventory Turnover: Comparing Supply on Hand Between U.S. and Japanese Companies

A company should use Figure 1–5 to compare their months' supply of inventory on hand in the United States with that of the Japanese.[3] In all but three of the industries listed the Japanese do better. Look at the data in two ways. First, how does your industry do in comparison with the Japanese? Second, is your company's overall months' supply on hand more—or less—than your American competitors'?

INDUSTRY	UNITED STATES	JAPAN
DRUGS	1.8	3.3
TOILETRIES AND COSMETICS	2.2	6.4
MACHINE TOOLS	2.3	2.5
PRECISION EQUIPMENT	2.6	3.3
AGRICULTURAL EQUIPMENT	2.8	4.2
CONSTRUCTION MACHINERY	3.2	3.0
ELECTRONICS	3.2	6.0
TIRE AND RUBBER	3.6	6.0
HOME APPLIANCES	3.7	6.5
AUTO PARTS (OEM)	3.9	11.3
TEXTILES	4.1	5.0
ELECTRICAL EQUIPMENT	4.5	3.6
FOOD PROCESSING	5.4	6.5
AUTO AND TRUCK	5.6	11.9
FOREST PRODUCTS AND PAPER	5.8	5.7
PLASTICS ACCESSORIES	8.7	12.2
OVERALL	3.7	5.7

FIGURE 1–5: Inventory Turnover—U.S. Versus Japan

CASE IN POINT: Profits and Cash Flow Improvements Possible

These examples just cited suggest that substantial financial improvements can be made with effective inventory management. Not only can company profits increase, but considerable cash can also be made available if the company can achieve the same sales at a lower inventory investment. Based on the R.G. CEPT Company statistics, the reduction to only six weeks' inventory investment from the present 19 weeks on hand (at 16 percent carrying costs) increases pretax profit 21 percent by reducing safety stock, unused inventory, scrap, and unfavorable variances, as illustrated in Figure 1–6. At the same time, a $1,786,000 increase in available cash is achieved.

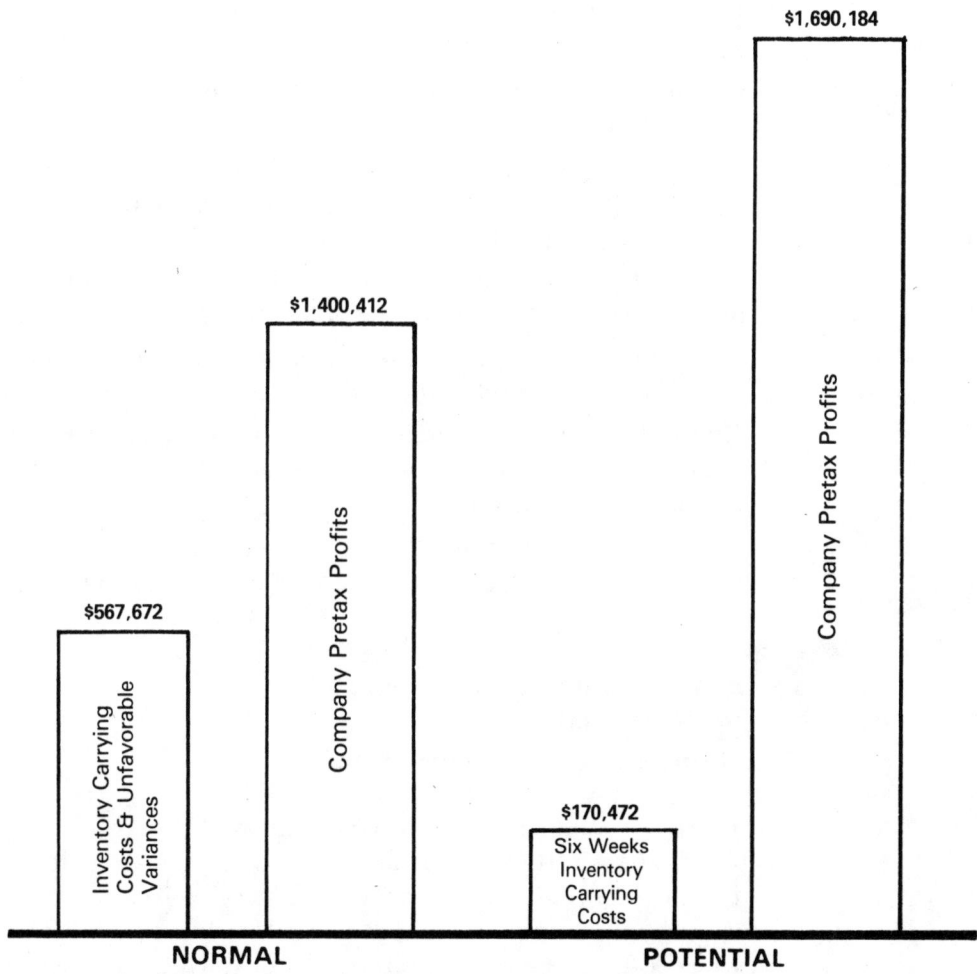

FIGURE 1–6: Normal Versus Potential Company Profits

NINE STEPS TO IMPROVE YOUR INVENTORY MANAGEMENT

Substantial improvements in inventory levels can be achieved, given executive support, adequate time, and considerable patience. There are nine steps necessary:

1. Utilize the company's strategic marketing plan to develop an inventory management program.
2. Establish inventory objectives to achieve an atmosphere of aggressive inventory management.

3. Publish an inventory policy statement to guide all employees in the company.

4. Create an inventory organization which delineates executive, managerial, and technical responsibilities.

5. Determine that the proper type of inventory control information system is installed using a control center containing computer CRTs with manual and computer-produced reference documents.

6. Obtain, from the Sales Department, a forecast in manufacturing units of at least 70 percent of sales in forthcoming months.

7. Determine that manufacturing and purchasing reorder decisions are based on a finite master schedule using accurate inventory records.

8. Establish inventory reports tied to position responsibilities with quantitative inventory budget targets based on the inventory policy and then monitor compliance monthly.

9. Utilize task-force groups to reduce any and all inventories that exhibit warning signs and/or that exceed established targets.

Step 1:
Establish a Strategic Inventory
Management Plan
Based on Marketing Expectations

The inventory management process begins with a study of the company's Business Plan, and then the Strategic Marketing Plan is developed from this initial plan. Figure 1–7 is a conceptual flow chart of the entire company's resource planning and control process.[1] The Inventory Program is then created based on the marketing input, thereby tying all aspects of this process into a cohesive plan. To prepare the plan, use an inventory worksheet which highlights over the next three to five years the conceptual goals under a number of options such as the following:

Possible Options

Option I: Continue present inventory management policy of gradually writing off obsolete inventory, using up passive inventory and closely controlling new inventory purchases.

Option II: Modify present policy to write off obsolete inventory over next four years, use up passive inventory, and closely control new purchases.

Option III: Change present policy, writing off all of the obsolete inventory next year, use up passive inventory, and closely control new purchases.

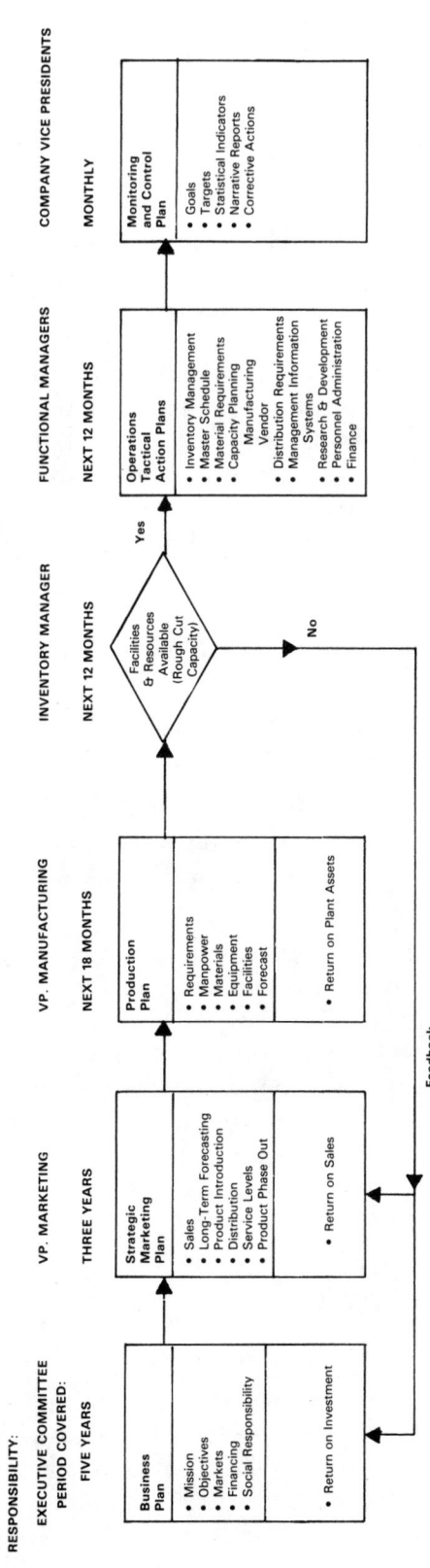

FIGURE 1-7: Company Resource Planning and Control Conceptual Flow Chart

Step 2:
Determine Inventory Objectives
with a Long-Term Perspective

Part of the problem today is that inventory appears to executives and managers to be too complex to control. Thus, companies take either a very superficial approach or attempt a very sophisticated control. Neither of the two extremes is correct. Some companies team with customers and with vendors to free inventory dollars using a coordinated approach. Other companies are successful in zero-based inventory budgeting, starting each year with the establishment of a new inventory target. Still others try to use inventory through planning with input/output controls, which they believe are better than safety stock.

Inventory is created, controlled, increased, and decreased by the following four characteristics:

1. on a very low level of corporate management, such as an inventory controller
2. on a continuous, day-to-day basis
3. gradually up and gradually down with a few quick reduction methods as well as a few immediate increasing methods
4. through hard work, dedication, very close attention to detail, and continuous self-criticism of previously made decisions

There are five objectives in successful inventory management: (1) to improve service to the customers by minimizing stock-outs, (2) to maximize investment in inventory, (3) to improve cash flow by timely shipment and invoicing of customer orders, (4) to provide accurate and timely information on inventory status, and (5) to improve the manufacturing efficiency by using inventory to level manpower; that is, to use the inventory as a buffer.

Step 3:
Initiate an Inventory
Management Policy Guide
for Employees

Inventory systems want to answer the three basic questions of what, how much, and when. This control and answering is not an easy task but should be done through the establishment of inventory management policy. This policy—which should be issued under the chief executive's signature—should address the items listed in Figure 1–8.

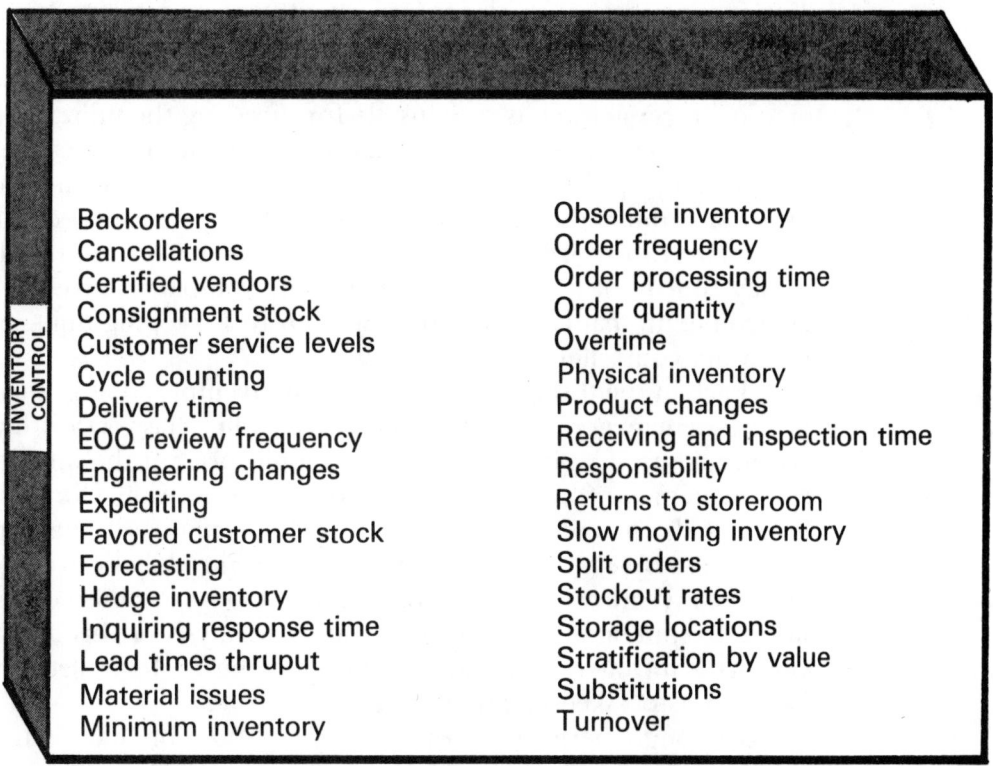

Backorders
Cancellations
Certified vendors
Consignment stock
Customer service levels
Cycle counting
Delivery time
EOQ review frequency
Engineering changes
Expediting
Favored customer stock
Forecasting
Hedge inventory
Inquiring response time
Lead times thruput
Material issues
Minimum inventory

Obsolete inventory
Order frequency
Order processing time
Order quantity
Overtime
Physical inventory
Product changes
Receiving and inspection time
Responsibility
Returns to storeroom
Slow moving inventory
Split orders
Stockout rates
Storage locations
Stratification by value
Substitutions
Turnover

INVENTORY CONTROL

FIGURE 1–8: Inventory Management Policy Contents

Step 4:
Delegate Responsibility Among
Three Major Levels

The important point to consider when establishing an inventory organization for the enterprise is to place carefully the functional responsibility and authority. Irrespective of the type of organization used to control the asset called inventory, three major levels must be present within the organization.

Level	Position	Responsibility	Information Needs
I. Executive	President or Vice President	Measurement and Monitoring	Overall Totals
II. Managerial	Inventory Manager	Management and Direction	Commodity Group Summary
III. Technical	Inventory Controller	Execution and Control	Component Part Detail

The first of these is the inventory investment monitoring function, which is normally performed by an executive within the enterprise. This executive establishes the inventory policy (as described in step three). The second person, on a managerial level, is responsible for directing the utilization of the inventory and watching various trends in the investment. It's often easier to manage by breaking up the inventory by product line or by common items, called inventory commodity groups. This individual performs a check-and-balance control over the third person, the inventory controller, who performs the day-to-day control of a substantial part of the company's inventory. In a larger environment, that is with more than 500 stock-keeping units, more than one inventory controller is involved.

Each of the three levels interested in inventory, that is, the executive, the inventory manager, and the inventory controller, has very distinct information requirements. The inventory system should present the information about a specific item for continuous or spot review as necessary for each of the three levels of the inventory management. The executive is concerned about the overall totals regarding inventory, such as the dollars in slow moving and obsolete inventory. The inventory manager looks at slow moving and obsolete items by commodity groups to guide the analysis of this inventory. The inventory controller wants to see slow moving and obsolete information by inventory stock-keeping units (SKUs).

Although there is no one inventory organization that will fit all companies, the five most common manufacturing organizations are illustrated in Figure 1–9.

Step 5:
Install an On-line Computerized
Inventory Service Center
to Control Information and Analyze Costs

The proper management of the asset called inventory can be improved dramatically through the use of a computerized system, especially with the on-line display capability of a CRT. This technique uses a managerial CRT for the company executive, the inventory manager, and the inventory controller to do analytical work to help improve the operations. This use of a computer for inventory control is heightened by a carefully devised plan to utilize this equipment in the company. The on-line computerized inventory service center, once installed, presents a selectively used CRT screen shown in Figure 1–10. The actual inventory information system configuration depends upon the size of the company, complexity of products, and number of parts controlled.

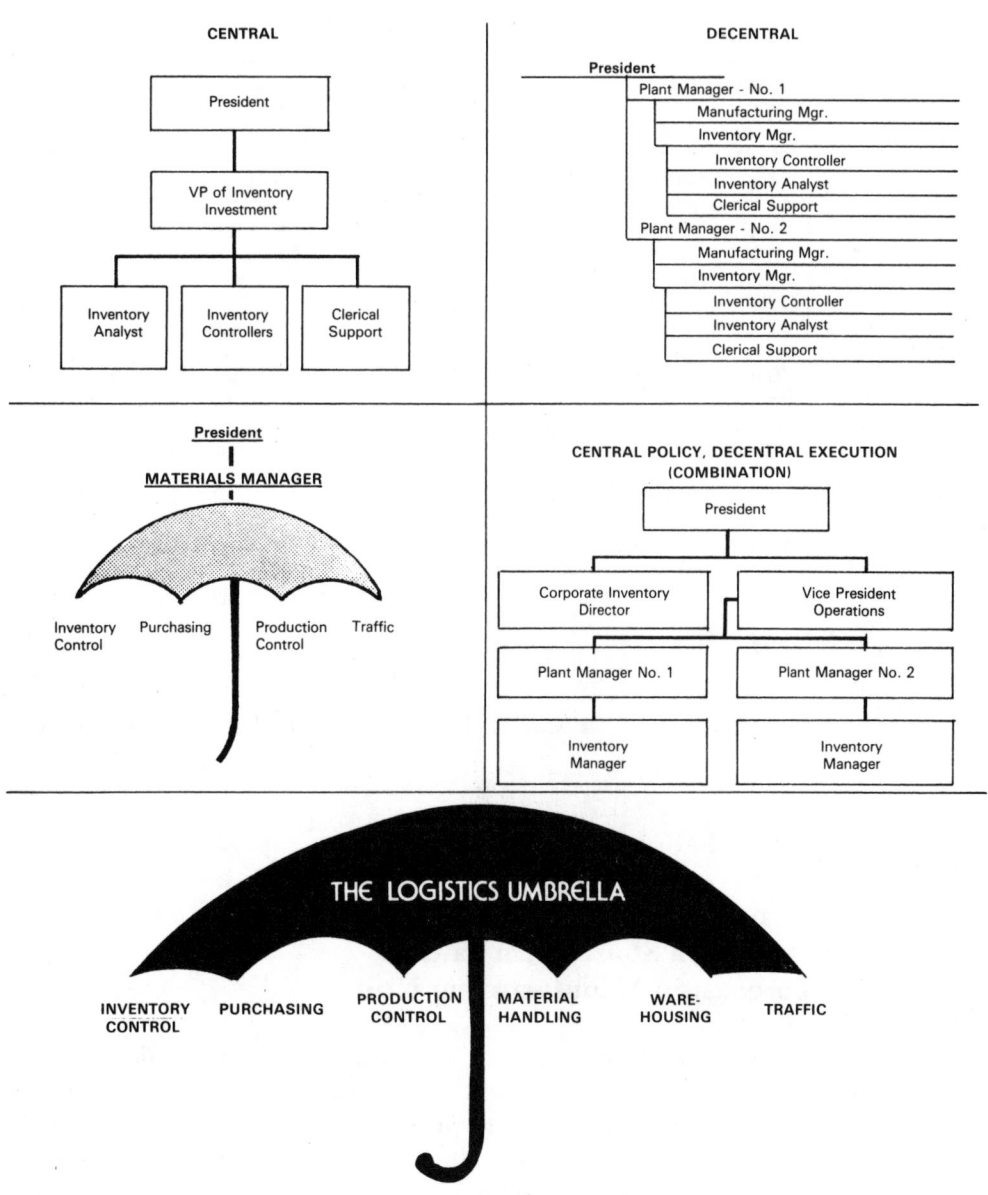

FIGURE 1–9: Five Inventory Organizations

RESPONSIBILITY	PRESIDENT	VP. INVENTORY	INVENTORY CONTROLLER
INFORMATION TYPE	EXECUTIVE	MANAGERIAL	TECHNICAL
DESCRIPTION	OVERALL TOTALS	COMMODITY SUMMARY	PART DETAILS
REPORT CATEGORY	CEPTMOBILE	STEERING ASSEMBLY	STEERING WHEEL
REFERENCE NOS.	PRODUCT LINE A	COMMODITY GROUP 38	PART 7097
INVENTORY VALUE	$33649	$11641	$1316
MONTHS SUPPLY	4.7	2.9	1.1
TURNOVER CURRENT	2.6	4.1	10.9
FORECAST ANNUAL USAGE	291	232	73
"A" CLASS VALUE	$21611	$9684	$1250
SLOW MOVING ITEMS	43	643	0
OBSOLETE VALUE	0	1716	0
STOCK OUTS YTD.	17%	9%	4%

FIGURE 1–10: Inventory Data Base Browser

Step 6:
Develop a Short-Term Sales
Forecast in Manufacturing Units

To achieve effective inventory management, the Sales Department must develop a forecast for at least 70 percent of the customer's needs. This forecast must be in manufacturing production units. Once achieved, adequate lead-time pressure is relieved so that manufacturing can more easily meet the other 30 percent less predictable customer orders.

Step 7:
Create a Master Finite Schedule

This step follows step six very closely using the forecast as the input to develop a finite master schedule, limited to the practical capacity of the plant and also of the vendors. Once developed, the net requirements to create inventory must be carefully established based on this schedule.

Step 8:
Establish and Monitor Statistical
Inventory Targets

There are two measures of inventory control. The common approach is to ascertain the dollar worth of the goods on the accounting records by comparing it to the amount counted during the annual physical inventory. This traditional accounting procedure calculates the net book-to-physical difference, such as

Category	*Calculation*	*Error*
Book to Physical:	$2,000,000 Book Value	
	− $1,960,000 Actual Count Value	
	= $ −40,000 "Net" Difference	= 2%
	$2,000,000 Book Value	

However, the true measure of an inventory control system's effectiveness is what is called the "absolute" or total error. This is determined by ignoring the minus sign and summarizing all the dollar errors, both over (plus) and short (minus):

Record Accuracy:	$2,000,000 Book	
	$ 270,000 + Adjustment	
	$ 310,000 − Adjustment	
	= $ 580,000 Absolute Difference	= 29%
	$2,000,000 Book Value	

Thus, it is possible to have a satisfactory result from a financial perspective but a poor one from the manufacturing operations standpoint—a fact too often true because you cannot rely on the inventory record accuracy when planning a production schedule.

Once this main absolute measure has been established, statistical inventory targets should be established. The choices are numerous, but should include at least all the measures in the Inventory Policy Statement plus performance against the established inventory investment targets.

Step 9:
Assign Task Forces

The three key persons in the inventory organization—executive, inventory manager, and inventory controller—must work in concert for aggressive, daily inventory management. Sometimes the achievements will be below the desired level; in this case an Action Program may be necessary to bring inventory

STEP NO.	DETAILS OF TASK	RESPONSIBILITY	TARGET DATE
1.	Create Inventory Policy Statement.	President	March
2.	Write manager job description.	VP, Mfg	March
3.	Appoint inventory investment manager.	VP, Mfg	April
4.	Establish turnover targets for inventory investment and service levels by location.	VP, Mfg	April
5.	Define duties of inventory/forecasting group.	VP, Mfg	April
6.	Establish "months supply," lot size (EOQ) by ABC class and by manufacturing location.	Inventory Mgr.	May
7.	Publish an EDP report of all parts with more than one year's supply on hand.	EDP Mgr.	June
8.	Conduct inventory training seminar on inventory control.	Inventory Mgr.	July
9.	Develop an inventory analysis matrix by product line.	Inventory Mgr.	July
10.	Define lead time by product line, by location and update quarterly.	Plant Mgr.	August
11.	Design standard inventory documents.	Inventory Mgr.	September
12.	Create a slow moving inventory disposition program.	Marketing Mgr.	September
13.	Modify inventory reports for exception basis.	Inventory Mgr.	October
14.	Evaluate "pros and cons" of real time vs. batch processed on-line CRT data.	EDP Mgr.	October
15.	Write Inventory Systems Information Requirements.	Inventory Mgr.	November
16.	Report key indicators for inventory control monthly.	Inventory Mgr.	November

FIGURE 1–11: Inventory Improvement Action Program

investment, customer service levels, and/or manufacturing efficiency into line. Figure 1–11 suggests ingredients of a medium-sized company Inventory Improvement Action Program.

THE INVENTORY CYCLE: AN AGGRESSIVE ATMOSPHERE

All of these nine steps, which help establish the inventory policy and determine the appropriate organization, system and targets, are part of "The Inventory Cycle." The aggressive approach is coordinated through the chain of command so that proper adherence to the policy and the system assist you in achieving the goal of meeting customer requirements with efficient manufacturing at minimum inventory investment.

The need for closer attention to inventory is aptly illustrated in Figure 1–12, which shows the present emphasis of executive efforts is not balanced

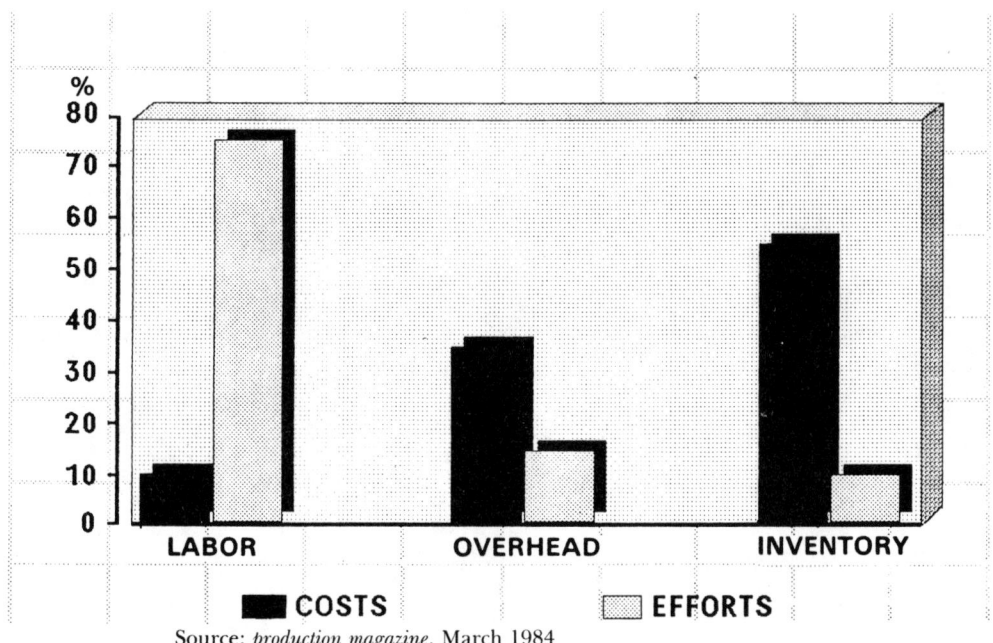

Source: *production magazine*, March 1984

FIGURE 1–12: Cost Versus Executive Efforts

to the company costs. As this survey illustrates,[5] even though inventory represents 55 percent of the cost of sales, it receives only 10 percent of top management's attention.

CHAPTER REFERENCES

1. *Federal Reserve Bulletin*, Domestic Financial Statistics, Federal Reserve Bank, 1953–1985.

2. *Annual Statement Studies*, © Robert Morris and Associates, Philadelphia, PA, 1985.

3. R. E. Fox, "Keys to Successful Materials Management Systems," APICS *Conference Proceedings*, American Production and Inventory Control Society, Falls Church, VA, 1980.

4. James H. Greene, *Production and Inventory Control Handbook*, 2nd ed. (New York: McGraw-Hill, 1987). Reprinted by permission.

5. *Production Magazine* (March 1984).

Establishing Inventory Characteristics: How to Specify Items Maintained in Stock

2

CHAPTER HIGHLIGHTS

This chapter describes the various characteristics comprising the inventory items maintained in stock. Before you can understand the inventory cycle, the characteristics of each inventory item must be clarified. This includes establishing each inventory item with its own identity such as part number, description, specifications, lead time, historical usage, and other important data.
You will learn

- Why the item master file is considered the "heart" of your recordkeeping system
- how to calculate and analyze lead times
- why Mean Absolute Deviation (MAD) is important
- the importance of maintaining a desired service level for safety stock
- eleven lot-sizing techniques and how to determine the most economical order quantity for your company

You will also find time-frames for updating your inventory item information and six different types of requisition forms to use.

THE ITEM MASTER FILE:
HEART OF YOUR RECORDKEEPING SYSTEM

The item master file is the heart of the inventory management data base. It contains identification and specifications of the item's raw material, component parts, and/or assembly relationship. All the items discussed in this chapter are contained on the item master record. Figure 2–1 shows a CRT master record presenting, on three screens, the more important information for an axle used by the R.G. CEPT Company.

- Screen 1, the Header Data, assists the CRT user to input information that helps establish the part record on the computer.
- Screen 2, the Ordering Data, collects information which permits the computer to calculate a suggested reorder point and reorder quantity.
- Screen 3, the Management/History Data, obtains information for future analysis of an item's activity in order to make best use of the dollar investment in inventory.

However, a wide range of information can be placed on the Item Master File, on its companion Inventory Stock Status File, or on numerous other screens and/or reports.

ITEM SPECIFICATIONS:
THE IMPORTANCE OF CLARITY
AND DETAIL

There must be a common way of establishing the specifications in any enterprise. To do this, a department—usually an engineering function but it could be the requisitioner—provides a carefully stated explanation of the item (including the tolerances and dimensions) using language and terminology that are not ambiguous. For a manufactured part these blueprints, or dimension sheets as they are sometimes called, may originate from one of the following:

1. customers' drawings or specifications
2. company specifications file
3. users who prepare the requisition

Whenever any requisitioner is requesting new or replenishment material, it is the responsibility of this person to detail carefully and completely the specifications of the item as well as the quantity and timing of the need. These specifications should be clearly stated on the requisition provided to the Pur-

SCREEN NO. 1

HEADER DATA

Part Number.	2361	User Department	Assembly
Description:	Axle	Planner	Corman
Unit of Measure (Issue)	Each	Commodity Code	11
Part Family	Wheel Assembly	A,B,C Classification	A
Blueprint Number	C6791	Unit of Packaging	Each
Old Part Number	A271WX	Purchased or Manufactured	P
Alternate Part Number	71387	Standard Cost per U/M	101.00
ECO Revision Number	0	Material Cost	—
Revision Date	00/00/00	Labor Cost	—
Part Effectivity Date	10/16/00	Overhead. Cost	—
Cost Effectivity Date	7/15/00	Total Actual Cost	103.86

FIGURE 2–1: Inventory Control Computerized Item Master Record Screens

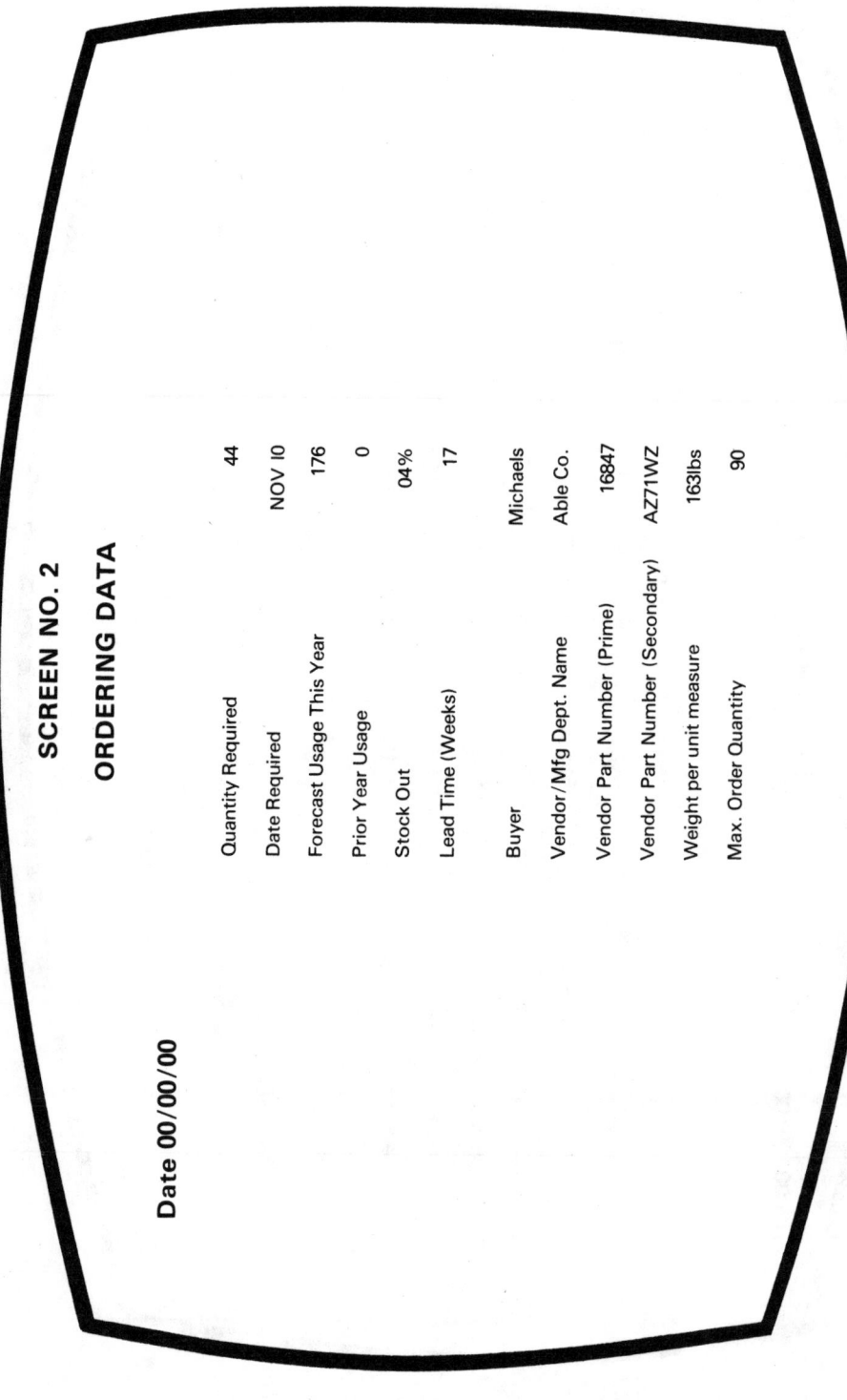

SCREEN NO. 2

ORDERING DATA

Date 00/00/00

Quantity Required	44
Date Required	NOV I0
Forecast Usage This Year	176
Prior Year Usage	0
Stock Out	04%
Lead Time (Weeks)	17
Buyer	Michaels
Vendor/Mfg Dept. Name	Able Co.
Vendor Part Number (Prime)	16847
Vendor Part Number (Secondary)	AZ71WZ
Weight per unit measure	163lbs
Max. Order Quantity	90

FIGURE 2–1: Inventory Control Computerized Item Master Record Screens (cont'd)

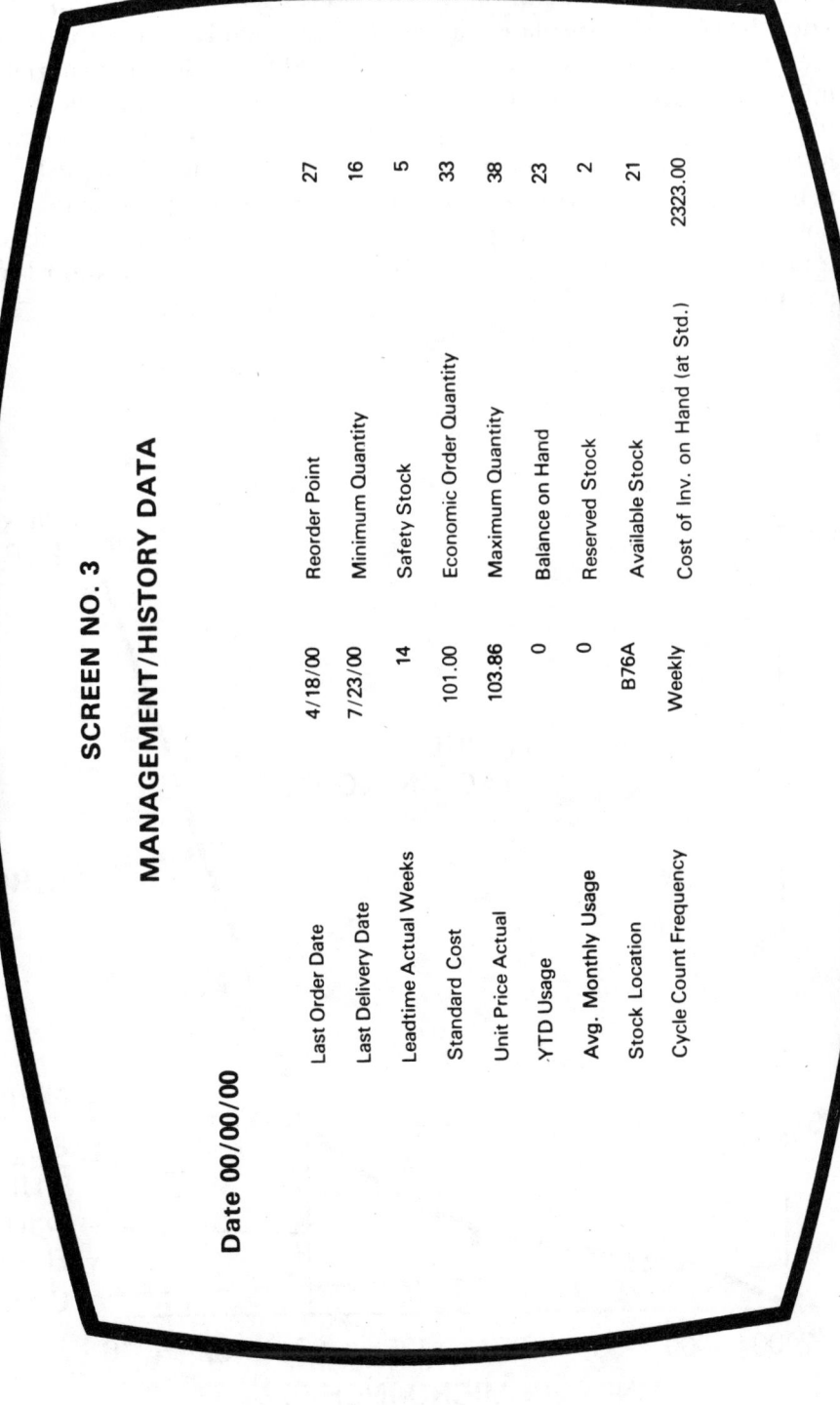

SCREEN NO. 3

MANAGEMENT/HISTORY DATA

Date 00/00/00

Last Order Date	4/18/00	Reorder Point	27
Last Delivery Date	7/23/00	Minimum Quantity	16
Leadtime Actual Weeks	14	Safety Stock	5
Standard Cost	101.00	Economic Order Quantity	33
Unit Price Actual	103.86	Maximum Quantity	38
YTD Usage	0	Balance on Hand	23
Avg. Monthly Usage	0	Reserved Stock	2
Stock Location	B76A	Available Stock	21
Cycle Count Frequency	Weekly	Cost of Inv. on Hand (at Std.)	2323.00

FIGURE 2–1: Inventory Control Computerized Item Master Record Screens (cont'd)

chasing or the Manufacturing Department. An item specifications should consider the current information about the part, that is, a description of the item, the production process, how the item should be made, the material to be used in the manufacturing process, along with the primary and secondary uses of the item and possible substitutions. Optional factors are the demand, both historical as well as the current for this product, what might be the future demand, the current competition, and the overall supply situation. Sometimes potential new suppliers and political trends that could impact availability, price, transportation costs, cost system used, and even the relationship to other products are specified.

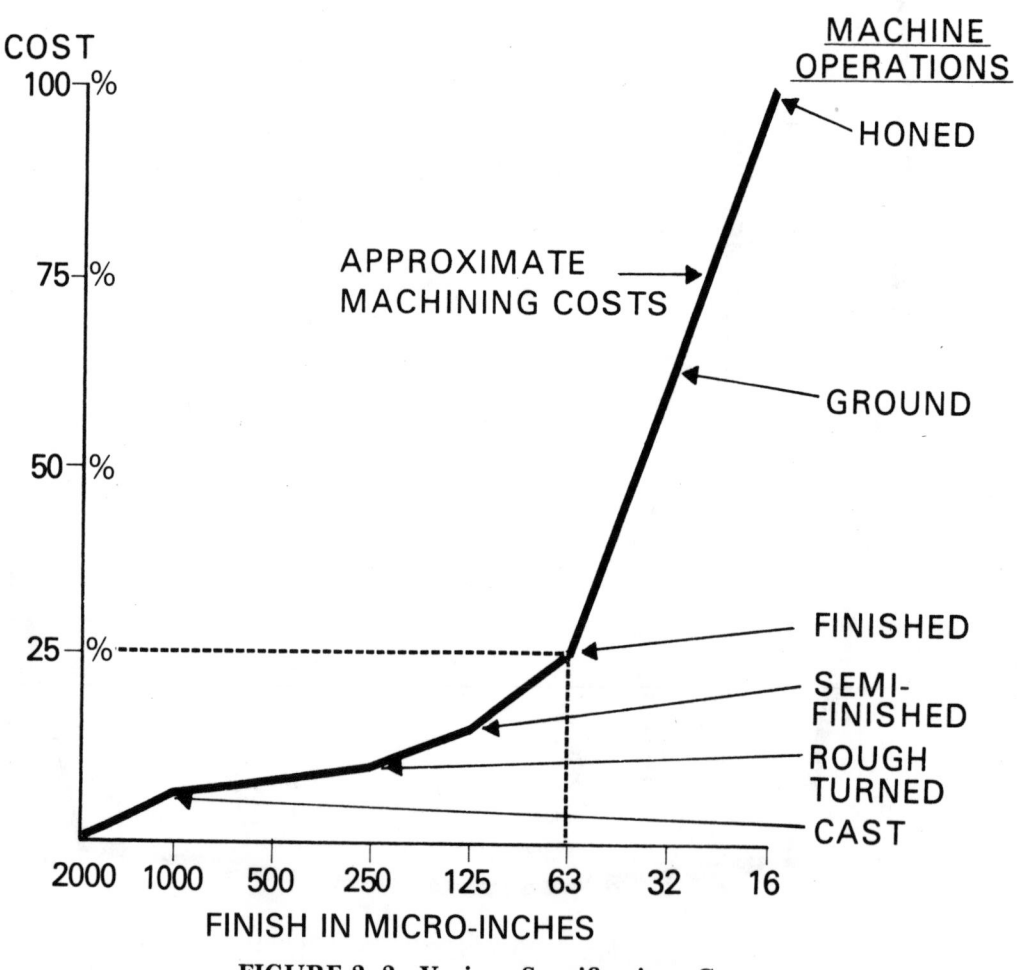

FIGURE 2–2: Various Specifications Costs

STANDARDIZATION: THREE WAYS TO CONSOLIDATE AND MINIMIZE INVENTORY INVESTMENT

In looking at the item's specifications, a designer should try to standardize using materials that are in ample supply, thus eliminating those that are difficult to obtain or from a critical geographical area. It is also important to eliminate from the specifications extreme tolerances that may not be necessary for the functioning of the product. Figure 2–2 shows the increase in the cost of a casting due to various surface finishes. The challenge is to design the product with as many commonly available parts as possible. This is done to lessen the number of different parts in several similar products while retaining the marketability of each individual product—thus minimizing the inventory investment.

Particular requirements of certain industries and the efforts of industry groups have developed material specifications that become the industry standard. Such standards are frequently outlined in sufficient detail and with enough exactness to make it satisfactory to refer to them as part of the purchase specification. Standardization can be facilitated by three related actions:

- Form a company Product Standardization Committee with members from Sales, Production, Engineering, and Purchasing.
- Identify for this committee's review, those parts or products with high scrap rates, long lead times, and long setup times.
- List parts, within commodity group, where there are numerous similar parts so design standardization can be encouraged.

COMMODITY CODES: THE ADVANTAGES OF IDENTIFYING A GROUPING OF LIKE ITEMS

Along with carefully delineated specifications and other specially selected information in the inventory management system, commodity codes should be established that identify a grouping of like items. These codes—which are used company wide, in Engineering, Sales, Inventory Control, and Purchasing—are established to

1. provide a coded list to the requisitioners, engineering, and others of like items for standardization purposes
2. control the investment by inventory groups
3. determine the dollar value of manufactured or purchased items for subsequent make or buy analysis

4. set up numerical codes for ease of computer summarizing purchases by type of item group (commodity)

5. identify control groups for both inventory controller and buyer

6. use in controlling the inventory and purchasing budget

Normally one of two types of commodity codes can be used. The first is a uniquely established sequence that groups items together based primarily on items controlled in a similar fashion. This is commonly called a "company" commodity code. The advantage of this type is the limiting of vendors to one buyer and to one inventory controller. Figure 2–3 is an example of this style for the R.G. CEPT Company. The second type uses an established government sequence that groups items together based on similar type products. The U.S. Government Producers Price Index and/or the U.S. Government Standard Industrial Classifications (SIC) can be used as models for this sequence. The advantage of this type is the ability to obtain government price trends and other statistics. Commodity codes should not be confused with the part num-

Number	Raw Materials (10-20)
11	Aluminum
12	Canvas
13	Chemicals
14	Colorants
15	Forgings
16	Resin
17	Rubber
18	Steel Bars
19	Steel Sheets
20	Wire
21	Miscellaneous

Number	Purchased Components (30-49)
31	Batteries
32	Brakes
33	Bumpers
34	Electric Motors, Controls and Parts
35	Grills
36	Hoods and Sides, (Polyethylene)
37	Seats
38	Transmissions
39	Wheels and Hub Caps
40	Miscellaneous Components

Number	Subcontracted Services (50-59)
51	Heat Treating
52	Plating
53	Miscellaneous Services

Number	Prod. Supplies and Services (60-69)
61	Dies, Molds and Tools
62	Equipment Rental Repair and Parts
63	Gasoline and Lubricants
64	Packing and Shipping Supplies
65	Paints
67	Transportation Services
68	Miscellaneous Production Services

Number	Office Supplies and Services (70-79)
70	Building Maintenance
71	Office Equipment Rental
72	Paper and Forms
73	Miscellaneous

Number	Capital Equipment (80-89)
80	Computer Hardware
81	Office
82	Plant

Number	Utitilies (90-99)
91	Electricity
92	Gas
93	Telephone
94	Water

FIGURE 2–3: Commodity Codes

ber; they are an additional inventory master file descriptive information field. In preparing commodity codes it may be useful to consider the most common manufacturing commodity groups in the United States. These particular commodities are

Automotive	Fuel oil	Office supplies
Castings	Furniture	Paints
Chemicals	Hardware	Paper
Coal	Instruments	Plastics
Construction	Lumber	Printing
Containers	MRO (Maintenance	Rubber
Electrical	Repair, and	Textiles
Electronics	Operating Supplies)	Steel
Foods	Nonferrous metals	

CALCULATING AND ANALYZING LEAD TIMES

Lead time is easily defined and consists of many days used for numerous activities. Consider the following chronology of an order that required a total of 137 days:

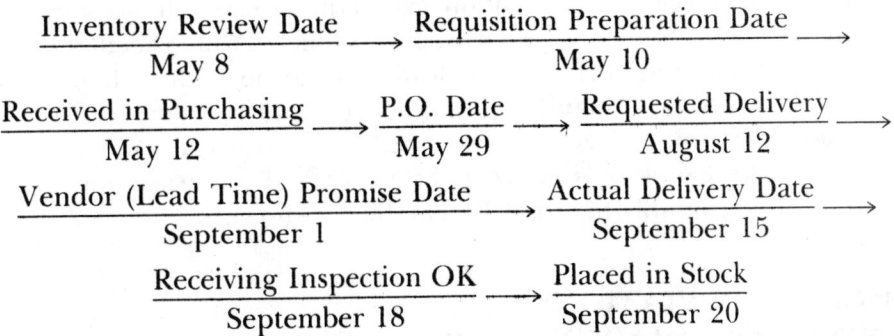

It is often useful to analyze the actual lead time by vendor compared to the delivery promise and the lead-time promise. The lead time usually represents a bell-shaped curve somewhat different from the standard curve. Usually about 60 percent of the items are delivered later than promised, that is, later than the vendor or factory quoted lead time. In a manufactured part, the wait time or queue time is a function of the backlog. Setup time and movement time are consistent from month to month. However, as more orders are put into the system, the backlog or work-in-process increases the queue time; thus, the lead time is lengthened.

A lead-time analysis report is especially useful for purchased parts; its characteristics depend on whether it is an "off the shelf" or a "made to order" item. If it's off-the-shelf, the order processing cycle, which is how long it takes to mail the order to the vendor, the vendor's entry process, warehouse process and transportation, plus the vendor's planned customer service percentage, are critical to lead time. The customer service percentage is what percent of the time the vendor plans to have inventory in stock. While the normal inventory system uses a 5 percent stock-out, many vendors will intentionally or unintentionally keep a 10 percent stock-out or a 90 percent stock-in level. The higher stock-out means more things have to be produced to make up the items needed on the shelf. The larger the vendor's backlog is, the greater the work-in-process that will result. This causes a longer lead time and, ultimately, a more inaccurate lead time. This should be determined in discussion with the vendor if an item is a shelf item and what is the "stock-in" percentage. Figure 2–4 represents a CRT Lead Time Analysis Screen for a manufactured part.

For products that are made to customer order, the lead time is the same as in your own company, that is run time, queue time, move time, setup time, plus the procurement of raw material and, of course, any kind of backlog in the vendor's plant for these items.

Before the recession of 1974–1975, many vendors were quoting 12 to 16 months of product lead time. Yet, three months after the recession began, lead time dropped by 75 percent, or to three to four months, in many cases. The reason this happened was as a longer lead time kept being quoted, more customers were placing orders. In fact, they were often placing duplicate orders at more than one location. When the recession hit, companies cancelled the duplicate orders as well as reduced their existing needed orders, ending up with a chaotic process and lead-time evaporation. Chapter 11 discusses another method of handling the lead time, but for now, you should calculate lead time and analyze it as indicated here. You can estimate an assembly's overall lead time by following the purchased materials and manufacturing lead-time example for the CEPTmobile as shown in Figure 2–5.

MEAN ABSOLUTE DEVIATION: DETERMINING HOW "MAD" YOU ARE

The purpose of "safety stock" is to have a little extra inventory on hand just in case you cannot forecast accurately enough your customers' requirements. While the concept is simple, it is often difficult to determine how much that "little extra" amount is! Of course, if you could predict exactly what customers want, you would never need any safety stock at all! However, since the real world of inventory control is much less certain, let us discuss how to determine the amount of safety stock for the items your company keeps.[1]

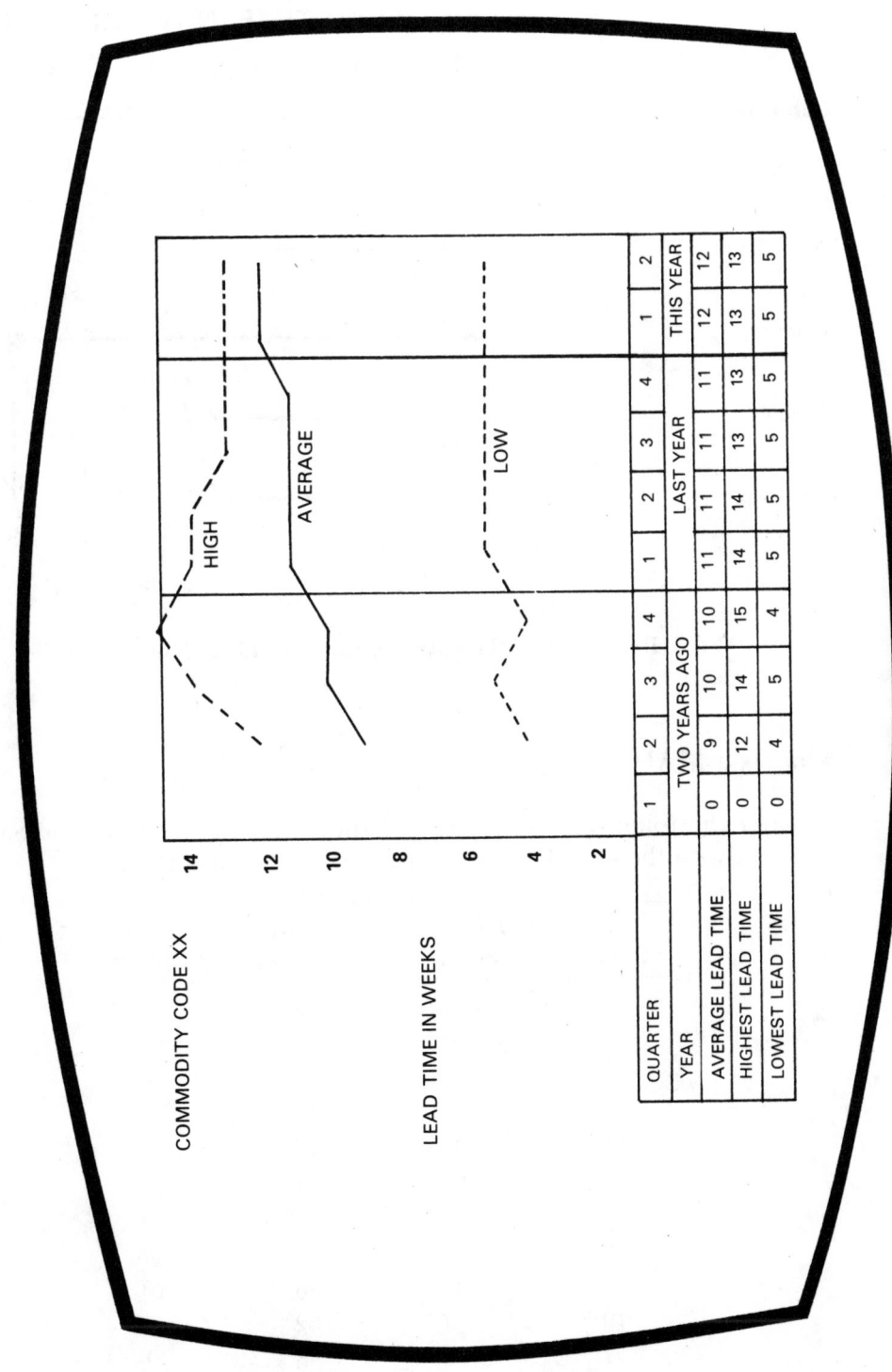

FIGURE 2–4: Lead Time Analysis Screen

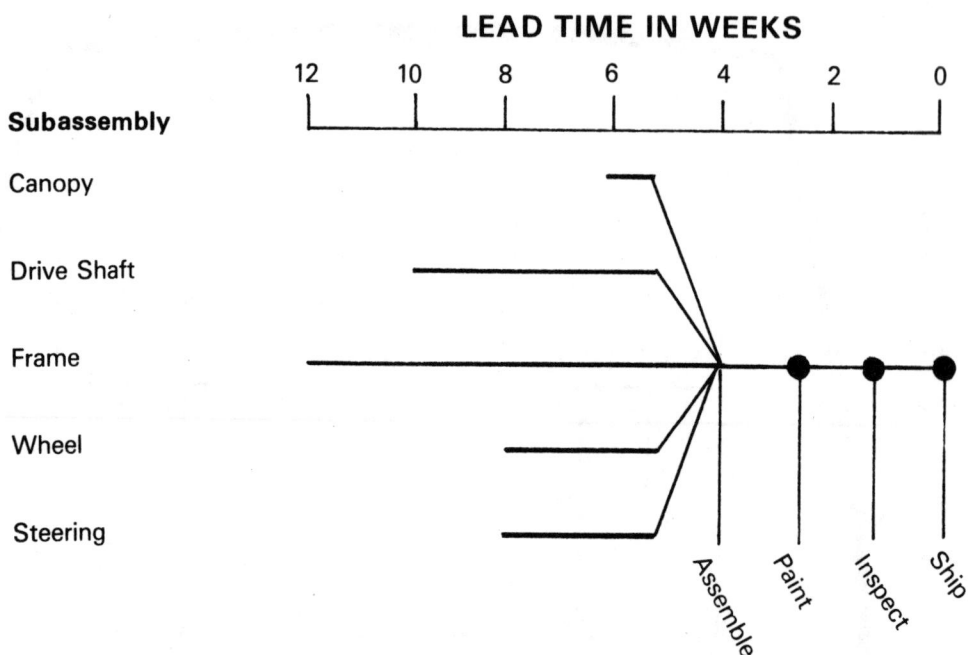

LEAD TIME IN WEEKS

FIGURE 2–5: CEPTmobile Cumulative Lead Time Example

What Is a MAD?

Consider the following comparison of the "forecast" made by the Sales Department with the actual quantity ordered by the customer:

Month	Forecast	Actual	Deviation
	PART NO. 76831 BEARING		
1	76	82	6
2	93	70	23
3	67	87	20
4	106	117	11
5	133	122	11
6	62	91	29
7	73	83	10
8	65	57	8
9	38	48	10
10	71	62	9
11	89	88	1
12	88	82	6
TOTAL	961	989	144

In the first month, the forecast was for 76 bearings but the customer ordered 82. If we had produced only the forecast, we would be short six bearings to complete the last order. To forestall this occurrence, we produced the 76 forecast plus a "little extra" since we know from experience the customer's orders may differ. To determine how many extra to produce, we should study each of the last 12 months' forecast, actual and the difference or deviation between the two sets of figures.

In looking at this set of data, the monthly forecasts ranged from a low of 38 to a high of 133, while the actual orders were from 48 to 122 and averaged 82 per month. The month-to-month forecast compared to the actual orders deviation ranged from 1 to 29 pieces. When added up, the total difference of 144 is called the "absolute" deviation, since the minus sign is ignored. If we divide the total 12 months' deviation of 144 by 12, we learn that the average deviation was 12. Because statisticians use the term "mean" for average, the deviation of 12 is designated the "Mean Absolute Deviation." Since inventory controllers like to use abbreviations, it is called "MAD."

For practical purposes one MAD is roughly equivalent to one standard deviation. For those statistical purists—or just the curious—while one MAD is the arithmetic average of the absolute difference, one standard deviation is calculated by squaring each of the forecast errors, summing the squares (2430 for these 12 months), and dividing by the number of errors (12) to obtain the average squared error (202.5), and finally taking the square root of the average squared error. For the previously described part number 76831, the standard deviation is 14.23. Because it is easier for manual inventory management, the MAD formula is more frequently used. However, in a computerized system the standard deviation should be calculated since it is more accurate.

How to Determine Desired Service Levels

One of the major decisions in inventory management for stock items is what percent of the customer demands is to be met from having inventory on hand. This is called the "service level," designated as the "K" factor, which is the number of standard deviations from the mean required to meet the desired service level:

Desired Percent of Orders Without a Stock-Out	"K" Factor Needed
50%	0.00
84%	1.00
93%	1.50
97%	2.00

Desired *Percent of Orders* *Without a Stock-Out*	*"K" Factor Needed*
99.9%	3.00
99.999%	4.00

By using one MAD (or standard deviation) 84 percent of the time, adequate inventory will be on hand to meet anticipated customer needs, but the other 16 percent of the time there will be an out-of-stock condition. Now let us assume we want to meet a higher percentage of customer needs, so we will have two MADs' worth of safety stock. Now we can meet 97 percent of the demands. However, if we kept three MADs of safety stock on hand, we could even meet 99.9 percent; so, why not keep four MADs on hand so we can meet almost all of the needs? The reason against four MADs would be the heavy investment due to the cost of carrying all of this inventory! This situation can best be understood by referring to Figure 2–6, which is based on 12-month data for an axle part number 2361, and having a MAD of 12. If we look at the first line ("0" MAD) for any given customer order, there would be a 50 percent chance of filling the order from stock. At a 1.5 MAD, there would be a 93 percent service level and a 7 percent stock-out frequency. The carrying cost of the various MAD levels are shown in the last column in Figure 2–6. For 1.0 MAD—which is a common service level—the annual carrying cost would be $171.00 for the average quantity on hand of 95 items. However, if we want to increase to a very high service level of 4.0 MADs (99.999 percent), the carrying cost of $235.80 would be 38 percent more than a 1.0 MAD carrying cost.

The fictitious R.G. CEPT Company, which is used as the basis of these calculations, had annual sales of $15,671,983 and $2,591,000 investment in inventory on a LIFO (last-in, first-out) basis. The company uses an average 1.0 MAD service level policy. Pretax profits last year were $1,102,000. Should company management wish to meet any and all customer needs—which means a 99.999 percent service level and 4.0 MAD—inventory would have to increase by 38 percent to $3,575,580. At 24 percent inventory carrying costs, there would be an additional expense of $236,299, which would decrease pretax profitability by 21 percent.

When Historical Input Is Unavailable:
An Alternate Formula for Estimating Safety Stock

The key ingredient necessary to calculate a MAD is the historical average difference between the forecasted and actual customer orders. This deviation of one MAD (and also 1.0 K for safety stock) is often called the "Forecast

"K" Factor	Service Level	Stock Out Frequency	Replenishment Lead Time Usage	Safety Stock	Reorder Point	Economic Order Quantity	Average Quantity On Hand	Average Value of Inventory	Annual Inventory Carrying Costs
0 MAD	50%	50%	123	0	123	166	83	$622.50	$149.40
1.0 MAD	84%	16%	123	12	135	166	95	$712.50	$171.00
1.5 MAD	93%	7%	123	18	141	166	101	$757.50	$181.80
2.0 MAD	97%	3%	123	24	147	166	107	$802.50	$192.60
3.0 MAD	99.9%	0.1%	123	36	159	166	119	$892.50	$214.50
4.0 MAD	99.999%	0.001%	123	48	171	166	131	$982.50	$235.80
Notes:		(1)		(2)	(3)	(4)	(5)	(6)	(7)

38% Increase

NOTES:

1. Based on vendor six week lead time.

2. "K" factor times one MAD of 12.

3. Replenishment lead time plus safety stock.

4. Based on annual usage of 989, ordering cost of $25, 24% carrying cost and $7.50 unit cost.

5. One half of EOQ plus safety stock.

6. Average quantity on hand times $7.50 unit cost.

7. At 24% carrying costs.

FIGURE 2–6: Increase in Carrying Costs Due to Service Levels

35

Error." At least six months of forecast and actual history are needed to determine the MAD. But what do you do if this historical information is not available, such as for a new part or when you are just starting to have safety stock? When this happens, an alternate method can be used to determine safety stock. This is accomplished by using the "Normal Distribution" formula to determine the safety stock in units.[2] All that is necessary is for you to estimate the average quantity per storeroom requisitions, the vendor lead time in months, and the average number of units the customer will order in the forthcoming months (called "Average Monthly Demand"). It is important to note that the storeroom requisition quantity used in this calculation is not the usual reorder quantity (EOQ or lot size) but is the amount withdrawn (issued) from the inventory on hand. The formula and calculations using our earlier part number 2361 example are:

$$\text{"K"} \times \begin{array}{c}\text{Average Quantity}\\\text{Per Storeroom Requisition}\end{array} \times \sqrt{\dfrac{\begin{array}{c}\text{Average Monthly Demand}\\\times \text{ Lead Time in Months}\end{array}}{\text{Average Quantity per Storeroom Requisition}}}$$

$$\text{Safety Stock} = 1.5 \times 3 \times \sqrt{\dfrac{82 \times 1.5}{3}} = 28.8; \text{ use } 29$$

Remember: The purpose of all this explanation is to help you decide how to calculate the MAD and then, using service level guidance from management, set safety stock as necessary. It's important to realize the small return on excessive investment in inventory safety stock. Each equal investment of safety stock beyond one MAD (standard deviation) gives less additional protection to the company than the previous increment. Although many companies set the same MAD "K" factor (and service level) for all parts, this should not be done. You should use a higher 3.0 MAD for very important long lead-time "A" class parts and a 1.0 MAD for items that you can replenish rapidly. Safety stock helps for those instances when the forecast is too low but is of no value when the forecast is too high; so, if you could improve your forecasting you could substantially decrease the safety stock—but that's a subject discussed in Chapter 6.

THE ORDER QUANTITY: DETERMINING THE MOST ECONOMIC LOT SIZE FOR YOUR COMPANY

Literally thousands of words have been written and hundreds of formulas proposed for use to calculate the order quantity, more accurately defined as "lot size." Theoretically, the most economic order quantity occurs when the acquisition costs equal the carrying costs. The purpose of these calculations is to determine the value where the sum of the inventory carrying costs and the ordering costs are the lowest total. For example, for the following eight order quantities, the total costs can be compared in order to find the lowest total cost.

Order Quantity	Carrying Costs	Acquisition Costs	Total Costs
100	$ 50	$800	$850
200	100	400	500
300	150	267	417
400	200	200	400
500	250	160	410
600	300	133	433
700	350	114	464
800	400	100	500

The most economical order quantity is a quantity of 400.

It is difficult to justify an order quantity that exceeds a six-month supply of material. The purpose of these calculations is to determine a "suggested order quantity," which should be judgmentally reviewed, since humans often know facts not available to the computer or equations. If a company has thousands of items to control, then manually review only those parts that exceed certain control limits, such as a "new EOQ being 50 percent higher or lower than the old EOQ."

Eleven Lot-Sizing Techniques to Consider Using

There are eleven main order quantity or lot-sizing techniques. These are listed below in sequence of popularity:[3]

1. Judgmental
2. Fixed Order Quantity
3. Reorder Quantity
4. Economic Order Quantity (EOQ)
5. Lot for Lot (Replacement Amount for Amount Used)
6. Fixed Period Requirement
7. Period Order Quantity

8. Least Unit Cost (LUC)
9. Least Total Cost (LTC)
10. Part Period Balancing (PPB)
11. Wagner–Whitin algorithm

The first three are used primarily in Reorder Point system, the last seven in MRP systems, and the fourth (EOQ) in both systems.

Calculating the Economic Order Quantity (EOQ)

The economic order quantity—because it is a mathematical calculation—seems to cause considerable confusion. The formula is clear enough and the actual calculation for a bearing is

A = 139,000 units per year
S = \$40 ordering cost
i = 25% carrying cost (expressed as a decimal .25)
C = \$.20 cost per unit

$$\text{EOQ} = \sqrt{\frac{2AS}{iC}} = \sqrt{\frac{2 \times 139,000 \times 40}{.25 \times .2}}$$

$$\text{EOQ} = \sqrt{222,400,000}$$

$$\text{EOQ} = 14,913, \text{ use } 15,000$$

However, to save time and facilitate order quantity decisions, an EOQ matrix can be calculated by the computer similar to the Figure 2–7 example which uses a 24 percent carrying cost and a \$50 cost per order.[4] To use this method, find the crossroads where the unit cost (such as \$10.00) meets the annual usage line (such as 1,000) for an EOQ of 204.

Tips for Calculating EOQ and POQ Lot Sizes

- A POQ is "Purchased Order Quantity," same EOQ formula but the ordering cost will be different from the manufacturing setup cost.
- An order quantity can be tailored to achieve an overall turnover of an established number of months' supply, such as three months.
- When the order quantity is small (like three weeks) but the lead time is

Annual Demand Quantity	Unit Cost								
	.50	1.00	5.00	10.00	25.00	50.00	100.00	250.00	500.00
5	65	46	20	14	9	6	5	3	2
25	144	102	46	32	20	14	10	6	5
50	204	144	65	46	29	20	14	9	6
100	289	204	91	65	41	29	20	13	9
500	645	456	204	144	91	65	46	29	20
1000	913	645	289	204	129	91	65	41	29
10000	2887	2041	913	645	408	289	204	129	91
100000	9129	6455	2887	2041	1291	913	645	408	289
500000	20412	14434	6455	4564	2887	2041	1443	913	645
1000000	28868	20412	9129	6455	4082	2887	2041	1291	913
1500000	35355	25000	11180	7906	5000	3536	2500	1581	1118

Carrying Cost .24
Cost per Order $50.00

FIGURE 2–7: EOQ Selection Matrix

long (like four months), use blanket orders with monthly shipment releases.

- Many parts that belong to similar "die sizes," production machine setups and/or even from the same raw material should be considered for joint order reviewing for so called related "family" items.

Remember: The EOQ breaks down if the part has a long lead time, so consider a time-phased reorder quantity, releasing against blanket order.

REVIEW FREQUENCY OF INVENTORY ALLOCATIONS AND ISSUES: CONTINUOUS VERSUS PERIODIC

One advantage of a computerized inventory system is that it permits more frequent review of inventory allocations and issues. The on-line, real time computer systems are, of course, "continuous" systems since transactions are posted instantaneously as soon as they are received. An on-line inquiry system processes in a batch mode, usually once each night, though some systems process the batches semiweekly or once a week. The "periodic" manual review systems post all accumulated transactions once a week or even as little as once a month. The trade-off is more clerical cost for more frequent reviews compared with less inventory safety stock in a continuous system. The periodic method has greater clerical efficiency but more inventory on hand as protection for customers' demand as there is a longer time between inventory reviews. By comparing a continuous real time computer review with a monthly manual periodic, we have the following inventory investment:

Units	*Continuous*	*Periodic*	*Difference*
Cycle stock (½ EOQ)	4.5	4.5	0.0
½ of the average monthly demand	0.0	12.5	12.5
Safety stock	45.0	45.0	0.0
Average inventory	49.5	62.0	12.5
Months' supply	1.98	2.61	.63

TIME-FRAMES FOR UPDATING THE INVENTORY ITEM INFORMATION

Lead Time: This critical information should be updated manually at least once a quarter, based on the last six to twelve months vendor or manufacturing actual time required to furnish material ordered. If a computer program exists, continuous updating should be performed.

Safety Stock: Probably one-half of safety stock inventory is never used. Thus, by observing customers "under" demand or by calculating forecast error, the safety stock quantity should be manually updated semiannually. A computer program should be measuring continuously (1) changes in weekly usage and (2) parts where demand is *less* than forecast.

Average Quantity Used Per Week: This should be updated semiannually on a manual system or continuously with a computer.

Item Unit Cost: Update the actual costs semiannually on a manual system or continuously from the computer. Note: standard costs should be updated only periodically in either type of system.

Inventory Carrying Cost: Modify, if appropriate, annually or whenever the prime interest rate changes (plus or minus) by more than 3 percent.

Cost to Place an Order: Change annually based on budget for forthcoming year.

REQUISITIONS: SIX MANUAL AND COMPUTER
FORMS TO COMPLEMENT YOUR INVENTORY SYSTEM

Six different types of requisitions may be used in an inventory control system. Although the general intent of this book is to describe a computerized inventory system, often the input to the system is a manual inventory requisition. These manual and EDP requisition options include the following:

1. A "general purpose" requisition, often called a "hand-written" requisition, which is to be used for less frequently purchased, nonstock, special items. This requisition should be completed carefully so that it specifies clearly the material required as engineering specifications may not be available.

2. A "traveling requisition," which after being prepared by the requisitioner, "travels" to the Manufacturing or Purchasing Department to order the goods and then is sent back to the requisitioner for filing until more material is needed. These requisitions are printed on heavy paper, which can be reused. Over time this document provides a history of the use and cost of the item. A traveling requisition is used primarily for stock and other items that are ordered three or more times a year. These requisitions are useful because they require less time on the part of the requisitioner and help reduce mistakes, since much of the information of repeat nature has been placed previously on the form.

3. A "bill of material," which often can be used as a requisition to the Purchasing or Manufacturing Department. In this procedure, a standard bill of material is used, annoted to indicate the number of assemblies required to make a finished item. Then the number of units or materials needed for each assembly can be ascertained.

4. A computer requisition, which, as an output from the computer system, lists the information necessary to replenish adequately the inventory balance on hand.

5. A more complicated "capital equipment" requisition specifies the unique needs and descriptions of these special assets for the company.

6. The CRT screen, which is used in on-line, real time computerized inventory systems, is illustrated in Figure 2–8. This screen is helpful because prelisted items are identified by specific part numbers (as shown on the side of the screen). This requisition is intended to minimize mistakes by lessening the number of written words as well as providing edits for validating against selected fields on the screen.

Take a good look at each characteristic of the inventory items, making certain the data are correct. This data base will receive considerable use—and its accuracy will be most valuable to you.

The figure shows a CRT (cathode ray tube) screen displaying a requisition:

Req'n No.   674
Date   03/03/xx
Order No.   6396   Assembly Number   16719
Description Frame   Assembly Quantity 10

Part No.	Description	Quantity	Required
1671	Frame	10	03/14
0401	Hood, Steel	10	03/14
0402	Side, Steel	20	03/14
0911	Grill, Aluminum	10	03/14

FIGURE 2–8: CRT Requisition

CHAPTER REFERENCES

1. R. L. Janson, "How Mad You Are," *Midwest Purchasing* Magazine (October 1983).
2. Modified by Sanford A. Jaffe and George A. Harris.
3. Joseph Orlicky, *Material Requirements Planning* (New York: McGraw-Hill, 1975). Reprinted by permission.
4. Created by Gerhard T. Schmidt, 1985.

Inventory Accounting: How to Evaluate and Control Costs

3

CHAPTER HIGHLIGHTS

This chapter expands on the characteristics of items explored in Chapter 2 by telling how to determine the costs for those items. The standard and actual costs of materials are compared, as are cost component percentages for over-head rates. Costs of goods and carrying costs are explored in-depth, with guidelines for anticipating and offsetting your losses. Also explained are the three major accounting methods used to determine inventory cost, with special emphasis placed on the LIFO inventory valuation method.

Once the characteristics have been established for each item maintained in inventory, a methodology must be set to determine a cost for that item. Inventory accounting is a byproduct of the Cost System, for better or for worse; it must be done carefully so that the value of the inventory to the financial enterprise can be adequately determined.

The concern in inventory management goes beyond the number of pieces purchased, used and ultimately shipped to the customer. All this material requires money to obtain, to store, to convert, and to ship. Effective inventory managers consider the inventory just like money in the bank—to be invested and controlled.

Any discussion of inventory accounting must consider and answer these questions in order to help inventory control personnel comprehend the financial information:

- How can the company operate with only one common inventory accounting system, recording the manufacturing perpetual control, the actual balances in the storage areas, and the accounting "book" information?

- What ways are used to determine the inventory aspects of the product cost—standard and actual—since inaccurate costs have significant impact on inventory valuation and possibly on the selling price?

- What are the five main areas to consider when estimating the selling price?
- How can the correct carrying cost for this inventory be determined considering the cost of money, storage, insurance, obsolescence, and so forth?
- Which of the inventory costing techniques is most appropriate for your enterprise—FIFO, Average Cost, or LIFO?
- How do you keep track of inventory during the year on a FIFO basis yet understand the influence of the year-end LIFO adjustment?

In recent years it was unfortunate to note great losses in profits, and even bankruptcy for some companies, because of their inability to handle the abrupt changes in customer requirements, inventory levels, and cost of money with the attendant variability in prices paid for purchased components and raw material.

A NOTE OF CLARITY ON THE LIFO CONFUSION

The use of the LIFO inventory valuation method will be explained later in this chapter. However, a word of clarification is pertinent to help lessen the confusion. During the course of the year, for operating (not financial) purposes, inventory transactions and statistical reporting are on an Average Cost, FIFO, Standard Cost basis, or some other system. Thus, for day-to-day practical inventory management, LIFO calculations are not visable. It is only when financial statements are prepared (usually at year-end) that the LIFO method (if utilized) becomes apparent.

The real effect of LIFO is on the Income Statement, as explained by R.G. CEPT's last year's Consolidated Income Statement, shown in Table 3-1.

PROBLEMS INVOLVED WITH USING MORE THAN ONE ACCOUNTING SYSTEM

Numerous companies (unfortunately) operate with two or three different inventory accounting systems, such as a perpetual inventory record for manufacturing purposes, the periodic general ledger record maintained in the Accounting Department, and the actual stockroom balances for daily receipts and issues. This causes problems since different quantity, and ultimately dollar, balances are maintained in each system, without reconciling the difference. Many times the daily updating and transaction error corrections made to the manufacturing inventory perpetual record are not completely made to the accounting general ledger periodic inventory file; neither record may indicate

Table 3-1: FIFO vs. LIFO Income Statements

	FIFO Basis		Calculated on LIFO Basis			
	(For Day-to-Day Operations) Values in $000	*Percentage*	*(For Year Ending IRS Purposes)* Values in $000	*Percentage*		*Differences*
NET SALES	$15,672		$15,672		100	—
Cost of Sales:						
Material	6,463		6,979	61%	44	$(516)
Labor	1,258		1,258	11	8	—
Variable overhead	1,373		1,373	12	9	—
Fixed overhead	1,831		1,831	16	12	—
COST OF SALES	10,925	70%	11,441	100	73	(516)
Gross margin	4,747	30	4,231		27	—
Expenses:						
General, selling, and administrative	2,587	17	2,587		17	—
Interest expense	542	3	542		3	—
Operating margin (income before taxes)	1,618	10.3	1,102		7	516
Income tax expense	724	4.6	487		3	237
NET INCOME	$ 894	5.7%	$ 615		4%	$ 279

the actual balance in the storeroom. The rule of thumb is to have any manufacturing material transactions or adjustments also be the accounting transaction, so one account balance is utilized by both parties, manufacturing in terms of 103 pieces and accounting in terms of 103 pieces worth 10¢ each or $10.30.

STANDARD AND ACTUAL COSTS OF MATERIALS

The purposes of a cost system are to value inventory and determine the company's cost of sales—similar to a manufacturing system dollarized. A company should have two views of costs for each item produced. The first is called the "standard cost" and is compared as a benchmark base price during the year, measuring actual prices paid for materials against the standard cost. The second cost is the "actual or current cost," which is the latest price paid for a purchased item or actual cost of a manufactured item. This information is recorded on a computerized standard cost report such as the one shown in Figure 3–1.[1]

Here are some points to consider about cost systems:

- The manufacturing documents form the foundation of a cost system, especially the bill of material, route sheets, and the production plan/master production schedule.

- The objective of a direct material cost system is to identify materials as closely as possible to the actual end product identification number.

- Two tests can be used to make this identification: (1) is the material listed on the bill of material, and (2) is it too expensive to measure (such as fasteners).

- Four ways (listed from easiest to hardest) can be utilized to set the material cost standard: (1) "last actual" price paid for the material, (2) "average actual" price paid last year, (3) "anticipated cost," that is, what average price purchasing expects to pay for the material (usually the midyear price) or (4) the "negotiated annual price" for the forthcoming year.

- Material price determination can be varied using the A, B, and C inventory item classification; "A" items can be set via negotiated prices, "B" using anticipated cost, and "C" from the last actual price paid.

- If the part is manufactured, the material price should be submitted by the Purchasing Department, direct labor costs from Manufacturing, and the overhead expense through Accounting input.

- Overhead allocation is considered the art of cost accounting.

SUMMARY STANDARD COST REPORT
* * * * SIMULATED COSTS * * * * *

PART NUMBER	PART DESCRIPTION	U/M	STANDARD COST					REVISION DATE	TARGET SELLING PRICE	BASE SELLING PRICE	GROSS PROFIT PERCENT	REVIEW BASE PRICE
			RAW MATERIAL	LABOR	OVERHEAD	TOOLING	TOTAL					
CEPT-STD	STD CEPTMOBILE	E	1,218,180	60,905	99,971	67,370	1,446,426	4/09/86	1,686.21	1,995.00	27.5	
0011	CANOPY	E	9,520	2,334	4,459	.000	16,313	4/09/86	16.31	.00		
0113	DRIVE SHAFT	E	11,920	1,166	2,041	3,250	18,377	4/09/86	18.38	.00		
0149	SUPPORTS	E	.010	1,429	2,251	.000	3,690	4/09/86	3.69	.00		
0401	HOOD-STEEL	E	3,640	4,000	7,125	11,620	26,385	4/09/86	26.39	.00		
0402	SIDE-STEEL	E	2,520	3,200	5,700	2,710	14,130	4/09/86	14.13	.00		
0986	INDUCTION MOTOR	E	28,960	1,416	2,478	8,330	41,184	4/09/86	41.18	.00		
1394	DROP WINDSHIELD	E	6,500	1,429	2,394	.000	10,323	4/09/86	10.32	.00		
1397	SIDE CURTAINS	E	8,020	1,250	2,094	.000	11,364	4/09/86	11.36	.00		
1671	FRAME-WELDED	E	16,480	1,600	3,025	12,380	33,485	4/09/86	33.49	.00		
1683	GEAR SHIFT	E	2,220	2,800	5,350	4,160	14,530	4/09/86	14.53	.00		
2361	AXLE	E	12,840	1,600	3,025	7,110	24,575	4/09/86	24.58	.00		
3334	TRANSMISSION	E	18,160	1,778	3,166	6,960	30,064	4/09/86	30.06	.00		
5549	BUMPER ALUMINUM	E	14,000	1,750	3,344	.000	19,094	4/09/86	19.09	.00		
6171	HUB CAPS-ALUMINUM	E	4,200	1,750	3,063	.000	9,013	4/09/86	9.01	.00		
7118	STEERING TILLER	E	8,380	1,166	2,228	1,030	12,804	4/09/86	12.80	.00		

FIGURE 3–1: Computerized Standard Cost Report

Many years ago a typical overhead rate was 45 percent of the labor rate. Today, due to the considerable increase in factory automation and decrease in indirect costs, many overhead rates are 400 percent or four times the labor cost. Seven comparisons of five cost component percentages are

	(1) Direct Material	*(2)* Direct Labor	*(3)* Indirect Labor	*(4)* Overhead	Sub-Total	*(5)* Research S,G&A	Total Cost
Years ago	25%	10%	20%	40%	95%	5%	100%
Another part	15%	20%	20%	35%	90%	10%	100%
Typical	45%	7%	3%	30%	85%	15%	100%
Toys	15%	3%	2%	25%	45%	55%	100%
Labor intensive	34%	21%	10%	28%	93%	7%	100%
Material intensive	66%	6%	4%	14%	90%	10%	100%
Future	15%	5%	5%	60%	85%	15%	100%

Symptoms of an aging Cost System are high inventory price adjustments (in contrast to quantity adjustments), high overhead rates, large variation in overhead rates, and uneven gross profit margins for similar products. Now, and in the future, overhead allocations may be based on machine hours, departments, finished goods handling, material acquisition, material handling, and even multiple overhead rates. Thus, the cost buildup is a process of cascading costs upward on a step by step or part by part basis through the bill of material to obtain the total product cost.

The "roll-up" method keeps the identity of individual material, labor, and overhead costs at each level of the buildup as well as the cumulative costs at each level, then totaled to obtain the final cost. A portion of a computer printed roll-up is illustrated in Figure 3–2.

COST OF GOODS SOLD: FIVE MAIN AREAS TO CONSIDER WHEN ESTIMATING SELLING PRICE

In establishing the cost to manufacture and sell an item, certain categories used are explained below and illustrated in Figure 3–3. It must be emphasized that, since the R.G. CEPT Company uses the LIFO Inventory Accounting method, all of these figures reflect this procedure.

1. *Material:* This refers to all material that goes directly into the product including scrap allowances for machining, cutting, and waste as charged to the material category. For the R.G. CEPT Company, this amounts to 61 percent of the cost of sales and 44 percent of the total company sales.

R.G. CEPT COMPANY
PROGRAM# OE1316

STANDARD COST REPORT
SIMULATED COSTS

DATE 4/09/
PAGE   1

PART NO.	DESCRIPTION	PROD CLASS	U M	FINISHED WEIGHT	SELLING PRICE/E	CUSTOMER NUMBER	PRICE CODE	STANDARD MARKUP% MATL.	LAB OVH	TOOL	PIECES PER CARTON	ROUGH WEIGHT/E	COST REVISION DATE
CFPT-STD	STD CEPTMOBILE	AAAA	E	800.00	1,995.00			15.0	25.0	25.0	1	.00	4/09/86

OPER NO	WGT BASED	OPER TYPE	FG CD	LEAD TIME	MACH NO	CREW SIZE	WORK CTR HRS/E	LABOR HRS/E	UNITS/HR					
01	S	01		01		1.00	.2000	.2000	5.00					

CONSTRUCT FRAME

	QTY/E	UNIT COST	MATERIAL	LABOR	OVERHEAD	TOOLING	LINE TOTAL
				------COST OF THIS OPERATION------			48,600
PART# 1671 FRAME-WELDED	1.00		16.480	1.600	3.025	12.380	33.485
PART# 0401 HOOD-STEEL	1.00		3.640	4.000	7.125	11.620	26.385
PART# 0402 SIDE-STEEL	2.00		5.040	6.400	11.400	5.420	28.260
MATL# 0911 GRILL-ALUMINUM	1.00	43.0000/E COST/E	43.000			.000	

OPER NO	WGT BASED	OPER TYPE	FG CD	LEAD TIME	MACH NO	CREW SIZE	WORK CTR HRS/E	LABOR HRS/E	UNITS/HR
02	X	01		02		1.00	.3333	.3333	3.00

ASSEMBLE AXLE

	QTY/E	UNIT COST	MATERIAL	LABOR	OVERHEAD	TOOLING	LINE TOTAL
				------COST OF THIS OPERATION------			205,333
			196,000	4.000	5.333	.000	
PART# 2361 AXLE F	2.00		25.680	3.200	6.050	14.220	49.150
MATL# 0398 WHEEL-FRONT	1.00	33.0000/E COST/E	33.000				
MATL# 7614 WHEEL-BACK	2.00	41.0000/E COST/E	82.000				
PART# 6171 HUB CAPS-ALUMINUM	3.00		12.600	5.250	9.189	.000	27.039
MATL# 9601 BRAKES-DRUM	3.00	27.0000/E COST/E	81.000				

FIGURE 3–2: Standard Cost Roll Up

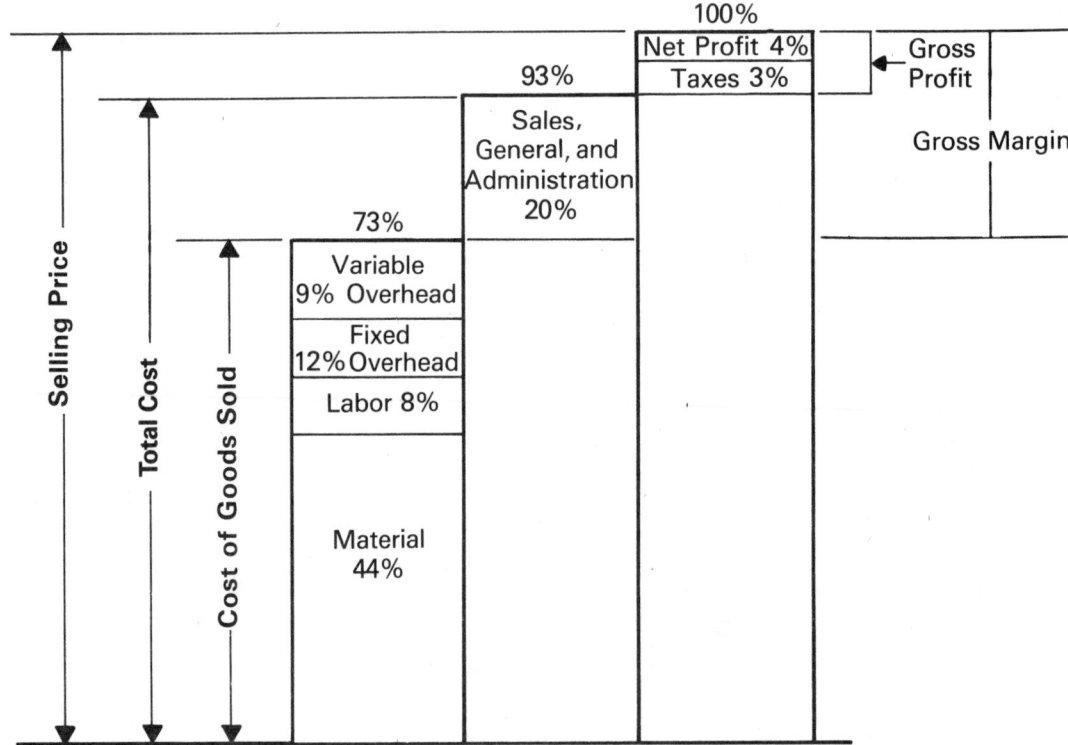

FIGURE 3–3: Elements in Cost Estimate

2. *Labor:* This means all work called "direct labor," which can be directly attributed to an individual product including fabrication, assembly, and finishing operations (11 percent of the cost of sales and 8 percent of total sales).

3. *Overhead:* This consists of fixed and variable indirect costs, which can be attributable to manufacturing, research, and engineering. This includes indirect labor wages and support expenses for such individuals as foremen, inspectors, material handlers, inventory controllers as well as such factors as depreciation, repairs and factory space, heat, light, and power (28 percent of cost of sales and 21 percent of total sales).

The sum of material, direct labor, and overhead are called "cost of goods sold," constituting 100 percent of the manufacturing cost of sales and 73 percent of total selling price. The balance is called the "Gross Margin" from which the company pays SG&A expenses, taxes, and hopefully, makes a profit.

4. *Sales, General, and Administrative Expenses:* While this category is similar to overhead, it includes expenses for areas less closely related to production, such as sales and administration. This grouping includes salespeoples'

compensations and expenses, advertising, sales office space, equipment and supplies, executive compensation as well as insurance, taxes, interest, legal expenses, clerical support personnel, and the like. All these expenses (commonly called SG&A) are usually accumulated in various indirect cost groups and then distributed among products or departments on a pre-selected, prorated basis (17 percent of total sales).

5. *Profit:* 3 percent of the gross goes as taxes, leaving 4 percent as net profit.

Overhead can be allocated to the Cost of Goods Sold as a percentage of direct labor costs (by far the most popular), a dollar amount per production unit, or several other ways.

All of these items go together toward making the estimate of the selling price. Naturally, as the quantities on an item increase, the percentage of these cost elements can change. As the quantity goes from 1 piece to 100 pieces, the percent cost for direct materials may increase (assuming a lowering of the selling price due to the larger volume), while labor decreases and overhead stays the same. Thus, it is not only germane to know the exact cost, but also the quantity in reviewing the cost buildup.

CARRYING COSTS: HOW TO ANTICIPATE AND OFFSET YOUR LOSSES

As the old saying goes "TANSTAAFL—There ain't no such thing as a free lunch." There is also no such thing as free inventory. The company must buy this inventory using hard-earned company money to pay for raw material, purchased goods, manufactured, and/or assembled items. Then it costs the company money to hold or "carry" the inventory. The term "carrying cost" means that amount of money the company must invest to continue carrying this inventory time after time, month after month, year after year. Even if you "expense" the cost of the inventory when it is received, you still have lost the use of the money. If the company did not have any excess money, it would have to go out and borrow the money in order to "buy" the inventory, whether from its own Manufacturing Department or a vendor. The cost of borrowing money is one of the prime ingredients in inventory carrying costs. Thus, at a minimum, inventory on hand costs you at least as much as what you could get as interest if you put the money in a bank. However, you can use two times the prime interest rate as your total inventory carrying costs to include other inventory carrying expenses such as storage costs, labor to move material, and so forth. Or, you can calculate what percent of the inventory value is the actual cost.

While you might put out a million dollars to buy the inventory for the R.G. CEPT Company, you may have to keep this inventory dollar level to support production and meet customer demands. If you did not have the $1 million tied up in inventory, you could invest the money at prime interest rate and get that return on the investment. Whether you have to pay for the material or not, you lose money by having to pay for the interest rate and carrying cost of this inventory, either by borrowing money to have the inventory or by losing the interest on the money if you already have adequate cash.

Four Main Carrying Cost Elements

1. Operational Costs

- *Equipment depreciation and maintenance:* The actual amount of depreciation for the operations is determined by accumulating the book depreciation for the lift trucks and other material handling equipment mainly based on historical experience.

- *Electricity:* This cost is distributed on a basis of some type of survey that takes into account the amount of electricity required to operate each piece of equipment. Then the electricity costs may be broken down for the individual areas located in inventory storage areas.

- *Stock handling:* This covers all labor and nonlabor costs related to the movement, storage and warehouse recordkeeping such as wages paid to receiving and shipping personnel, lift truck operators, company truck drivers, warehouse supervisors, and clerical help all involved in stock handling. Not only is the actual payroll included, but fringe benefits, office expenses, and even warehouse supplies are part of this cost.

- *Breakage and obsolescence:* Some allowance must be made for breakage of material due to handling, shrinkage of the inventory due to loss (unavoidable and intentional) by employees, and for the obsolescence that happens to inventory when the anticipated life cycle of the product has ceased.

2. Facilities Costs

- Building maintenance services
- Building depreciation and/or rent
- Fuel oil

3. Taxes and Insurance

- Personal property taxes
- Real estate taxes
- Liability and fire insurance

4. Cost of Money

- Corporate lending rate
- Investment earnings rate

CATEGORY	A. Operational Cost				B. Rent Costs			C. Taxes/Insurance			D. Interest	Total
	Equip. Dep.	Elec-tricity	Stock-handling	Bkge. & Obso-lescence	Dep. and/or Rent	Bldg. Mtnce. Services	Fuel Oil	Real Estate Taxes	Personal Propty. Taxes	Liab. & Fire Ins.	Cost of Money	Inventory Carrying Costs
All inventory storage areas	$6,031	$6,063	$83,611	$53,887	$64,296	$12,861	$6,311	$30,548	$32,831	$4,036	$341,788	$643,163
Percentage	1%	1%	13%	8%	10%	2%	1%	5%	5%	1%	53%	100%

$$\text{Carrying Cost Calculation} = \frac{\text{Total Inventory Carrying Costs}}{\text{Inventory Investment}} = \frac{\$643,163}{\$3,107,167} = 20.7\%$$

FIGURE 3–4: Carrying Cost Calculation

The various costs of carrying inventory are shown in Figure 3–4 where an example of the cost for the R.G. CEPT Company for all inventory storage areas is shown. If this information is added up, you will see that the total inventory carrying costs are $643,163 a year for inventory valued at $3,107,018. Thus, the inventory carrying cost is 20.7 percent of the total inventory investment. Rounding off, the R.G. CEPT Company would use 21 percent a year as its inventory carrying costs.

Updating Carrying Costs and the EOQ

Carrying costs should be updated at least once a year or whenever the prime interest rate changes (increases or decreases) by 3 or more percentage points. However, it is not advisable to expend considerable time calculating an exact carrying cost percentage. As indicated in the table, the Economic Order Quantity changes (decreases) only about 29 percent when the carrying cost increases 100 percent (from 12 percent to 24 percent).

| | | | EOQ | | |
Item Cost	Ordering Cost	Annual Usage	@12%	@24%	Difference 12% vs. 24%
		1,000	420	297	−29.3
$5.00	$53	10,000	1329	940	−29.3
		100,000	4203	2972	−29.3
		1,000,000	13292	9399	−29.3

Do not be overly concerned about needing extreme accuracy for the ordering cost, annual usage, carrying cost, and even the unit cost when calculating the EOQ. The impact on EOQ of a 200 percent increase in carrying cost is only about 42 percent, for instance:

| | IMPACT ON EOQ | | | |
Increase of	Ordering Cost	Annual Usage	Carrying Cost	Unit Cost
50%	+22%	+22%	−19%	−19%
100%	+41%	+41%	−29%	−29%
200%	+73%	+73%	−42%	−42%

The same comparison can be used for unit cost in the EOQ formula; doubling the unit cost reduces the EOQ only about 29 percent. The converse is true for the ordering cost and the annual usage—if these data bits are doubled, the EOQ increases about 41 percent. It should be noted that this example is based on increase in one variable at a time with other variables held constant.

You can also use variable carrying cost percentages. For three different raw materials and purchased parts, the R.G. CEPT Company uses:

Category	Characteristics	CARRYING COST	
		Annual	Per Month
I	Inexpensive, standard, durable, cannot be pilfered, small-size parts.	18%	1.5%
II	Medium cost, somewhat breakable, some losses, specially designed items.	24%	2.0%
III	Expensive, fragile, frequent engineering changes, material can be pilfered.	30%	2.5%

Ordering Costs

Another ingredient in the EOQ formula is the cost to place a factory or purchase order, called the "ordering cost." Figure 3–5 illustrates one method to determine the purchased material and manufacturing ordering costs.

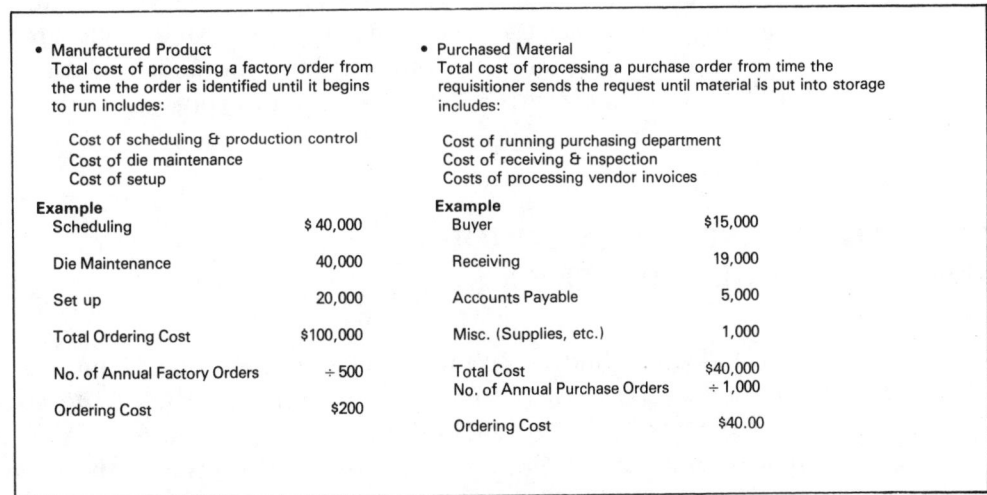

- Manufactured Product
  Total cost of processing a factory order from the time the order is identified until it begins to run includes:

  Cost of scheduling & production control
  Cost of die maintenance
  Cost of setup

Example	
Scheduling	$ 40,000
Die Maintenance	40,000
Set up	20,000
Total Ordering Cost	$100,000
No. of Annual Factory Orders	÷ 500
Ordering Cost	$200

- Purchased Material
  Total cost of processing a purchase order from time the requisitioner sends the request until material is put into storage includes:

  Cost of running purchasing department
  Cost of receiving & inspection
  Costs of processing vendor invoices

Example	
Buyer	$15,000
Receiving	19,000
Accounts Payable	5,000
Misc. (Supplies, etc.)	1,000
Total Cost	$40,000
No. of Annual Purchase Orders	÷ 1,000
Ordering Cost	$40.00

FIGURE 3–5: Calculating Ordering Cost for EOQ Calculations

THREE MAJOR ACCOUNTING METHODS AND THEIR IMPACT ON INVENTORY INVESTMENT

There are three major methods used to determine inventory cost. These include FIFO (First-In, First-Out), Weighted Average Cost, and LIFO (Last-In, First-Out).

FIFO

The FIFO method figures that the price of the item is the oldest purchase price on the assumption that the goods that first came into the plant are also the first to go out of the plant. One problem in using FIFO cost prices is that they may not reflect the quickly changing value of a dollar in inflation and may actually distort company income by showing more profit.

Weighted Average Cost

An average cost system computes the cost of inventory using a weighted average based on the prices paid (multiplied by the quantity) each time an order is made for purchased or manufactured material.

LIFO

LIFO considers the price of the last (most recent) item placed into inventory as the first one used in production. This means that the price paid for the last unit purchased or manufactured becomes the cost of material in the current production. In periods of inflation, LIFO yields a higher cost of goods sold since the more recent costs are the ones that are allocated to production. This results in higher costs reflected more immediately into the selling price and shown as a corresponding decrease in profit.

LIFO: THE CONSERVATIVE CHOICE OF MANY LARGE INDUSTRIES

The LIFO method of accounting has received great interest during recent inflationary periods, even though over two-thirds of the companies in the United States still use a FIFO or average cost method. Although LIFO was first permitted in 1938, a number of discussions and challenges, particularly by the Internal Revenue Service (since this method lessens profits and thus income taxes paid), kept it from being accepted until the 1940s.

Today many people believe that LIFO reporting is more conservative accounting and allows them to match more fairly current cost with current revenues. The dollar value LIFO method was conceived in 1941 by H.T. McAnly of Ernst & Ernst (now Ernst & Whinney).[2] LIFO was adopted by a number of large industrial companies and large department stores in 1941. It is now a commonly accepted, though complicated, method of determining inventory costs. Today multiple versions of LIFO are used.

The Dollar Value Method calls for treating inventory as a composite in terms of dollars and computing an index of price changes contained in the ending inventory compared to the beginning inventory. This index or price change applied to the end-of-year inventory costs makes possible the determination of inventory equivalents at beginning-of-year price levels. If there is an increase in the actual quantity of inventory measured in terms of the beginning-of-year cost dollars, the increase will be valued at current-year costs by adding a price increase factor to such increments.

There are two main problems with LIFO. First, if future price levels recede to a point below the beginning-of-the-year costs, the LIFO cost becomes a price "floor" in determining taxable income. The lower of LIFO or market costs is not permitted by the IRS and, in deflationary times, this can be to the detriment of the company. Second, the IRS code requires that LIFO be used for financial reporting in order to be acceptable for tax accounting purposes, a stringent requirement because one may not always be useful for the other. There are other limitations to LIFO. A serious one is that it may weaken a company's credit standing because of the adverse effect on earnings since profit is decreased and therefore earnings are less. However, a plus point is that by lower profits the company pays less tax and therefore it has more cash to use to maintain the enterprise. Figure 3–6 shows a typical profit and loss comparison under LIFO and FIFO for the R.G. CEPT Company.

Three Points of Caution in Using the LIFO System

- Irrespective of what financial system is used to cost the inventory, any operational measures of inventory must not be on a LIFO basis since this can distort the statistics by giving incorrect information.

- Sometimes financial managers at year-end wish to have additional material brought in to protect the LIFO investment. This is a trade-off. See Figure 3–7 for a conceptual illustration.

- To implement the various aspects of inventory accounting requires help from product engineers who design the item correctly, manufacturing engineers who specify the material lists, inventory controllers who store and issue the items, and foremen who accurately report production information.

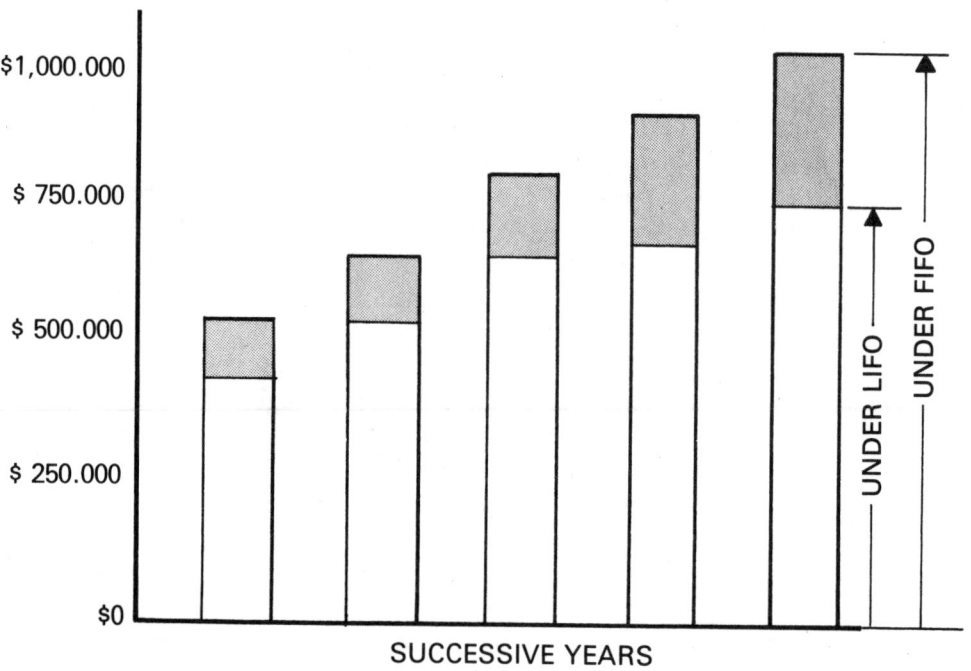

■ "INVENTORY PROFITS"

□ PRETAX EARNINGS ON LIFO BASIS

FIGURE 3–6: Comparison of LIFO and FIFO Profits

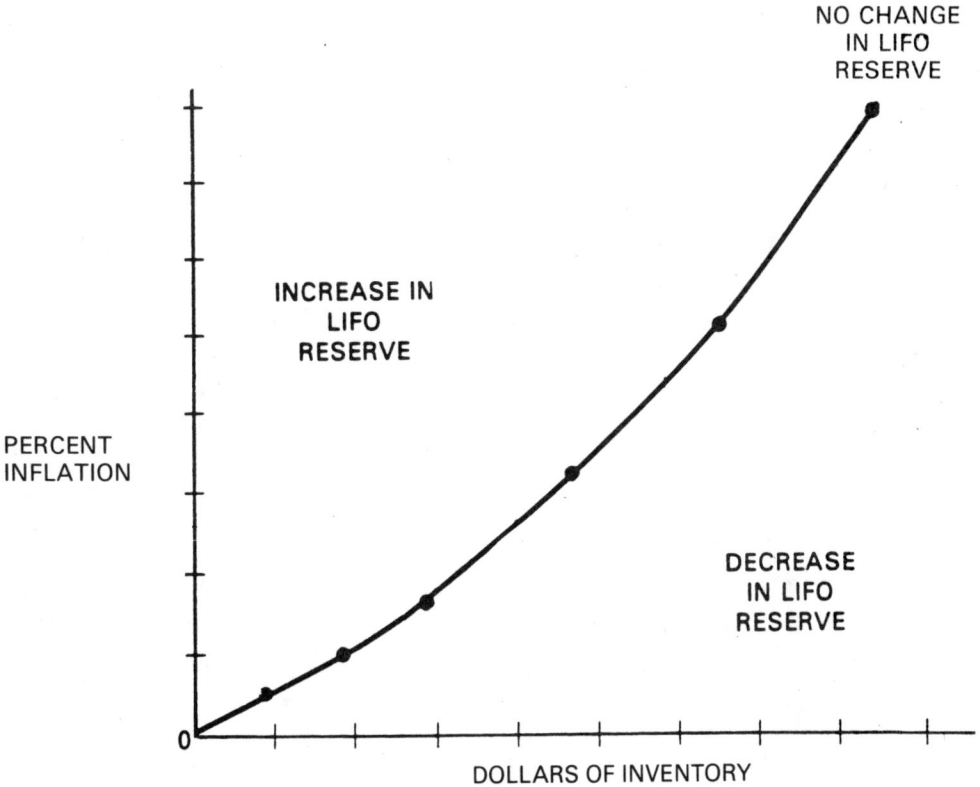

FIGURE 3–7: LIFO Versus Inventory Reduction Trade-off

CHAPTER REFERENCES

1. The Plastics Advisor Computer Software Program, Ernst & Whinney, Cleveland, Ohio, 1985.
2. H. T. McAnly, "How LIFO Began," *Management Accounting*, Copyright May 1975 by National Association of Accountants. All rights reserved. Reprinted by permission.

How to Target Problem Areas for Improvement: The Inventory Management Operations Appraisal

4

CHAPTER HIGHLIGHTS

Inventory systems, because of the inventory process and difficulty of predicting customer demand, are always in a state of flux. You should never be satisfied with the inventory management procedure in your company. In fact, good companies should perform—at least once a year—a review of their inventory function.

This chapter tells when to consider a reappraisal and pinpoints specific "symptoms" of an unhealthy inventory system. You'll learn how to measure the effectiveness of your inventory management and find 20 questions for gauging how well your system now functions. A detailed appraisal program featuring nine steps to identify the real problems behind the "symptoms" is also given. Finally, you'll learn how to turn the recommendations made in your inventory analysis into action with an 18-step improvement program.

WHEN TO CONSIDER A REAPPRAISAL: SYMPTOMS OF DISSATISFACTION

Certain symptoms (what *appears* to be wrong) can indicate problems (the root *cause*) in inventory management, such as

- inability to meet delivery promises
- periodic, extensive backorders
- growing inventory investment while customer order input remains constant or decreases
- high rate of customer turnover and/or order cancellations
- uneven production with frequent layoffs and rehirings
- considerable splitting of production run quantities to meet customer delivery requirements
- excessive machine downtime because of material shortages or changeovers
- periodic lack of storage space
- substantial differences between perpetual record and actual inventory balance on hand
- varying rates of inventory turnover among various inventory items within inventory classification for the same commodity group
- extensive disposals of obsolete or slow-moving stocks
- consistently large write-downs at annual physical inventory taking

As a result, several major inventory issues arise where management

- ponders the significant economic cost of carrying inventory, given high interest rates and inventory levels
- desires to know how to establish reasonable and attainable inventory management goals and measurements by division and product line
- likes to know how the company compares to other companies in similar businesses and to widely accepted inventory management practices
- questions informal inventory management goals and measurements without significant company direction
- wonders if production scheduling, based on short-range needs, takes precedence over forecasting of customer demand and sound inventory management practices
- suspects the desire to meet production quotas, safety stock levels, and production lot sizing is causing high inventory levels and inventory imbalance problems

HOW TO MEASURE THE EFFECTIVENESS OF YOUR INVENTORY MANAGEMENT

These symptoms and management's concern should initially be met head-on with a self-appraisal of the inventory function. Figure 4–1 lists 20 major measures of inventory management. Complete all 20 questions. Calculate the points earned for each question (it is permissible to interpolate a partial score), then add up the total point score for your Inventory Department. Any total in excess of 80 points is "very good news"; this score indicates well-run inventory management. A total from 60 to 79 is in the "good" range but suggests the need for some fine tuning. A rating from 40 to 59 is an "average" (fair) score and steps should be taken immediately to correct any poor scoring characteristics. Any organization that scores below 40 points (a "poor" rating) is in need of drastic steps—probably through the aid of internal auditors or outside consultants.

A NINE-STEP DETAILED INVENTORY APPRAISAL PROGRAM FOR PINPOINTING TROUBLE SPOTS

If the initial appraisal of inventory management results in less than a "good" rating, then a more detailed appraisal is warranted. A nine-step program should be followed to identify the problems behind the symptoms, obtain quantitative measures concerning the use of the inventory investment, and perform selected qualitative observations. Then, using the information obtained, develop an Implementation Plan to obtain the proper inventory control.

Step 1: Make an appraisal of the following areas:
   a. Organization structure
   b. Overall results
   c. Policies
   d. Objectives
   e. Planning techniques
   f. Adequacy of control methods
   g. Effectiveness of various departments

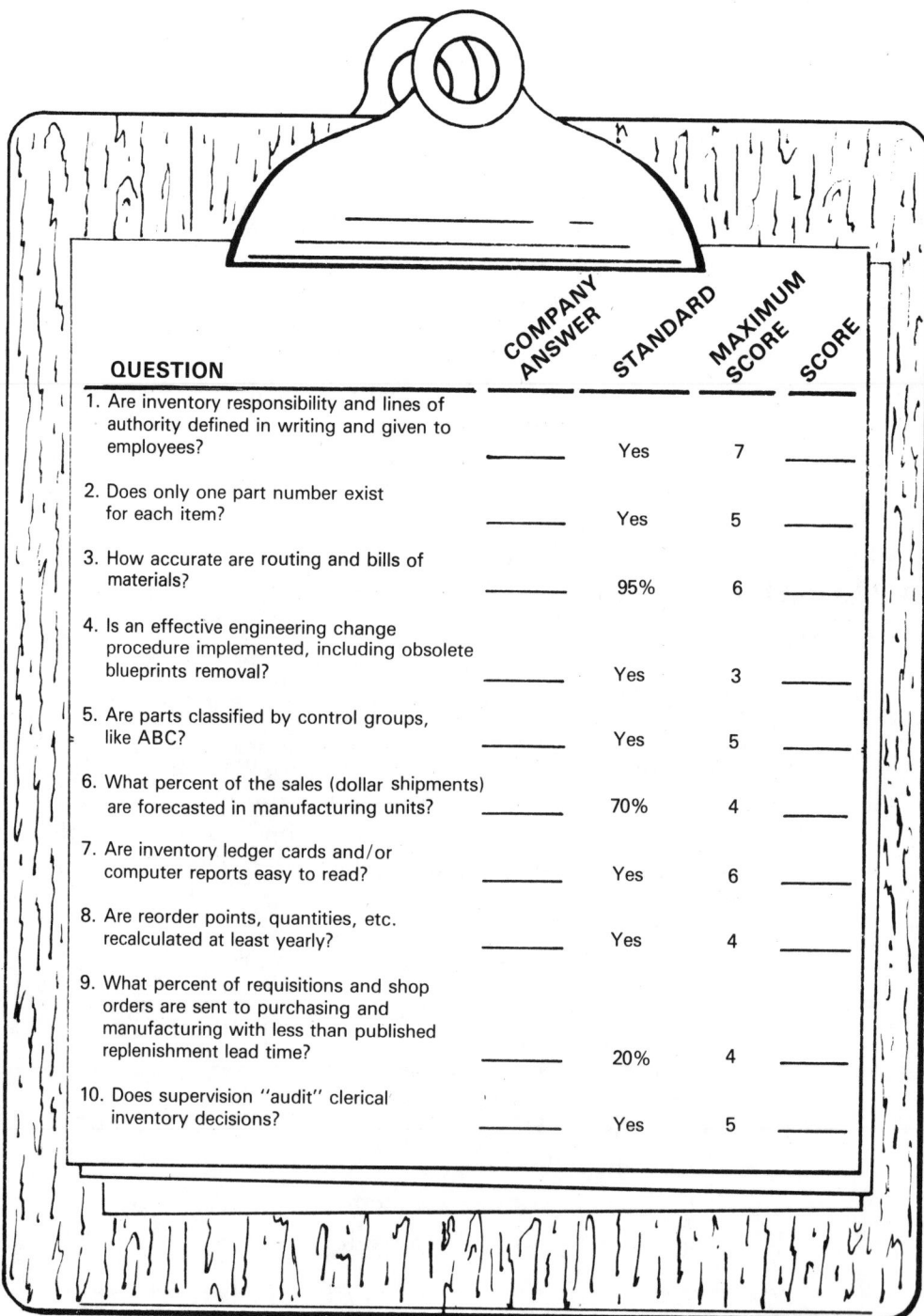

QUESTION	COMPANY ANSWER	STANDARD	MAXIMUM SCORE	SCORE
1. Are inventory responsibility and lines of authority defined in writing and given to employees?	____	Yes	7	____
2. Does only one part number exist for each item?	____	Yes	5	____
3. How accurate are routing and bills of materials?	____	95%	6	____
4. Is an effective engineering change procedure implemented, including obsolete blueprints removal?	____	Yes	3	____
5. Are parts classified by control groups, like ABC?	____	Yes	5	____
6. What percent of the sales (dollar shipments) are forecasted in manufacturing units?	____	70%	4	____
7. Are inventory ledger cards and/or computer reports easy to read?	____	Yes	6	____
8. Are reorder points, quantities, etc. recalculated at least yearly?	____	Yes	4	____
9. What percent of requisitions and shop orders are sent to purchasing and manufacturing with less than published replenishment lead time?	____	20%	4	____
10. Does supervision "audit" clerical inventory decisions?	____	Yes	5	____

FIGURE 4–1: Twenty Major Measures of Inventory Management

QUESTION	COMPANY ANSWER	STANDARD	MAXIMUM SCORE	SCORE
11. Are material in process identification tags used?	_____	Yes	4	_____
12. Are storerooms controlled, clean, absent of rust and papers?	_____	Yes	8	_____
13. Are shop and purchase orders older than 120 days cancelled or rescheduled?	_____	Yes	5	_____
14. How many receiving reports are forwarded to inventory control within 24 hours?	_____	90%	4	_____
15. Is rejected material (purchased and manufactured) quickly reprocessed?	_____	Yes	4	_____
16. Are early or overshipments returned to vendors?	_____	Yes	4	_____
17. Does a Shop Order Completion form account for all pieces including scrap?	_____	Yes	5	_____
18. Are slow moving models, assemblies and parts lists forwarded periodically to sales?	_____	Yes	4	_____
19. Are reports available of inventory by groups in units and dollars?	_____	Yes	6	_____
20. Has turnover increased in the past three years?	_____	Yes	7	_____

FIGURE 4–1: Twenty Major Measures of Inventory Management (cont'd)

Step 2: Use the following techniques to determine how your inventory management rates:

    a. Interviews with key personnel

    b. Reviews of operations and physical layout

    c. Analysis of data and transactions

    d. Comparisons to industry and competitive data

    e. Evaluation of key indicators

    f. Analysis of trends

Step 3: Take a walking tour of the plant and inventory locations. Figure 4–2 can be used as an observation guide. The best indicators of a good inventory system are clean production areas and storerooms.

Step 4: Utilize internal and external standards for judging comparative performance.

Step 5: List strengths and limiting factors of the system.

Step 6: Develop conclusions, then system improvement recommendations.

Step 7: Review the recommendations with the inventory manager.

Step 8: Report the recommendations from the inventory appraisal to management.

Step 9: Establish an Implementation Plan and Schedule including task responsibility assignment and a progress monitoring report.

HOW TO IMPLEMENT THE PROGRAM: KEY AREAS

The key areas for implementing the program include the people involved, the policies and procedures used, the existing documentation, the statistical analysis, and the inventory analysis report.

Interview Staff and Assess the Key Personnel Positions

For the people aspects of the appraisal, you should

1. Acquaint yourself with the operating personnel.
2. Obtain an inventory organization chart.
3. Study job duty lists for the key positions.
4. Interview key materials control personnel and company executives.

	Observation Remarks	
	OK?	Statistics
✓ • Study capital equipment investment, age and condition. _____		
✓ • Check amount of unused space in storage areas. _____		
✓ • Estimate overall machine utilization. _____		
✓ • Determine percent of floor space used for storage; both official and casual. _____		
✓ • Watch creation and disposal of scrap; see if different kinds mixed together. _____		
✓ • Study quality of product produced. _____		
✓ • Look for existence of good housekeeping. _____		
✓ • Check condition of tools and die sets. _____		
✓ • Study flow and handling of material. _____		
✓ • Determine type of storage (fixed vs. random), fill density of area, and use of locked areas. _____		
✓ • Note doors to enter/leave the plant; both personnel and receiving/shipping. _____		
✓ • Ascertain type of material counting in receiving, issuing and shipping. _____		
✓ • Determine method to locate orders in process. _____		

FIGURE 4–2: Plant Walking Tour Guide

Determine How Current Policies and Procedures Are Utilized

1. Observe physical safeguards, housekeeping, and shipments leaving premises.
2. Study existing company operating policies, procedures, and goals as they apply to the materials system.
3. Flow chart the system, keying in the current forms and reports. (You may wish to use Figure 4–3 as a guide since it incorporates the main aspects of the inventory management system.)

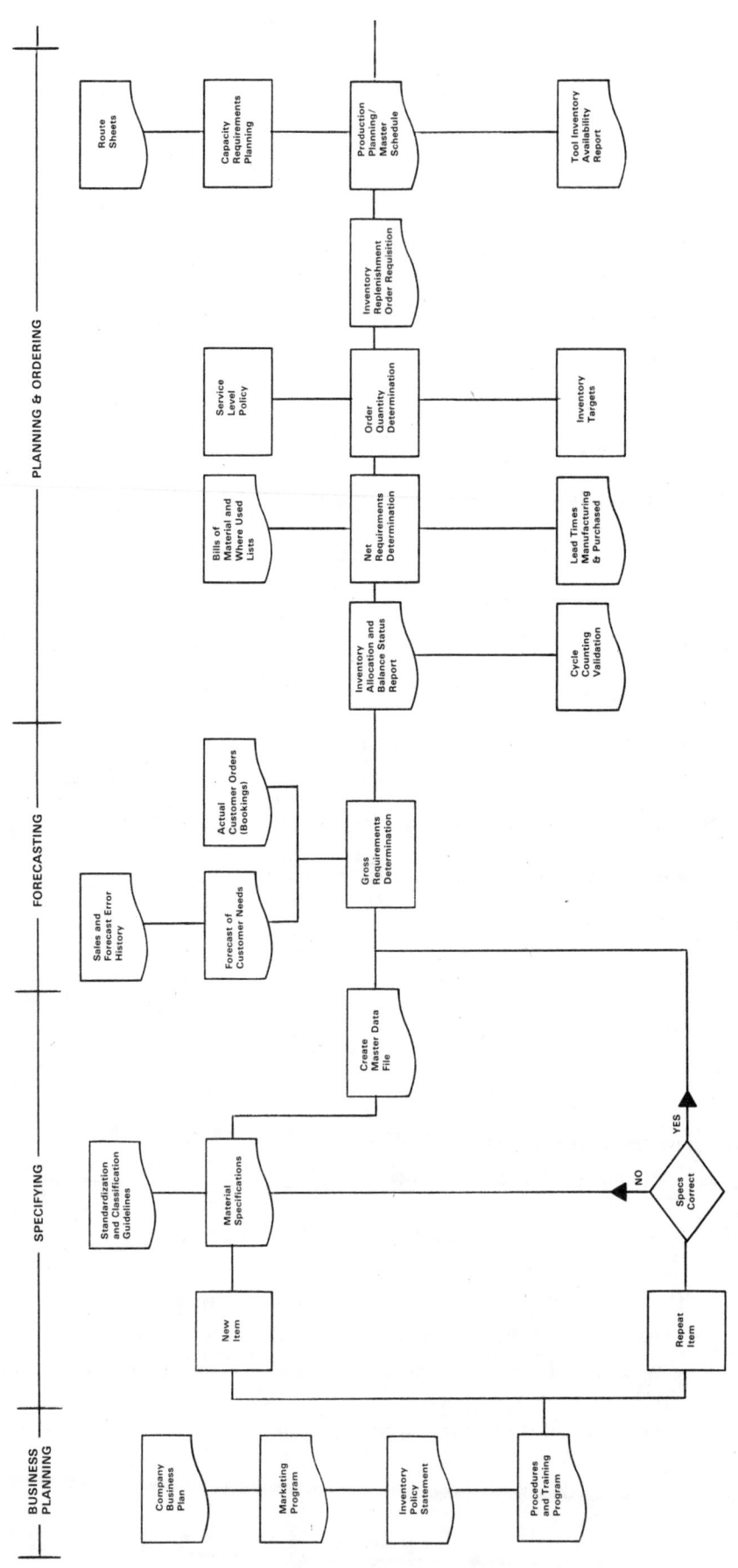

FIGURE 4–3: Inventory Management Cycle

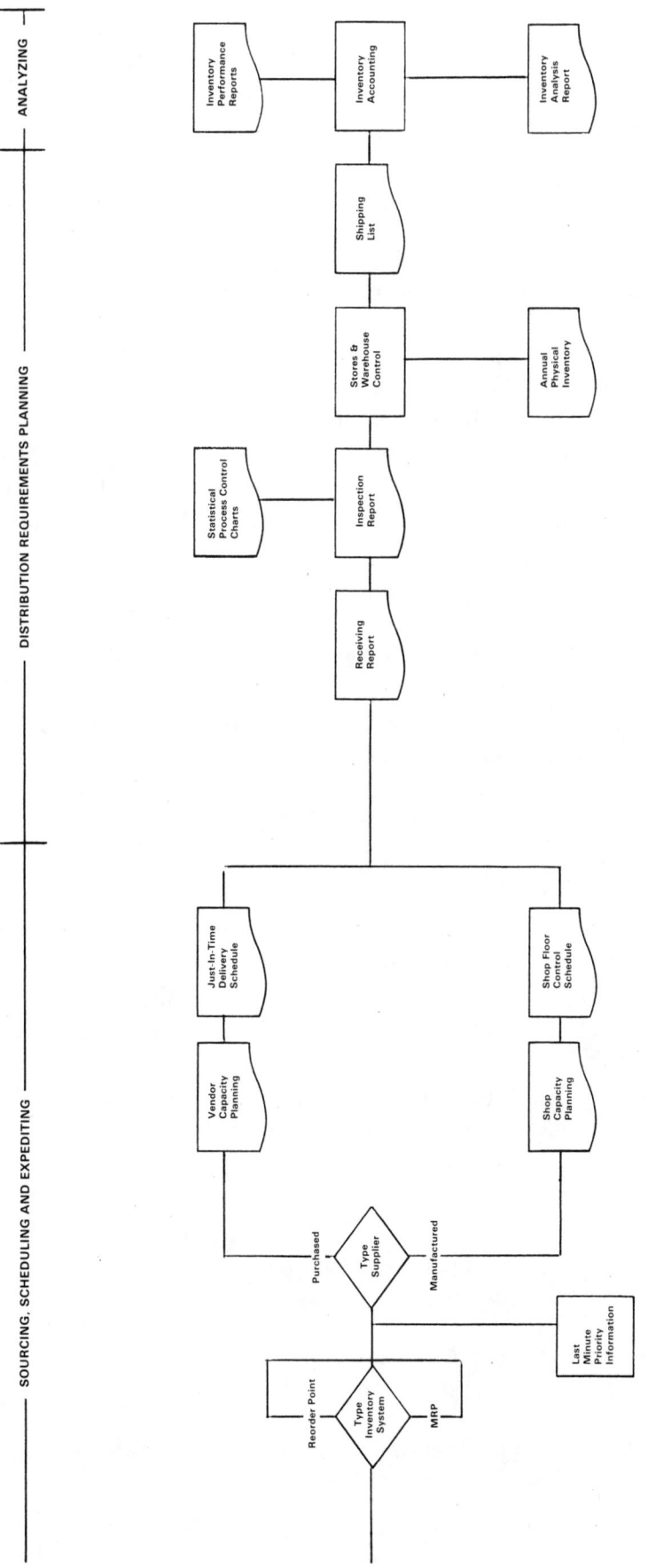

FIGURE 4–3: Inventory Management Cycle (cont'd)

4. Analyze current computer software programs and their inventory reports.

5. Identify the inventory management goals and measurement objectives for the company.

Review Existing Documentation

1. Make a general review of the physical inventory and the perpetual inventory listing.

2. Obtain physical book inventory details; review this summary, ensuring that someone has accounted for all types of reconciling items.

3. Obtain prior year physical to book inventory detail, compare adjustments and inventory totals between years, and study any large or unusual fluctuations.

4. Perform, through the use of sampling, tests of operating and control report contents.

5. Test mathematical accuracy of both the perpetual and physical inventory listings.

6. Request confirmation of significant amounts of inventory on consignment, undergoing outside processing or in outside warehouses.

7. Summarize inventories by location and type, comparing amounts and relationships of classifications with prior periods.

8. Test selected inventory items by physical count and compare with the perpetual record quantities.

9. Compare relationship of scrap cost with material put into production, and the level of scrap sales with prior periods.

10. Determine the existence of damaged, slow moving, overstocked, out-of-style, and obsolete inventories, looking for commitments of additional quantities of similar items.

11. Test accuracy of material quantities in work-in-process and finished goods by reference to bills of materials and requisitions.

12. Determine whether any previously written-off inventory (scrapped) is still on hand.

13. Compare and analyze inventory management performance by product line to other companies in similar businesses and to sound inventory management practices.

Prepare a Statistical Analysis of Inventory

One of the more important steps in the detailed appraisal is a statistical analysis of the inventory. This analysis should include one or more of the following:

1. Inventory turnover as contrasted to annual dollar usage. (See Figure 4–4 for correct method to calculate the overall turnover, note that it uses cost of sales, not sales dollars.)

2. Inventory months' supply on hand of finished goods by period for the major product lines.

3. Inventory component parts months' supply on hand by ABC classification (refer to Figure 4–5).

4. Raw material and work-in-process inventory versus production lead-time efficiency.

5. Book to physical absolute and net error.

6. Inventory investment as a percent of sales; watch for differences by major groups and industry.

7. Stockout, downtime, and overtime hours and dollars.

8. Inventory dollar carrying cost by month and by year.

9. Safety stock and obsolete/slow-moving inventory as a percent of cost of goods sold and of inventory level.

10. Customer order backlog in weeks as a percent of the production process cycle (lead time).

11. Customer order backlog as a percent of inventory by period.

12. Shipment performance to scheduled promise dates.

$$\frac{\text{PERIOD COST OF SALES}}{\text{PERIOD AVERAGE INVENTORY}} = \text{TURNOVER}$$

$$\frac{\$1,200,000 \text{ COST OF SALES}}{\$400,000 \text{ INVENTORY}} = 3 \text{ TIMES}$$

$$\frac{\text{CURRENT INVENTORY BALANCE}}{\text{AVERAGE PERIOD USAGE}} = \text{PERIOD SUPPLY ON HAND}$$

$$\frac{\$400,000 \text{ BALANCE}}{\$100,000 \text{ A MONTH}} = 4 \text{ MONTHS}$$

FIGURE 4–4: Inventory Turnover Calculation Method

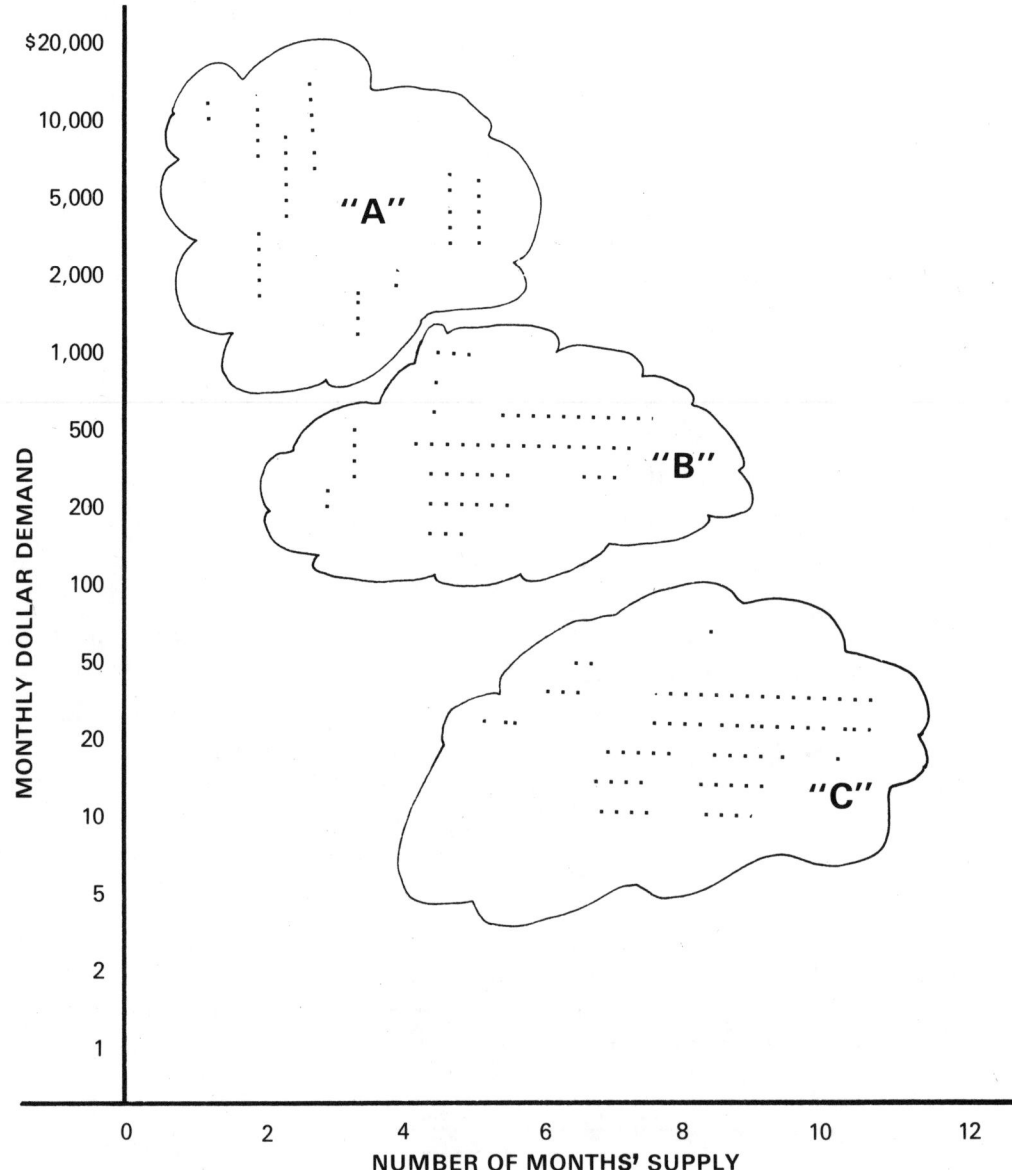

FIGURE 4–5: Scatter Diagram of Component Parts by ABC Class

Typical statistical results of problems

- Ten pages of computer input transaction errors a day for corrections.
- Bills of material are 28 percent incomplete.
- Three different bills of material exist for each item.
- 33 percent of the inventory dollars represent more than a one-year supply of parts on hand.

- 42 percent of factory space used for storage of material.
- 11 percent of stock status report balances on hand were negative.
- "A" class items had greatest months' supply on hand.
- Actual customer requirements were 27 percent of forecast.

Typical system observation

- Chrome-plated material received from outside vendors is not packaged in a manner to prevent surface damage.
- Numerous items were found lying on the floor because they could not be stacked.
- Same part number identifies a part throughout the manufacturing process even though the part changed in physical appearance during the various stages of completion.
- Multiple parts have the same item number.
- Part numbers of the material being scrapped cannot be identified.
- Material received is not counted or weighed unless a packing slip or a tag is missing.
- There is no reconciliation to the dollar value on the accounting books except during the annual physical.
- There are approximately 13 different storage areas; only one is fenced, locked, manned, and controlled.
- Batch controls are exercised over the number of inventory requisitions sent to EDP but not on the total quantity.

Tabulate Resulting Recommendations in an Inventory Analysis Report

When the above efforts are complete, the reviewer should tabulate the results of the study in a listing with two major sections. The first section includes the strong points of the department, that is, the items for which the reviewer believes no improvements are necessary. The second part includes all those limiting factors or problems for which improvements are necessary. For this latter category, and for each weakness identified, one or more methods should be listed by which this problem can be overcome.

Specific ways to overcome weaknesses are identified in a one-, two-, and three-priority sequence. This sequence is then used in an Implementation Schedule for follow-up of the work necessary to improve the function and, at the same time, to provide a monthly progress report. This report should list all recommendations in a short, clearly stated sentence. Then the reason for the change should be explained with supporting information.

DEVELOPING YOUR RECOMMENDATIONS
INTO ACTION:
AN 18-STEP INVENTORY MANAGEMENT
IMPROVEMENT PROGRAM

You should use the various information developed and recommendations made based on the inventory analysis to put together a plan that helps guide the establishment of correct methodologies and inventory investment for your company.

The following is a representative 18-step program. This program (summarized on the Implementation Schedule shown in Figure 4–6) is presented in sequential format that should help you in completing the tasks.

1. *Create a company inventory management policy statement* that would include service levels by type of product and, if a stock-out occurs, average number of days prior to having inventory available in order to meet customer demands.

2. *Clarify the existing inventory organization*, assigning one person with responsibility for all inventory investment, irrespective of the manufacturing or warehouse location. While it might be a corporate staff position, it would be necessary to have strong support of top management.

3. *Establish an inventory management control center*, a location where all inventory information from reports and questions could be funneled. This office would be run by the inventory management person previously appointed in step 2.

4. *Update the inventory item classifications* to make certain that these are the items you wish to give special attention. Then establish a control mechanism for the A, B, and C class items.

5. *Determine the inventory carrying cost and the order processing cost* that would subsequently be used in an economic order quantity formula.

6. *Calculate the economic order quantity* for each item or an EOQ matrix (refer to Figure 2–7), which may be used as a reference table.

7. *Update the forecast for the key parts* discussed in step 4. It is not necessary to have a forecast for every active item in the system. If 70 percent of the dollars sold are forecast accurately (within ± 10 percent of the actual) you have adequate information for a successful inventory management system.

8. *Measure any subsequent deviation* for these key parts regarding the forecast versus the actual orders from the customer. Revise the forecasts if the method is not performing well.

9. *Calculate the safety stock* that you wish to carry by type of item. Set up the safety stock manually, item by item, for all A class items and then by

STEP NO.	OBJECTIVE	RESPONSIBILITY	COMPLETION TARGET DATE
1	Policy Statement	President	February
2	Inventory organization	President	February
3	Control Center	Inventory Manager	March
4	Inventory Item Classification	Inventory Manager	March
5	Carrying and Ordering Costs	Inventory Analyst	March
6	EOQ Calculation	Inventory Analyst	March
7	"A" Class Part Forecasts	Sales Manager	April
8	Forecast vs. Actual Deviation	Inventory Analyst	May
9	Safety Stock Determination	Inventory Manager	May
10	Master Production Schedule	Production Manager	May
11	Inventory Investment Targets	President	May
12	Inventory Report Contents	Inventory Manager	June
13	Prepare Inventory Reports	Inventory Manager	June
14	Key Indicator Measures	President	July
15	Excess and Obsolete Indentification	Finance Manager	September
16	Gross Margin Analysis	Finance Manager	October
17	MRP/ROP Study	Inventory Manager	November
18	Training Seminars	Inventory Manager	November

FIGURE 4–6: Inventory Management Improvement Program

category for the B and C class items. In establishing safety stock, utilize the forecast to actual comparison to guide you as well as the vendor or manufacture lead time necessary for a replenishment order. If the forecast has a larger error and/or if the replenishment order lead time is longer, then greater safety stock should be maintained. Conversely, if the forecast is accurate and/or the item has a short replenishment lead time, then less safety stock would be required.

10. *Establish a master production schedule* based on the above information regarding replenishment orders with special emphasis on the key items.

11. *Calculate the inventory investment targets* utilizing the desired balance on hand, stock-out position, and safety stock policy. Use this as a budget by item and by product line grouping, as well as by plant and warehouse location.

12. *Modify the existing inventory management reports* to place more emphasis on an exception basis. These modified reports should show

    - The number of months' supply on hand sorted high to low by months and by dollars. However, all inventory on hand, with less than six months' supply and more than one, should be excluded from the report. Likewise, all lower dollar values on hand should be excluded so that emphasis is on the higher dollars in inventory.

    - Calculate turnover by product line and by location, as well as for the total company.

13. *Print these reports in both units and dollars* for the inventory controllers to work with on a quantity basis while the inventory manager and executives should be concerned on a dollar basis.

14. *Establish a monthly inventory management key indicator report* to show progress against previously set targets.

15. *Determine quarterly the excess and obsolete inventory* on hand measuring both the historical customer usage and anticipated demand by the forecasting system for items. Use this information to determine methods to eliminate slow-moving and obsolete inventory on hand, by product line if possible.

16. *Study the inventory turnover by gross margin* and use this as a method to ascertain the type of inventory you wish on hand. Stocking higher profit margin items for quick sale is often a wise inventory policy.

17. *Conduct a detailed study of the manufacturing system* to determine which of the five types of MRP and/or reorder point systems would be the best suited for your inventory and customer environment (refer to Chapter 5).

18. *Present training seminars on inventory management* which would explain many of these program points to selected executives, managers, and inventory personnel in your company.

Remember: All inventory situations are not created equal. Consider Figure 4–7, which shows the system characteristics of five different manufacturing companies.

COMPANY NO.	MFG. #1	MFG #2	MFG #3	MFG #4	MFG #5
• No. of Parts Active	150,000	35,000	10,000	5,000	1,000
• Daily Inventory Trans.	3,000	1,000	700	300	60
• Bill of Material Levels (Max.)	5	9	3	2	1
• Number of B/M	85,000	30,000	5,000	400	100
• Turnover (Annual)	4	2	5	7	8
• Month's Supply on Hand	3	6	2.4	1.7	1.5

FIGURE 4–7: Characteristics of Inventory System in Five Companies

Two Major Inventory Systems and the ABC Classification Procedure: How to Determine the Best Choice for Your Company

5

CHAPTER HIGHLIGHTS

This chapter presents the two major inventory systems with their numerous control techniques, then explains how to utilize an "ABC" part classification procedure. Specifically, Reorder Point (ROP) and Material Requirements Planning (MRP) systems are discussed. ROP involves rate of usage, while MRP considers both customer orders and forecast as well as usage. After you determine the inventory technique that's best for your company, you'll see the universal inventory technique that works for any company (large or small)—the ABC inventory classification system that determines control based on an item's value to your company.

INVENTORY CONTROL TECHNIQUES

Inventory control is difficult, full of uncertainties and variables. It must be done carefully and thoroughly, and it requires constant attention—day after day for thousands of parts. Yet all the items in inventory are not created equal. More often than not, more than one inventory control technique should be used in any given organization. Even in a sophisticated inventory system, certain items (hardware, for one example) may be directly expensed upon receipt of the goods and placed in a "free stock" area with sufficient safety stock to minimize stock-outs, thus lessening the need for frequent review and reordering actions.

Figure 5–1 lists the various inventory techniques of Reorder Point (ROP) and Material Requirements Planning (MRP) that can be used along with a brief explanation about each technique; Figure 5–2 shows the ROP and MRP relationship.

1. REORDER POINTS

- Visual; Recordless, Periodic Review

    - Stock Out; When none is there, order more

    - Replenishment; Whatever you use, request more of same

    - Minimum/Maximum; If at min, order up to max

    - Mark on Wall of Bin; If below the line, reorder

    - Two Bin Reserve; When first one empty, send a requisition

    - Cycle; Once a week (month), reorder as needed

- Writen Record; Periodic or Perpetual Review

    - Stock Out; When none is there, order more

    - Replenishment; What ever you use, request more of same

    - Minimum/Maximum; If at min, order up to max

FIGURE 5–1: Types of Inventory Control Techniques

- ABC Cycle; Review "A" items daily, "B" weekly, "C" monthly

- Reorder Point; Set a review level, then requisition when below

- Statistical Order Point; At a calculated reorder quantity, get more

- Phased Order Point; Key need to a calendar schedule

- Kanban; Use Japanese method of "card" ordering

2.   MATERIALS REQUIREMENTS PLANNING

- Manual Requirements; Calculating requirements by hand

- Single Level Explosion; Consider each item without indentures

- Gross Requirements Explosion Only; Do not worry about balance on hand

- Net Requirements; Do worry about what's on hand

- Time Series Planning; Involve period "buckets" in explosion

- Time Phased Order Point; Use forecast as requirements

- Explosion Forecasting; Reorder point merged with MRP

- Just-In-Time; Japanese daily period requirement delivery schedule

- OPT; Optimized Production Technology

FIGURE 5–1: Types of Inventory Control Techniques (cont'd)

CHOOSING TYPE OF TRANSACTION POSTING: TWO OPTIONS

Regardless of the technique used to control inventory, certain practices can be followed. The first choice concerns the type of transaction posting to the inventory records. Two options are available.

■ *Perpetual Inventory Method* maintains "continuous" balances by recording daily, and even hourly, additions to and reductions from raw materials, work-in-process, and finished goods. Since computerized systems have made it practical to record inventory movements instantaneously, the

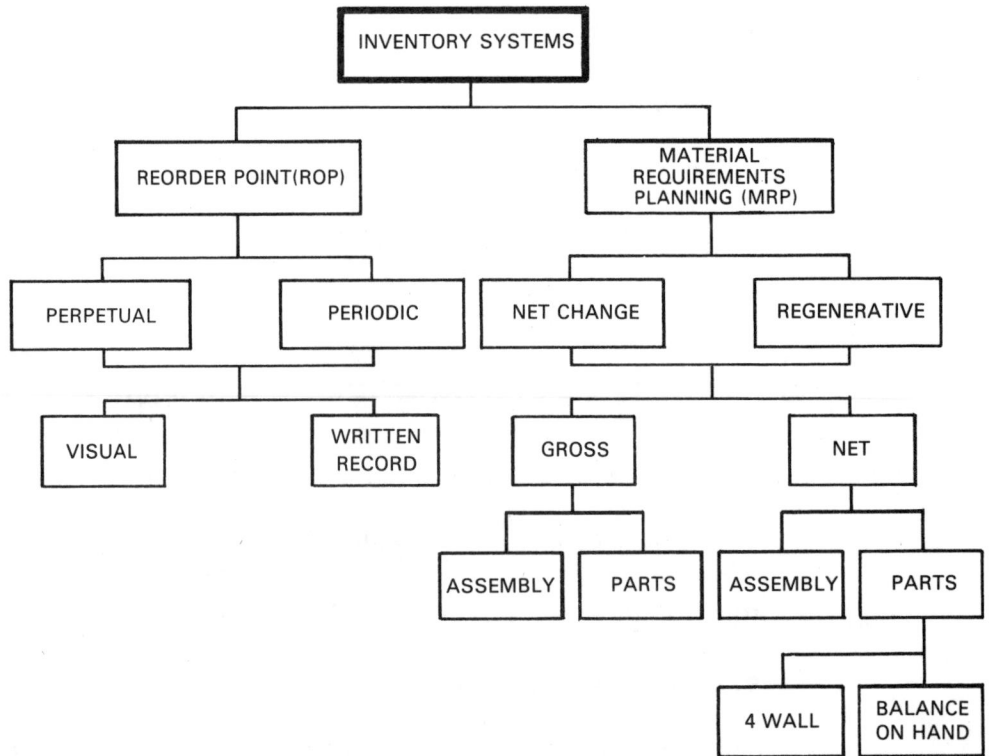

FIGURE 5–2: ROP and MRP Relationship

technique is applicable to updating the inventory records on manufacturing, as well as the accounting records.

- *Periodic Inventory Method*, as the name suggests, does not maintain continuous balances. Instead, the material is added to, or subtracted from, the previous period's ending inventory, resulting in a new inventory balance. Ending inventories, determined by a summary of inventory transactions or physical counts, are then subtracted from the available inventory and accounting balance to determine the cost of goods sold. Typically, the process is repeated weekly or monthly.

WHEN TO POST DATA FOR YOUR RECORDKEEPING SYSTEM

Once the type of information posting technique has been selected, and the kind of written record chosen, the next decision concerns the timing to "post" (type or write) data to the computer terminal or the manual record.

Three choices are available:

1. One-Step Actions

    "Prepost" Usage—This is done when the customer purchase order is received.

    "Post-post" Usage—The posting is accomplished after the transaction, when a reorder review is performed.

2. Two-Step Action

    "Reserve" or "allocate" the estimated period demand for the inventory; then post the actual usage later from the transaction slip.

The next decisions include the amount of detail necessary and the transaction accuracy required. The type of transactions include the actual demand for material, the receipt of the goods from the vendor or the company manufacturing department, and allocation or reservation of material for specific future demand.

TWO MAJOR ORDERING CONCERNS: WHEN AND HOW MUCH TO ORDER?

When to order concerns the reorder point, referred to as minimum lead time, sometimes using a planning/review cycle for joint or family items with common setups in manufacturing or bought from the same vendor. The reorder point equals expected demand during the lead time plus safety stock. The safety stock is a product of customer service desired and the standard deviation of forecast errors over time (see Chapter 2). The stock system sets a maximum stock level for each item at each bill of material level. Uneven customer demand, such as random demand variation for which no basic pattern can be determined, requires an extra quantity above the reorder quantity or bringing in material "X" weeks sooner (as a percent of lead time). This action can be based on ABC class.

How much to order considers an order quantity determined by some decision rule such as vendor minimum quantity (vendor price break), quantity discount, production lot size requirement, economic order quantity (EOQ), purchase order quantity (POQ), or some combination. The difference between a present maximum level and the current balance on hand are useful when customers have uneven order demand.

Four basic inventory demands should be considered:

1. Original pieces of equipment that are the primary items the company manufactures or assembles. This group usually has the longest lead time.
2. Special options which, by adding to the "original equipment," permit customers to customize the primary items. This lead time is less long.

3. Replacement parts, often called "service items," are those numerous parts ordered in small quantities that the customers require to maintain the "original equipment" and sometimes the "special options." These items usually are expected in short lead time.

4. Losses of those materials which, as a result of the process, cannot be sold.

REORDER POINT SYSTEM (ROP): FOCUSING ON RATE OF INVENTORY USAGE

A Reorder Point system—as well as an MRP system—helps the inventory controller determine (1) when to order, (2) what material, and (3) how much of it. The timing (when) is based on inventory balances. ROP estimates the requirements (what and how much) based on an average sales rate (usually expressed monthly) for both manufactured and purchased items. This type of system is based on continuous usage or sales pattern, usually based on historical information.

The definition of Reorder Point means that when the quantity of an item on hand in inventory goes below a predetermined level (the "Reorder Point," although sometimes this is called the "minimum"), a replenishment order is placed (for the "Reorder Quantity") with delivery requested at a specific date using the manufacturing or vendor stated lead time.

What You Need to Calculate ROP

The formulas necessary to make the Reorder Point system calculations require the following bits of information:

1. LT: item replacement lead time, in weeks
2. Qty: average quantity used per week in recent times or forecasted usage per week
3. SS: safety stock for unexpected customer requirements, expressed as so many weeks' usage
4. OC: cost to place an order
5. CC: inventory carrying cost percent (expressed as a decimal)
6. C: item unit cost
7. AL: allocations, material reserved for customer orders already received
8. BOH: inventory balance on hand in the various storage areas
9. OO: material already on a replenishment order
10. FQ: fixed reorder quantity, a preselected amount

Three Formulas for Determining the Reorder Point

The above information, once obtained, is used in one or more of three formulas. The first formula is used to determine the "Reorder Point"—that amount of inventory on hand at which you should order more material. This formula is as follows:

Reorder point = (LT × Qty) + (SS weeks × Qty)

$$(4 \times 300) + (2 \times 300) = 1,800$$

The second formula helps you to determine the "Reorder Timing"—a calculation that tells when to reorder. This formula is below; some companies do not record the allocations, so for these organizations delete this part of the formula. Reorder when the balance on hand less allocations plus on order is less than ROP.

$$\textit{Reorder Timing} = BOH - AL + OO < ROP$$

The third calculation involves determining the Reorder Quantity, usually abbreviated "ROQ." The two formulas described previously are fairly simple, with few variations in the formulas. However, to perform the ROQ calculation you may select from several formulas. The more frequently used ones include

1. Fixed Order Quantity = ROQ of 700
2. Order up to (maximum); Fixed Quantity less balance on hand:

    FQ − BOH = ROQ   700 − 161 = 539
3. Weeks Usage: WKS × Qty = ROQ   4 × 300 = 1,200
4. Weeks Usage by ABC Class: Weeks × Usage

    A =   4 weeks × 300 = 1,200
    B =   8 weeks × 300 = 2,400
    C = 16 weeks × 300 = 4,800
5. Economic Order Quantity (EOQ)

$$= \sqrt{\frac{2 \times (Qty \times 52) \times OC}{CC \times C}}$$

$$= \sqrt{\frac{2 \times (300 \times 52) \times \$25}{.24 \times \$1.25}}$$

$$= \quad 1,612$$

Your next concern: Once you understand the method by which to use the Reorder Point system, you should select which of the Reorder Quantity formulas is most appropriate for your needs. Whichever one is selected, keep in mind that the ROQ is only a guide to determine the actual quantity to be ordered. Always remember there is no substitute for a last-minute "human" review, which considers facts the formula does not know.

MATERIAL REQUIREMENTS PLANNING (MRP): BASING QUANTITIES ON BOTH CUSTOMER ORDERS AND FINANCIAL FORECASTS

MRP—like the Reorder Point System helps determine (1) when reordering is required, (2) what material to order, and (3) how much of it is needed. However, the production quantities (how much) are based on specific identifiable customer orders (in contrast to the continuous sales rate of ROP), and bookings (what) on a forecast presented in a monthly (weekly, quarterly, and so forth) time-phased manner. Material quantities (raw material and components) are based on specific planned production requirements taken from the master schedule. The timing (when) in a MRP system does not assume continuous (average) usage or sales since it reacts to specific, identifiable customer demands augmented by the sales forecast.

14 STEPS IN THE MRP PROCESS

The MRP procedure is complex and normally includes these 14 steps.[1] When reviewing this discussion you may wish to refer to Figure 5–3, an MRP flow chart.

Step 1: Determine Gross Requirements of Customers

The gross requirement is the total quantity taken from the actual quantities from sales orders as the customers wish the material shipped.

Step 2: Obtain Forecast from Sales of Other Customer Needs

This forecast should include any other anticipated needs and should be altered by management for purposes such as to smooth out production changeovers, account for vacations, and so forth.

Step 3: Add Customer Orders and Forecast to Get Gross Requirements

From this step you will have gross requirements by time period (also called buckets) and may be expressed as days, weeks, etc., depending on the type of items you are scheduling.

Step 4: See if Any Extra Finished Assemblies Are Available

It is possible that some available products are in the finished goods area.

Step 5: Calculate Net Requirements

The gross requirements obtained in Step 1 are adjusted by the amount of the inventory on hand for the various parts under consideration to obtain net requirements for finished goods. The actual calculation is as follows:

Gross Requirements − Balance on Hand Inventory = Net Requirements

Step 6: Prepare Master Schedule

By using the net assembly requirements for each time period as determined in Step 5, you can produce a master assembly schedule for what is called "Level 0," or the top level of this production document.

Step 7: Determine Bill of Material for Subassembly Level

There needs to be a bill of material available for each assembly item on the schedule. The gross requirements for a specific item on the next subassembly level (level 1) will be ascertained by multiplying the number of assemblies on the master schedule by the number of component or raw material items per assembly as given in the bill of material.

Step 8: Obtain Accurate Manufacturing and Vendor Lead Times

Since one of the characteristics of MRP is close timing as the expected production start and material required dates, very accurate manufacturing and vendor lead times must be obtained for use in the next step.

1. Order received for
   five Deluxe Model
   CEPTmobiles

2. Determine forecast from
   sales for other Deluxe Models

3. Add to above order to obtain
   "Gross" assembly requirements

4. See if any completed
   Deluxe models are
   "available" in finished
   goods

5. Subtract "available"
   inventory from "gross"
   requirements to get
   "net" requirements

6. Create Net Assembly
   master schedule

7. Obtain CEPTmobile
   bill of material
   and routing

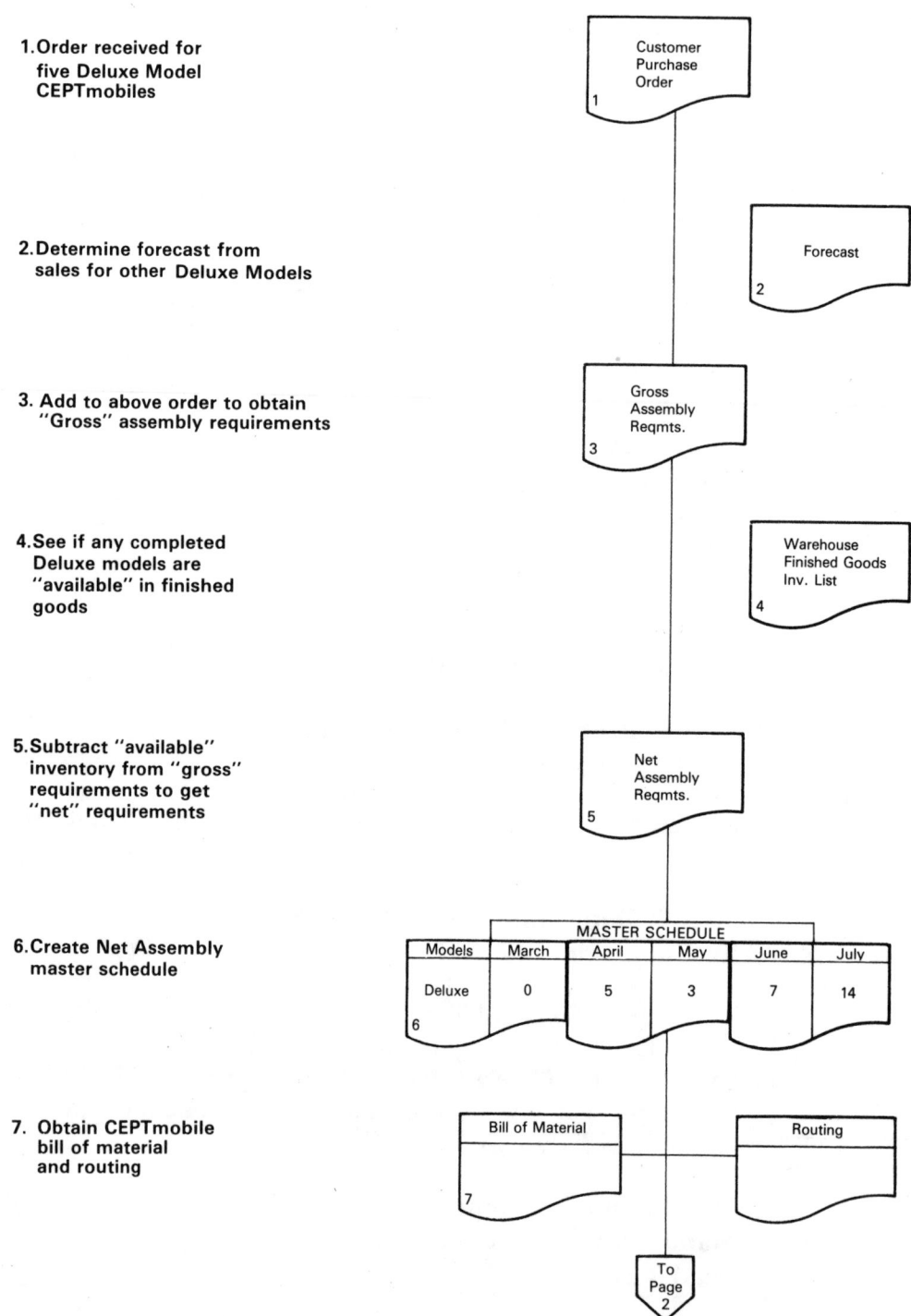

FIGURE 5–3: MRP Narrative Flow Chart

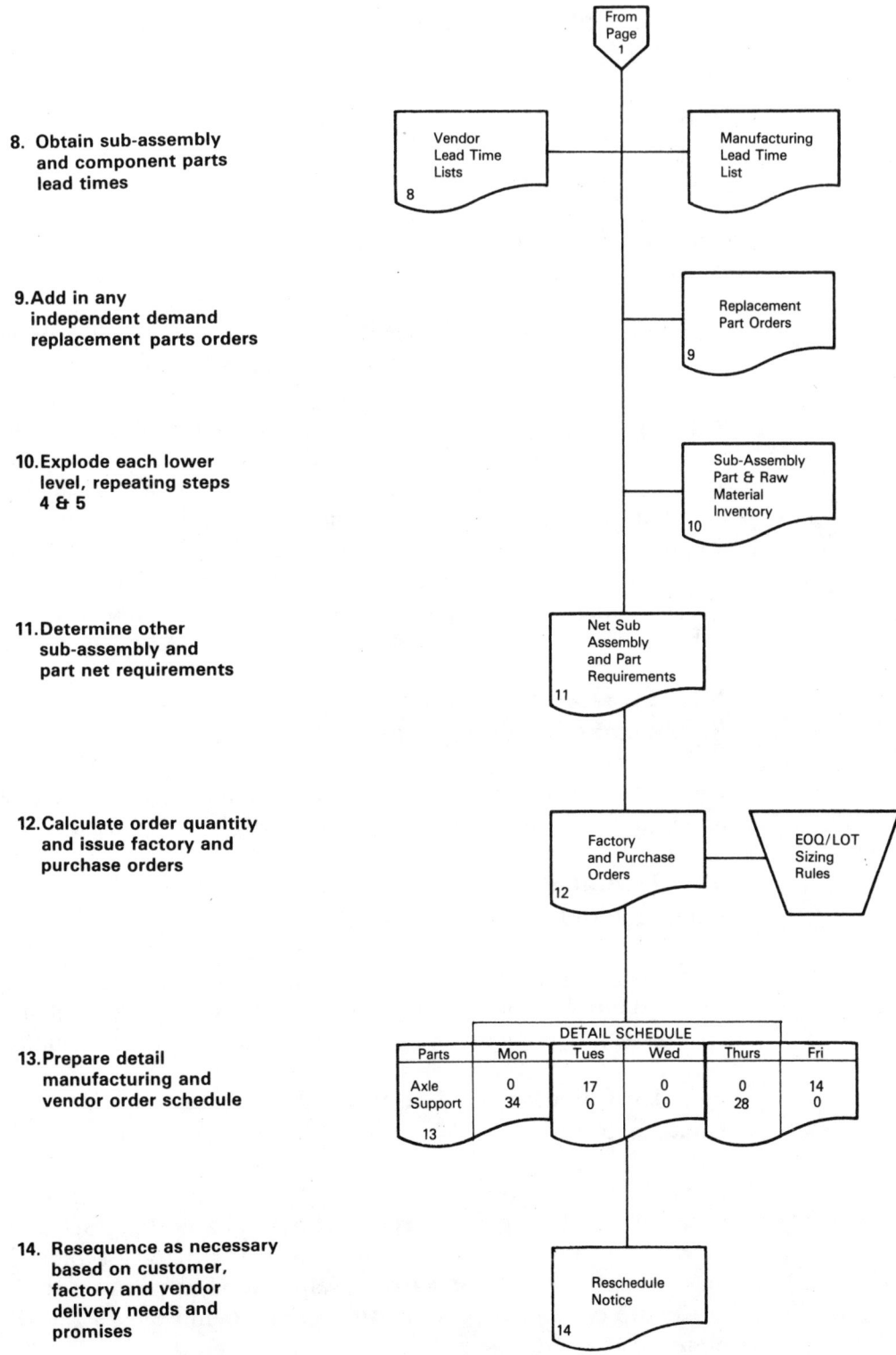

8. Obtain sub-assembly
and component parts
lead times

9. Add in any
independent demand
replacement parts orders

10. Explode each lower
level, repeating steps
4 & 5

11. Determine other
sub-assembly and
part net requirements

12. Calculate order quantity
and issue factory and
purchase orders

13. Prepare detail
manufacturing and
vendor order schedule

14. Resequence as necessary
based on customer,
factory and vendor
delivery needs and
promises

FIGURE 5–3: MRP Narrative Flow Chart (cont'd)

Step 9: Add Any Replacement
Part Orders

It is possible that some replacement (service) parts are needed by these customers. Such needs should be added to the requirements. These needs are called "independent" demand.

Step 10: Explode All Lower
Levels

The entire assembly is not exploded at one time but it is done level by level (e.g., line by line on the bill of material) after all previous steps are completed. Therefore, it is necessary to repeat steps 4 and 5 until each level has been exploded (e.g., quantity required per item multiplied by number of assemblies), time phased and required quantities have been determined. During all of the previous steps it might be discovered that one item is needed in a number of assemblies, at various levels, and even for an independent service requirement. Rather than place an order for each time an item appears, the procedure calls for waiting until the demand is developed for all items and then totaling this demand so just one replenishment order is placed. The information can be displayed on two kinds of MRP reports (Figure 5–4).

Step 11: Determine Other
Subassembly or Part Needs

Any needs for lower-level subassemblies and/or parts should be obtained on a net basis, e.g., deducting any available finished items.

Step 12: Calculate Order
Quantity and Issue Orders

A number of lot sizing order quantity determining rules, such as EOQ, should be considered to obtain the factory or purchase order quantity. Then the appropriate documents (Factory and Purchase Orders) should be printed.

Step 13: Calculate a Time-Phased
Detail Schedule

After the net quantity and lead time for an item is determined, it is necessary to detail schedule it. This process is time phased (e.g., scheduled using necessary lead time) so that the items will be ready for assembling based on the master schedule. The offset represents the usual accumulation of lead times needed to obtain the product on time. Remember, all items do not have the same offset (lead time).

NET MATERIAL REQUIREMENTS PLANNING WORKSHEET

PART NO.	DESCRIPTION	LOT SIZE	LEAD TIME (WEEKS)	UNIT OF MEASURE	B/P AND REV. NO.	MFG'D/PURCH.	INV. CLASS	UNIT COST
RECORD REVIEW DATE	ON HAND	TOTAL ON ORDER	BACK ORDERED QTY.	PRODUCTION USAGE/WK	SERVICE USAGE/WK.	STORES LOCATION		

Step / Description	PAST DUE	WEEK OF 4/30	WEEK OF 5/6	WEEK OF 5/13	WEEK OF 5/20	WEEK OF 5/27	WEEK OF 6/3	WEEK OF 6/10	WEEK OF 6/17	WEEK OF 6/24	WEEK OF 6/31	WEEK OF 7/7	WEEK OF 7/14
1. Forecasted Gross Requirements													
2. Inventory Balance-Start of Period													
3. Net Requirements													
4. Replenishment Order Due In													
5. Balance on Hand-End of Period													

ORDER PLANNING

6. Replenishment Order Start Date													

FIGURE 5–4, Part 1: Net MRP "Bucket" Report

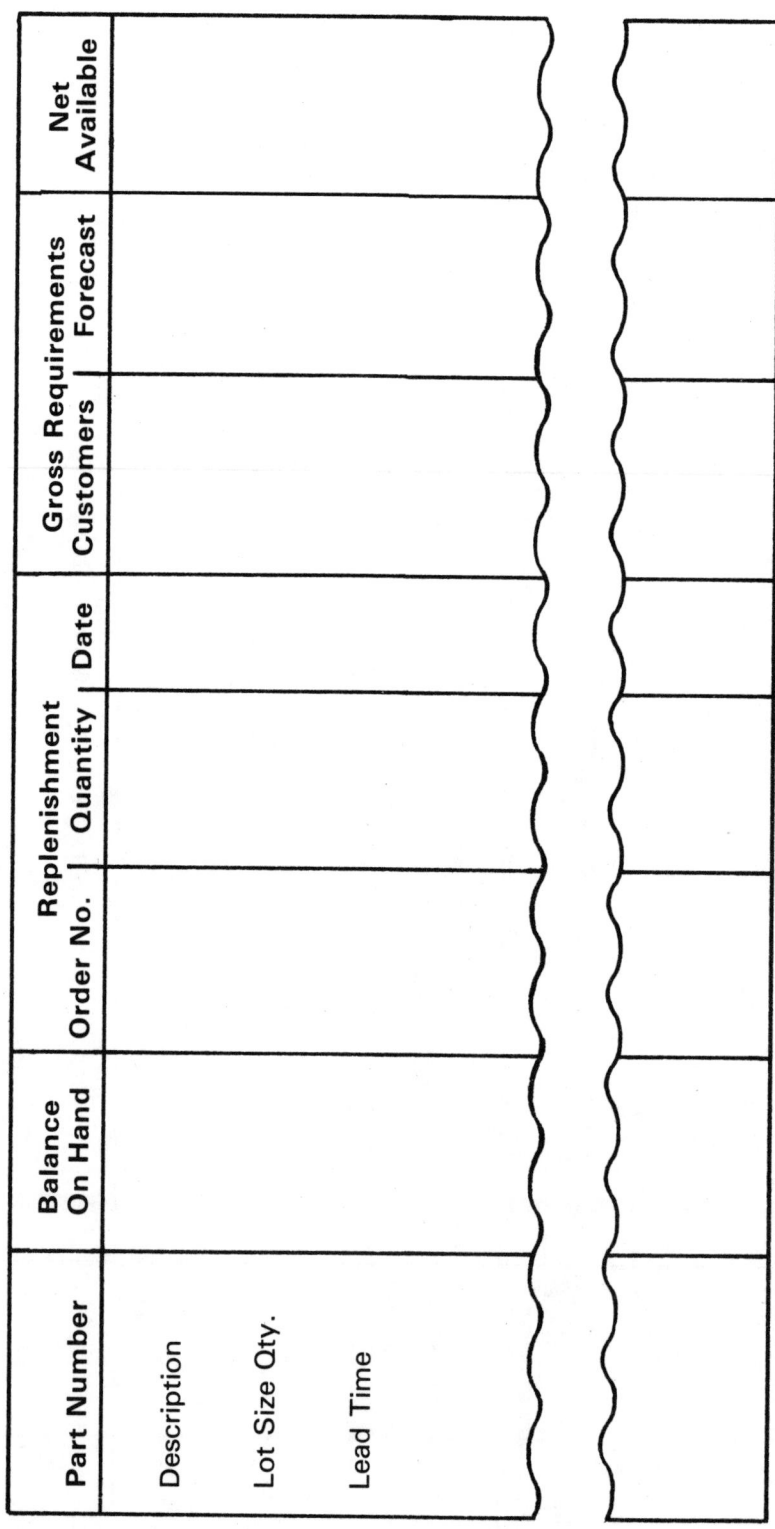

FIGURE 5-4, Part 2: Net MRP "Vertical" Report

The previous net requirements calculation and the lead time offsetting provide the exact quantity needed by time periods, usually weeks. However, you may not wish to produce or order these exact quantities, so then a lot size must be determined.

Step 14: Resequence the Schedule if Necessary

Production planning is dynamic since customer delivery dates change as do production schedules. Thus, whenever appropriate, change the schedule to meet revised priorities. This is needed since MRP is a combination inventory and scheduling technique. The quantities and schedule have been determined from the previous steps and from now on it will be a matter of expediting and revising schedules to meet the customer's requirements. The process is not completed until the product arrives in the customer's hands at the time desired.

MANUFACTURING RESOURCE PLANNING SYSTEMS (MRP II)

How MRP and MRP II Differ: Inventory vs. Manufacturing Systems

MRP is Material Requirements Planning; an inventory system, while MRP II is Manufacturing Resource Planning; what we formerly called a manufacturing system. An MRP II system can use for the inventory control procedure a Reorder Point, an MRP or a combination of both systems.

There are five types of MRP II systems, all worthy of consideration. Since the success of MRP depends on a higher degree of inventory record accuracy than an ROP system, the inventory system designer should select the least complicated level considering the current inventory accuracy, complexity of product and future manufacturing plans. The concept and value of MRP is now commonly accepted, so from the least to the most complex, these levels include:

1. Gross Assembly
2. Gross Parts
3. Net Assembly
4. Net Parts: Four-wall
5. Net Parts: Controlled Stock Areas

DOCUMENTS/RECORDS	1 ASSEMBLY	2 PARTS
BILL OF MATERIAL		
SINGLE LEVEL	YES	– –
INDENTED	– –	YES
RAW MATERIAL	YES	YES
MASTER SCHEDULE LEVEL	0 or1	1
INVENTORY RECORD		
NECESSARY	NO	NO
ACCURACY	– –	– –
RECEIPTS	YES	YES
RESERVATIONS	– –	– –
STOREROOM REQUISITIONS	– –	– –
BALANCE ON HAND	– –	– –
CYCLE COUNTING	– –	– –
SHOP/PURCHASE ORDER		
BLUEPRINTS ONLY	YES	– –
OPERATION ROUTE SHEETS	– –	YES
STANDARD LABOR HOURS	– –	– –

FIGURE 5–5: Gross Manufacturing Resource Planning (MRP II) Systems

Figure 5–5 lists the main ingredients and documents of the two "gross" types of MRP II; Figure 5–6 lists aspects of the three "net" kinds. In making the selection, remember that an MRP system does help reduce inventory and improve on-time customer delivery, but it requires an investment in computerized systems along with the need for highly accurate information.

Two Major Groupings—Gross and Net Systems

As noted previously, the five types of MRP II systems are comprised of two major groupings, gross systems and net systems. The terminology "gross" is used in the classical MRP sense in that these are the total requirements of the customer, irrespective of whatever inventory balance there might be on hand that could be applied against these gross requirements. The "net" term is also

DOCUMENTS/RECORDS	**3**	**4**	**5**
	ASSEMBLY	PARTS	
		4 WALL	BOH
BILL OF MATERIAL			
SINGLE LEVEL	YES	— —	— —
INDENTED	— —	YES	YES
RAW MATERIAL	— —	YES	YES
MASTER SCHEDULE LEVEL	ONE LEVEL ABOVE PLAN	DETAILED AS NECESSARY	DETAILED AS NECESSARY
INVENTORY RECORD			
NECESSARY	YES	YES	YES
ACCURACY	97%	90%	97%
RECEIPTS	YES	YES	YES
RESERVATIONS	YES	YES	YES
STOREROOM REQUISITIONS	YES	NO	YES
BALANCE ON HAND	YES	AVAILABLE BUT LESS ACCURATE	YES
CYCLE COUNTING	POSSIBLE	— —	YES
SHOP/PURCHASE ORDER			
BLUEPRINTS ONLY	YES	— —	— —
OPERATION ROUTE SHEETS	— —	YES	YES
STANDARD LABOR HOURS	— —	— —	YES

"FOUR WALL" - INVENTORY BALANCE KNOWN BY PART
      BUT NOT BY STORAGE LOCATION

BOH-(BALANCE ON HAND)-INVENTORY BY PART IS KNOWN ON A
      PERPETUAL BASIS BY STORAGE LOCATION

FIGURE 5–6: Net Manufacturing Resource Planning (MRP II) Systems

used in the classical MRP sense. It indicates that the net is obtained by taking the gross (or total) requirements and subtracting from it the balance on hand to obtain the net requirements. In a gross MRP system, more simplistic documents and controls are required. The bill of material is usually a single level, the master schedule is at the zero or one level of the assembly produced, and no detailed inventory records are maintained. This latter characteristic is the key to the gross system. In setting up this system, the planner does not worry about a detailed inventory master record since balances on hand are not calculated and they are not necessary. The planner is concerned only that the materials have been received as identified by receiving reports.

The net systems, in contrast to the gross system, do have balance-on-hand inventory records and thus the system is much more complicated. The key variable in a net system is the accuracy of the inventory information on record. Accuracy is defined as that percent of the records where the perpetual record level and the actual quantity in the stockroom are identical or within a close degree of accuracy. For an MRP system, this close degree of accuracy is plus or minus 5 percent for a total potential deviation of 10 percent; that is, the quantity on the inventory record (normally a perpetual quantity) is within 5 percent of the actual stockroom quantity, plus or minus. The rest of the net systems have varying document requirements, depending again on what actual level is selected.

THE FIVE MRP II SYSTEMS— FROM LEAST TO MOST COMPLEX

Let's now discuss the characteristics of each of these various systems.

1. Gross Assembly: How to Obtain the Advantages of MRP Without Extensive Recordkeeping

The purpose of a gross assembly MRP II system is to obtain the advantages of MRP (Material Requirements Planning) without all the complicated records as well as the extensive computer processing. The product being controlled must be a very simple assembly, but it can be in a made-to-order or made-to-stock environment. This system uses a single level bill of material. Any master scheduling is at the top or the number one (subassembly) level. Seldom are routing sheets used since this product is often just assembled and then shipped. A blueprint is normally used to explain the assembly operation. An inventory controller is usually concerned with vendor lead times for the bill of material explosion, but since shop lead time is minimal, normally it is considered just one week. Obviously, almost all components are purchased since there is usually very little manufacturing in terms of producing a part, as in a machine shop. It is possible (though quite difficult), if only a limited number of assemblies are involved, to manually operate a gross assembly level-one system without a computer.

2. Gross Parts: Keeping Track of Inventory for Manufacturing and Assembly Purposes Only

In a gross parts system, the complexity requires a fully indented bill of material so component parts can be identified for manufacturing and assembly purposes, but not for ordering purposes. In fact, the indented bill of material is treated as a single level bill of material when ordering material (refer to Figure 5–7). This complexity does not have balance-on-hand records because we are not concerned about tracking inventory. The first two systems use an abbreviated MRP report format usually produced by a computer (See Figure 5–8).

3. Net Assembly: Maintaining Balance-on-Hand Records

To use this system successfully, you do need an accurate bill of material at both the top level and the first indented level. Thus, the planner does have inventory balance-on-hand records for the top and subassemblies. Because more detailed inventory records are available, it is possible to allocate inventory to specific time periods based on the level controlled. Therefore, you do know the available balance on hand each period, if allocated, or just the total balance on hand in an unallocated system. The master subassembly and assembly schedules can be developed. Routing sheets are not required since they usually are controlling only a subassembly or assembly product. It is necessary to have assembly blueprints and usually these are in the assembly sequence. A computer is necessary, although manual procedures can be done if there are less

This structure may exist, for manufacturing:

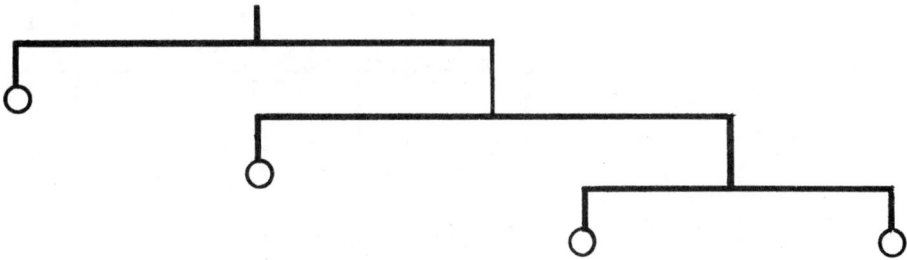

But for ordering it is treated the same as this structure:

FIGURE 5–7: Changing an Indented Bill to Single Level Bill

PART NO.	DESCRIPTION		LOT SIZE	LEAD TIME (WEEKS)	UNIT OF MEASURE	B/P AND REV. NO.	MFG'D/PURCH.	INV. CLASS	UNIT COST
RECORD REVIEW DATE	ON HAND		TOTAL ON ORDER		BACK ORDERED QTY.	PRODUCTION USAGE/WK		SERVICE USAGE/WK.	STORES LOCATION

CUSTOMER OR SALES ORDER NUMBER	GROSS REQUIREMENTS		SHIPPING DATE	BALANCE ON ORDER	ORDER DUE DATE	QUANTITY ON HAND
	ORDER	TOTAL				

FIGURE 5–8: Gross Material Requirements Planning Worksheet

than 50 subassemblies. Most subassemblies are purchased with a scrap allowance in the order quantity maintained at this level. The structure of the bill of material is very similar to that used in the level two complexity system.

The traditional MRP report format is used for this third system as well as for levels four and five.

Four-Wall Versus Balance on Hand

In a four-wall inventory storage system, such as used in the fourth system, the material is normally placed at any convenient spot within the factory when received. This could be in one or more designated storerooms plus at the point of usage or a combination of both. Irrespective of the storage procedure and locations, the inventory records show only that so many parts have been received and that so many parts are available, somewhere within the four walls of the company. Therefore, a four-wall inventory record does not indicate multiple locations of the material but only the total number available. In a balance-on-hand inventory procedure, the actual balance on hand for each storage location is known. Thus, if the identical part is stored in two different stockrooms, as well as having some in an assembly point of usage, the inventory records show the actual balance on hand for all three locations.

4. Net Parts Four-Wall: Numbers Rather Than Location Are Emphasized

In a net parts four-wall system, more inexpensive and numerous component parts are usually controlled. The only difference—but a significant one—between system four and five is the degree of inventory record accuracy. Level four requires a minimum of 90 percent record to actual accuracy. It is possible to control both manufactured and purchased parts and also to create both a master schedule and a detailed schedule. Routing sheets are required, blueprints usually exist detailing each part, and accurate vendor and shop lead times are a must. A computer is necessary.

5. Net Parts Balance on Hand: The Most Complex System Requiring Near-Perfect Accuracy

This is the most complex MRP II system. The "full cycle" MRP II system refers to the fifth system. An indented bill of material is necessary which must be very accurate, since it is exploded and netted level by level. Obviously this system is best suited for complex assemblies and more expensive component parts. The inventory records are the most complete of all five systems and—in contrast with system four—you know the balance on hand for each controlled location within the factory. Of course, allocations or reservations to specific customer orders by time period are possible. Cycle counting can be performed and you must achieve a high degree of record accuracy. Our studies indicate 97 percent is the minimum level required to make this system work. The concept of controlled stores does not necessarily mean locked stores but only that you can tell and reconcile through cycle counting the balance on hand at each location. Both manufactured and purchased parts can be controlled and, of course, a master schedule and detailed schedules are used. If the parts are manufactured, routing sheets are necessary as are blueprints for each part. As with the fourth system, detail vendor and shop lead times are a necessity.

HOW TO USE THE CLASSIFICATION TECHNIQUE TO HELP CONTROL INVENTORY ITEMS BASED ON VALUE

Once you have determined which inventory techniques you wish to use—keeping in mind that rarely will only one technique meet all your inventory control needs—then study the ABC inventory classification method. This is the one universal inventory technique for any company—large or small—and for any kind of manufacturing or service industry. All companies should use an inventory classification technique in some form or other.

Since all items in inventory are not created equal, some items are more valuable than others and deserve special attention. In the late 1800s, Vilfredo Pareto, an Italian economist and sociologist, came to the conclusion that income distribution patterns were basically the same in different countries and in different historical periods. Pareto's studies showed that a very small percentage of the total population always seemed to receive the bulk of the income. Then, in the 1940s, H. Ford Dickie of General Electric expanded on Pareto's concept and created what he called the "ABC" Inventory Classification.

Choosing Categories for Inventory Items

It matters little whether you use two categories or as many as five. The important point is that you look at your inventory items and classify them in some way. Then you control the items in inventory based on their value to you and your company. Our example here shows four groups, which we prefer to use.

> **"A" CLASS:** This refers to the one out of every ten items in inventory that usually comprises 70 percent of the dollar value of the inventory used. "A" items should get frequent attention, often daily.

> **"B" CLASS:** We call these the "20/20" items because they usually are 20 percent of the items in inventory and also 20 percent of the dollar value

of inventory used. While these parts should get less frequent consideration, they still are important and need intermediate level control.

"C" CLASS: The great bulk of items in inventory should be classified as "C," those less expensive and less utilized items. Attention should be much less frequent for these items because the safety stock protection is deliberately set high.

"D" CLASS: Some call these the "dogs," but you might prefer to refer to them as "dead" items. In any event, they have had no transaction usage (issues) for some period of time. You want to get rid of these items as quickly as possible if they will serve you no future purpose. As a rule of thumb, any item with no usage in the last six months should be classified "D" and no reordering permitted without special authorization.

Determining Inventory Classification Value

The traditional way of determining an item's inventory classification is to multiply the unit value of the item times the pieces used in a period of time (at least three months). Then, array the highest dollar summation obtained from the above, down to the lowest dollar value. Find the 70 percent of dollars issued, draw a line, and you have your "A" items that are usually the top 10 percent of the items. The next 20 percent of the items are the "Bs," and the remainder are "Cs" and "Ds," if there have been no recent issues. Figure 5–9 shows the traditional ABC Classification Report. However, a shortcut (see Figure 5–10) can be used, using only the dollar value of the item. For example, all items worth more than $100 can be classified arbitrarily as "A," those with unit costs from $25 to $99 as "B," and any item that costs less than $25 is a "C." Of course, an item with no activity in the last six months is a "D." Since these assignments are not fixed, you can later reclassify an item with ease. For example, some items that are lost through pilferage or are very fragile can be moved from a "C" to an "A" class for more special attention. Once the class has been finally established, it should remain unchanged for at least six months.

SIX WAYS TO USE THE ABC CLASSIFICATION SYSTEM

Determine Acceptable Accuracy Levels for Inventory Records

First of all, you must allocate the time spent on inventory items based on the classification. You need extremely accurate inventory records for "A" class items, that is, the perpetual record and the actual balances on hand in the stockroom should agree to a 98 percent accuracy level. For "C" items, only a

Page No. 1

ABC INVENTORY ANALYSIS

Part Number	Description	Ave. monthly usage	Unit Cost	Ext. $ amt. for period	Sequ. count	% of items accumulative totals	% of dollars accumulative totals
74–STB	Seat	501	$23.67	$11,859	1	0.1	1.86
16–YLM	Bearing	1886	3.03	5,714	2	0.2	2.79
55–BBU	Shaft	453	8.64	3,914	3	0.3	3.41

Page No. 6

PART NUMBER LISTING AND CROSS REFERENCE

Part Number	Description	Unit Cost	Sequence Reference
31–AY4	Bracket	0.66	683
74–B76	Bearing	2.43	168
98–AB9	Shaft	10.86	019

FIGURE 5–9: ABC Classification Report

SHORTCUT ABC ANALYSIS
USING PART VALUE

Standard Cost Value	$100	$25 to 99	Less than $25	Total
Percent of Parts	8%	17%	75%	100%
Number of Parts	241	510	2265	3016
Class	A	B	C	—

FIGURE 5–10: Shortcut ABC Determination

90 percent accuracy is required. For the "A" items, consider assigning one clerk to handle only these few but so important items in your inventory. You should also note that cycle counting and excess inventory identification frequency also varies depending on the class.

DESCRIPTION	*INVENTORY CLASSIFICATION*			
	A	*B*	*C*	*D*
1. Importance of record accuracy (versus actual balance)	Extremely (98%)	Good (95%)	Moderate (90%)	Good (95%)
2. Assign inventory clerks for one class only	Yes	Maybe	No	No
3. Cycle inventory counting frequency	Daily	Semimonthly	Quarterly	Yearly
4. Identification of excess inventory	Monthly	Quarterly	Semiannually	Quarterly

Approach Orders Based on Their Classification

You should work closely with your purchasing and/or manufacturing manager to set up blanket orders for "A" items and "spot buys" for "Bs" and "Cs." Remember not to order any "D" items, since you want to get rid of these "dogs." Other actions, of course, are predicated on the classification. Tell your suppliers (item 4) if it is an "A" or "B" class item because these are important to you. Observe the months' supply and turnover targets for each class.

	A	*B*	*C*	*D*
1. Basic method	Blanket Orders	Spot Buys	Spot Buys	Do Not Order
2. Frequency of orders/ releases per year	24	12	4	None
3. Maintain purchase price history record	Yes	Yes	Yes	No
4. Mark inventory class on purchase order	Yes	Yes	No	No
5. Months' supply on hand target	1	2	4	—
6. Turnover target, times per year	12	6	3	—

When to Order: Choose a Basic Method that Complements Your Inventory System

Studies indicate that at least 60 percent of all inventory systems use a blending of Reorder Point and MRP techniques. Thus, use a basic ordering method predicated on the type of inventory system necessary. Keep safety stock targets in mind and even review the frequency of the records according to the classifications.

	A	*B*	*C*	*D*
1. Basic method based on:	Forecast and MRP	MRP and Master Schedule	Reorder Point	None
2. Safety stock target	1 week	2 weeks	1 month	N/A
3. Record review frequency	Daily—as posting	Monthly	Quarterly	Semiannual

How Much to Order: Establish Guidelines According to Class

You should set up blanket orders for "A" items and release against them. Likewise, give your vendor a copy of your MRP forecast for "A" and "B" items, not necessarily a purchase order commitment, but tell your vendor what you think you will require. Consider having your inventory control supervisor review the inventory person's ordering decisions based on the class.

	A	*B*	*C*	*D*
1. Basic method	Release against blanket order	1 to 2 months' supply	2 to 4 months' supply	N/A
2. Provide forecast of requirements to vendor	Yes	Yes	No	No
3. Supervisor's review of ordering decision	Every requisition	Spot Check	None	Every requisition

Warehouse Location:
Keep "A" Items the Most
Accessible

Variations based on the class should be used in your stockroom/warehousing operations. Put those "A" items, which will have a high frequency of demand, close to the door within easy reach, your "dog" items way in the back (but still visible), and the other groups somewhere in between. Since the "A" and "B" items will have lots of receipts and issues, use random storage locations, while the "Cs" and "Ds" have fixed locations for each item.

	A	B	C	D
1. Storage location in warehouse	Near Door	Middle area	Distant area	Most distant area
2. Specific bin locations	Random	Random with locator file	Fixed by part number	Fixed by part number

---

CASE IN POINT:

Several companies had a composite inventory of $724,669, which represented 4.7 months' supply of inventory with an overall stockout rate of 9 percent. The use of the ABC (and don't forget the "Ds") brought this inventory turnover down to 2.5 months' supply or a 47 percent reduction. Stock-outs dropped from 9 to 5 percent. All of this certainly was worth the effort. The companies lowered inventory $340,000 and, at 24 percent carrying costs, saved $81,600 annually.

COMPARING ROP AND MRP:
HOW TO SELECT THE RIGHT SYSTEM
FOR YOUR COMPANY

A Reorder Point system is easier to administer; a Material Requirements Planning system, while demanding great record discipline to succeed, will permit better customer service with much less investment in inventory.

ITEM	REORDER POINT SYSTEM	MATERIAL REQUIREMENTS PLANNING
Mode	Fundamental	Advanced
Also called	Statistical inventory control	MRP
Implies	Timing based on average usage	Timing based on customer's need
Based on	Individual part	Product
Looks at	Past	Future
Requires	Manual	Computer
Plans	Have some inventory on hand and replenish as soon as depleted	Bases replenishment on master schedule
Safety stock	Higher	Lower
"How much to order" based on		
Production item	Historical or expected average usage rate	Actual current customer orders, time-phased forecast, or master schedule
Purchased item	Historical or expected average usage rate	Master production schedule
"When to order" based on		
Timing	Inventory balances	Date of actual customer or master production schedule, time-phased
Assumes	Continuous usage/sales rate in near future	Variable rate based on actual orders or forecast
Considers	Each item on its own, independent demand, individual part-oriented	Group of items, dependent demand, product-oriented
Demand	Smooth	Erratic, lumpy
Driven by	Usage	Master schedule

The traditional ROP approach has limitations. For example, requirements can be forecasted only over some fixed period of time. MRP, on the other hand, can determine and project requirements more exactly by subdividing the time period into a number of increments for which a separate forecast is provided. MRP also provides management with the ability to plan better and control inventories, maintain current open order priorities, and better determine capacity requirements. However, the following are necessary to operate successfully a Material Requirements Planning system:

1. *Computer hardware.* The volume of transactions in a large manufacturing organization cannot possibly be handled manually.

2. *Expertly designed Material Requirements Planning software.* Though the concept of MRP is extremely simple, the scope, diversity, and timing of the information to be accounted for makes the system and programming quite difficult.

3. *Accurate inventory records.* Replenishment orders generated through the system will fulfill time-phased shortages only if the shortage is projected from an accurate on-hand balance.

4. *Accurate bills of material.* MRP operates on the process of exploding the finished goods master schedule into all its component requirements to generate component replenishment orders where needed. If the bill of material is not accurate or complete, then excess component orders (or no order at all) will be generated and the master schedule of finished goods production cannot be met or excess inventories will be created.

5. *Forecast of a large percentage of customer requirements.* For most companies, at least 70 percent of the requirements for the lead time horizon must be forecasted accurately in manufacturing units.

6. *A realistic master schedule.* If finished goods and their related component requirements are in excess of capacity, it is physically impossible to meet master schedule commitments. Likewise, if MRP is building finished goods very efficiently, but the orders completed are for the wrong finished goods, nothing is accomplished except a building of overstock finished goods inventory. Therefore, considerable effort should be extended toward the forecasting and distribution techniques that will generate the master production schedule.

To select the proper system, see if you meet four basic tests for MRP—annual sales in excess of $2 million (so you can afford MRP), more than three levels on your bill of material (thus a more complex product), a forecast of 70 percent of customer requirements, and at least 90 percent perpetual book to actual balance accuracy. (Refer to Figure 5–11 for a decision tree.)

Question	Your Answer	Decision Guidelines
1. Are your company's annual sales at least $2 million a year?	----------	If "yes," go to Question 2. If "no," stop and use a Reorder point (ROP) system.
2. Does your product's bill of material have 3 or more levels?	----------	If "yes," continue to Question 3. If "no," use a ROP System.
3. Can the Sales Department provide a forecast of 70% of customer requirements, in manufacturing units, for the total lead time?	----------	If "yes," continue to Question 4. If "no," use a ROP System.
4. Is your inventory perpetual record accuracy, when compared to actual stock location quantity, at least 90%?	----------	If "yes," continue to Question 5. If "no," use ROP or a Gross (level 1 or level 2) MRP II system.
5. Is your inventory accuracy at least 97%?	----------	If "yes," select a "net" system, either level 3 or level 5. If "no," use MRP II level 4.

FIGURE 5–11: Inventory Management/MRP II System Selection "Decision Tree"

CHAPTER REFERENCE

1. Adapted from James H. Greene, *Production and Inventory Control Systems and Decisions*, 2d ed. (Homewood, IL: Richard D. Irwin, 1974), pp. 246–247.

The Art of Forecasting: Techniques for Coordinating and Controlling a Successful System

6

CHAPTER HIGHLIGHTS

Forecasting is worthwhile only if it is used properly. Although it is possible to evaluate a forecasting system by measuring its effect on related costs—carrying, ordering, and storage—misapplication of a forecast can provide unpleasant results for inventory management.

This chapter describes the key ingredients of a successful forecasting system. You'll discover why the forecast coordinator is an integral part of your system, the importance of input timing of demand, and the range of available systems. The need for feedback and management interpretation are emphasized as you review the 21 steps for preparing a productive forecasting system. You'll also learn how to select the best method of statistical forecasting for your company and how to interpret your results more accurately.

NINE KEY INGREDIENTS OF A SUCCESSFUL
FORECASTING SYSTEM

The premises of forecasting are

- The customer usage, called "demand history" for a particular item, is a good indicator of near-term future customer requirements.
- The more recent past is more significant than earlier periods.
- Whenever management knows of some factor that will significantly change the demand pattern of an item, the forecast for that item should be revised accordingly. Thus, the involvement of management is of paramount importance.
- Forecasts are required for short lead-time parts. However, for many long lead-time items, the customer bookings can be used as the actual requirement information for production planning purposes.
- Forecast errors, the difference between forecasted and actual demand, must be monitored to determine how much the forecasts are wrong and to help set extra safety stock as protection. This measure of accuracy cannot be ignored, for it helps guide forthcoming forecasts.
- A new forecast for an item should take into account the magnitude of the individual and cumulative forecast errors (+ or −) for the recent past, as well as the number of time intervals for which the accumulation of forecast errors has been consistently positive or negative.
- The demand history may exhibit a consistent pattern of increasing or decreasing volume, which is commonly referred to as a "trend"; this information must be considered. However, at least two years—and preferably three years of history—are necessary for most techniques to determine the trend.
- Rate of change and tracking are necessary elements that help make the decision to change a forecast.
- The forecasting system must monitor each item for unusual events and identify those items that require special, human intervention.

HOW THE MATRIX ORGANIZATION
FOR FORECASTING WORKS

It is impossible to have a single person, acting alone and without counsel, be successful as a forecaster. Too many variables, opinions, and events exist that preclude this possibility. In fact a good forecasting system is a classic communication system. However, a forecast coordinator is a necessary person as

I.   Overall Responsibility - The Forecast Coordinator is responsible for the coordination of sales forecasts with the manufacturing plans, while complying with company forecasting policies.

II. Responsibilities and Duties

   1. Establishes forecasts of sales and production.

   2. Coordinates forecast utilization by Sales, Manufacturing, Inventory Control and Purchasing.

   3. Establishes and recommends forecasting methods, operating policies, and procedures.

   4. Trains personnel in forecasting methodology and techniques.

   5. Keeps abreast of latest forecasting market research and publications.

III. Measures of Performance

   1. The obtaining of adequate and accurate forecasts from the Sales department by product line in manufacturing units.

   2. The discharge of responsibilities in such a manner as to publish a forecast of a majority of the customer's delivery requirements.

   3. The utilization of different statistical forecasting techniques, including seasonality and rate of change as appropriate, by product line and type of customer market.

   4. The measuring of forecast accuracy by product life cycles.

   5. The utilization of group consensus for a judgment forecast review.

   6. The creation of standard operating procedures for forecasting.

IV. Qualifications - The Forecast Coordinator should have a Bachelor's degree in Economics and a Master's in Finance, if possible. At least three years of experience as a forecast analyst and additional expertise in marketing are desirable. This person should be knowledgeable about the major types of forecasting techniques and econometric methods, including the use of forecasting procedures. The ability to understand computer programming and utilize a CRT terminal is desirable.

FIGURE 6–1: Forecast Coordinator Position Description

part of the system. Figure 6–1 provides a description of this position. Once established, this person works in a matrix organization environment considering

1. All forecasting activities should be a well-coordinated, joint effort of the primary functions involved, such as marketing and/or sales, production control, inventory management, purchasing, as well as manufacturing.

2. The methodologies used for forecasting production and inventory levels should be documented in standard operating procedures that are agreed to by all concerned departments.

3. The persons who participate in the decision process must clearly understand these procedures and their individual roles in this system.

4. All involved persons should sign off their agreement to the forecast and production plan as it is developed.

5. Use of variable (or updated) lead times by product line should be included in these calculations for adequate determination of forecast timing for the Material Requirements.

6. A statistical measurement system must be devised to determine at least quarterly the forecast error (actual sales to forecasted sales) to be used in safety stock determinations as well as identifying the need for different forecasting techniques.

7. The forecast should be made at the lowest level bill of material level where good accuracy can be obtained.

WHAT THE FORECAST COORDINATOR SHOULD KNOW ABOUT INPUT TIMING OF DEMAND AND RANGE OF AVAILABLE SYSTEMS

In addition to the above accuracy warnings and premises, the forecast coordinator must be aware of the input timing of demand (latest bookings, net shipments, or gross requirements) as well as the range of forecasting systems available. The coordinator does not have to obtain a forecast for all parts—in many companies only 70 percent of the sales need be forecasted. Many times these are the "A" inventory class items. This alone relieves enough of a burden on the production function so that the other 30 percent of less predictable customer requirements can be handled on a shorter lead-time basis with close management attention and the judicious use of safety stock. However, special company sales promotion demand should also be isolated and identified so as not to distort demand history.

In using forecasts the system should ignore small variances through the use of exception deviation control limits. Management should be sure that the program signals for human intervention when the forecast reliability drops below a predetermined level. This permits persons to use judgment on those items that are changing rapidly due to market fluctuations, promotions, or other causes. However, the system should routinely deal with the less volatile items. Blanket purchase orders and other special arrangements should permit increased flexibility in meeting customer requirements. Finally, the product life cycle must be understood since the type of forecast utilized—and the need for one—greatly depends upon this cycle timing. Figure 6–2 illustrates this cycle.

Forecasting techniques are influenced by the sheer volume of items that must be forecast. In a smaller manufacturing environment there are usually

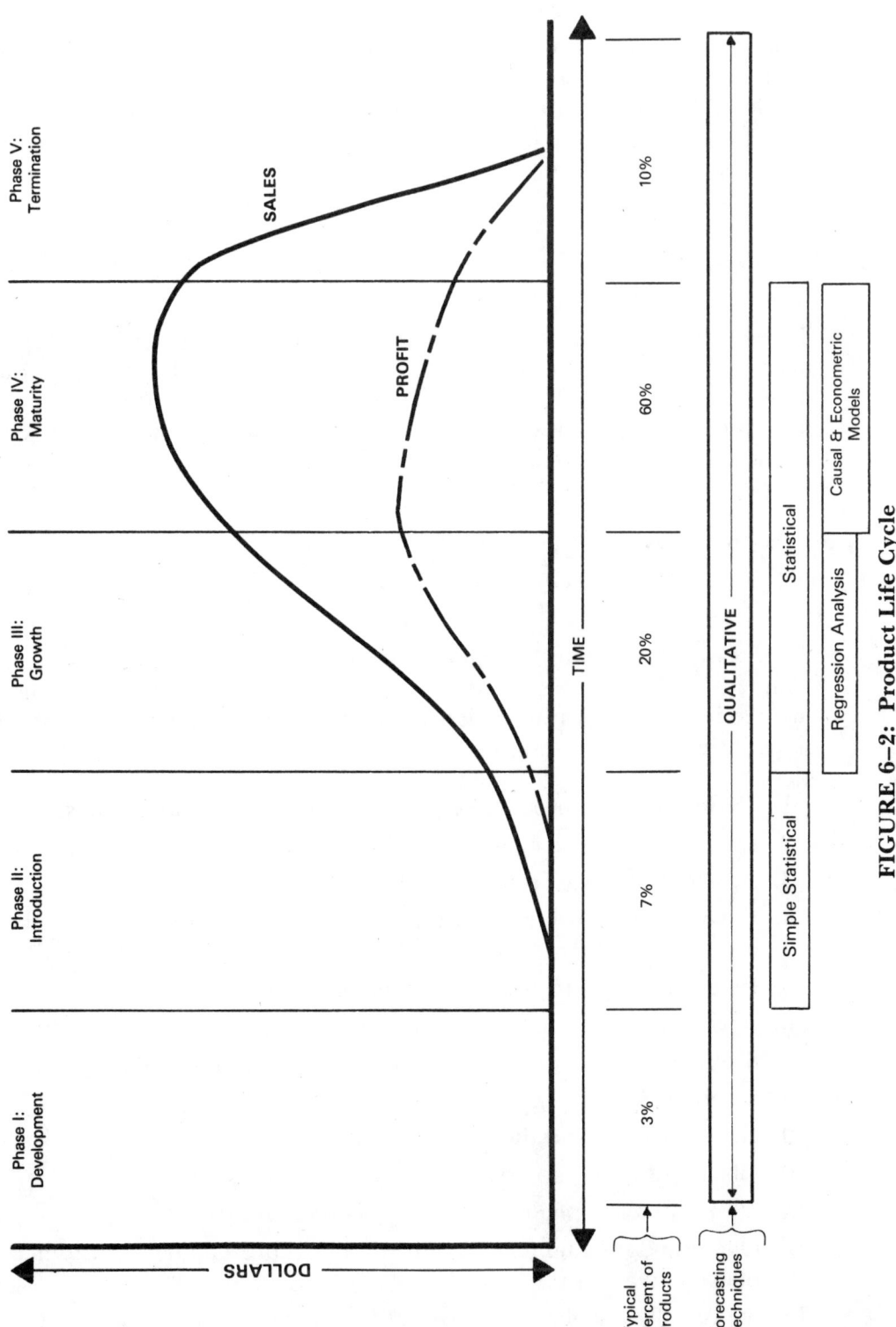

FIGURE 6–2: Product Life Cycle

a minimum of items to be forecast, perhaps no more than a few thousand, while in a large corporation some 50,000 SKUs (Stock Keeping Units) are involved. In a distribution environment, the number of items to be forecast is increased as the number of warehouse locations is increased, resulting in perhaps 100,000 or more SKUs to be forecast.

WHAT TO FORECAST

Three groups of items can be forecast: (1) sales of the product in dollars, by market and in total, (2) customer requirements in manufacturing production units, and (3) prices to be paid for materials purchased by the company. This discussion will stress procedures for group two—a forecast in pieces required by model and part number.

HOW TO PREPARE A PRODUCTIVE FORECASTING SYSTEM IN 21 STEPS

A successful forecasting system consists of a sequence of events with periodic planned feedback of results so management can use its knowledge and judgment to interpret the information and make any necessary adjustments. These steps include the following:

1. Understand the broad economic picture in the United States.
2. Establish a forecasting organization.
3. Appoint a forecast coordinator.
4. Develop and consider customer service and inventory management policies.
5. Determine the life cycle by product groups.
6. Review various forecasting techniques.
7. Select the right forecast technique(s) for your company.
8. Set timetables for input of data for forecast.
9. Get, structure, and then validate data.
10. Obtain 12 to 36 months of history to identify seasonality.
11. Study current open customer orders (bookings).
12. Obtain judgmental forecasts from sales representatives, customers, and management.
13. Statistically calculate a forecast at item detail level.
14. Analyze data obtained.

15. Study judgmentally to establish a sales and then a production forecast.

16. Measure the actual to forecast error (see Figure 6–3).

17. Interpret results, then modify the forecast.

18. Trace forecast errors, report to users, and calculate safety stock amounts.

19. Monitor the effectiveness of judgmental forecast modifications comparing to unchanged statistical forecast.

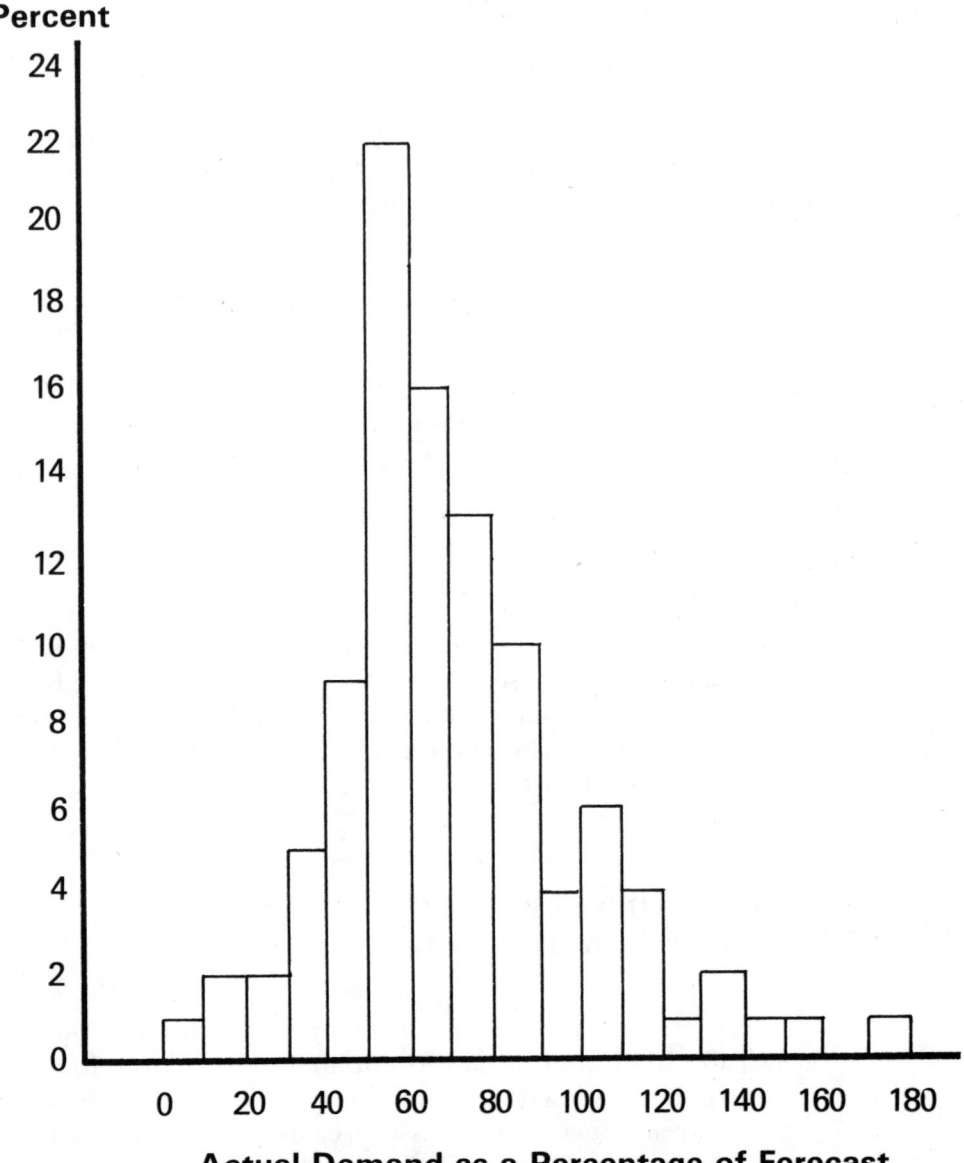

Actual Demand as a Percentage of Forecast

FIGURE 6–3: Forecast Error Analysis

20. Override forecast completely, if necessary, due to unforeseen events.
21. Input forecast information into master schedule.

TWO MAIN TYPES OF FORECASTING FOR INSIDE AND OUTSIDE COMPANY NEEDS

Two general types of forecasts can be considered.

Extrinsic (outside)

In this general type, marketing should provide an extrinsic (outside factors such as country wide economics) forecast to personnel so they can modify the intrinsic (inside characteristics like company plans) forecasts. Specifically, marketing should provide

1. forecasts for product groups, which are used to develop a production plan
2. forecasts for promotions and their impact on specific items
3. forecasts for new products
4. forecasts of the impact of competition on specific products

Intrinsic (inside)

Production should make intrinsic (inside) forecasts for specific items and options within the product groups to help detail the production plan by item as input to the master schedule. Production should quickly alert marketing if forecasts are not materializing as represented by actual customer orders. Then marketing should respond quickly by interpreting the information and helping to modify the forecasts.

THE TOP-DOWN AND BOTTOM-UP TECHNIQUES: TWO GENERAL APPROACHES

There are two approaches that may be taken from the types of forecasts available; they are called, appropriately enough, top-down and bottom-up.

In the top-down techniques, managers first forecast sales in total for the company and then divide this aggregate forecast among the various production lines and finally to individual products, thus obtaining a detailed forecast. In the bottom-up techniques, managers forecast each product or product line individually and then summarize the individual forecasts into an aggregate (total) forecast.

The top-down techniques are useful for forecasting expected annual sales of finished products and the annual usage of materials and components. This annual sales information can be used to develop the overall master production plan for items produced to stock. However, while these techniques generate information sufficient for planning inventory requirements on an annual basis, effective day-to-day control of inventory requires the more detailed forecasts of individual product lines derived from the bottom-up approach.

All of the possible forecast techniques fall into one or both of these two approaches. Figure 6–4 is a "pro and con" list of these techniques, identifying their main features. Figure 6–5 compares the cost of forecasting versus accuracy. These examples are organized by the three forecast families:[1]

1. "Qualitative" or judgmental decisions
2. Quantitative "Time Series," which are the statistical analysis
3. "Causal," those causes expressed in mathematical relationships

STATISTICAL AND MANAGERIAL FACTORS THAT CAN INFLUENCE FORECASTS

As with any automated system, characteristics of the forecasting must be specified, such as the following:

1. uses top-down and/or bottom-up forecasting
2. establishes proper level of product detail
3. incorporates management plans, such as special promotions into forecasting system
4. includes simulation capability
5. adjusts automatically and fine tunes system constants
6. updates seasonal factors
7. provides analytical reports
8. has capability to forecast new products
9. contains automatic data edit and substitution capability
10. forecasts distribution capability
11. has mass change capability
12. adjusts quickly to fundamental business changes
13. provides accurate error measurement
14. identifies extreme items that cause large forecast errors

Group	Technique	Useful for	Period Covered	Short Range Accuracy	Relative Cost	Indicates Turning Point
Qualitative (Judgment)	DELPHI	New Products & Phase Out	Short Range to Long Range	Fair to Very Good	Medium	Fair to Good
	Market Research	New Products	Short Range to Long Range	Excellent	High	Fair to Good
	Panel of Experts	New Products	Short Range to Long Range	Poor to Fair	Medium	Poor to Fair
	Visionary	New Products	Short Range to Long Range	Poor	Low	Poor
	Historical Analogy	New Products	Short Range to Long Range	Poor	Medium	Poor to Fair
Quantitative Time Series	Simple Average	Low Volume Inventory Control	Short Range to Long Range	Poor to Good	Low	Poor
	Moving Average	Production & Inventory Control	Short Range to Long Range	Fair to Very Good	Low	Poor
	Exponential Smoothing-Single	Stable Items Inventory	Short Range to Long Range	Fair to Very Good	Low	Poor
	Exponential Smoothing-Double	Trend Projection	Short Range to Long Range	Poor to Very Good	Low	Poor
	Adaptive	Trend Projection	Short Range to Long Range	Poor to Very Good	Low	Poor
	Experiencial Roughing	Trend Projection	Short Range to Long Range	Poor to Very Good	Medium	Poor
	Winters Model	Large Volume Inventory Items	Short Range to Long Range	Very Good	Medium	Fair
	Box-Jenkins	Large Volume Inventory Items	Short Range to Long Range	Very Good	Medium	Very Good
	X-II Routine	Forecasts of Sales	Short Range to Long Range	Very Good	Medium	Very Good
Causal	Regression Analysis	Phase Out Inventory	Long Range	Good to Very Good	Low	Very Good
	Econometric	Long Range	Long Range	Good to Very Good	High	Excellent
	Surveys	Long Range	Long Range	Poor to Good	High	Good
	Input/Output Models	Long Range	Long Range	N/A	High	Fair
	Econometric I/O Models	Long Range	Long Range	N/A	High	Good
	Diffusion Index	Long Range	Long Range	Poor to Good	Medium	Good
	Leading Indicators	Long Range	Long Range	Poor to Good	Medium	Good
	Life-Cycle Analysis	Long Range	Long Range	Poor	Medium	Poor to Good

FIGURE 6–4: Comparison of Forecasting Techniques

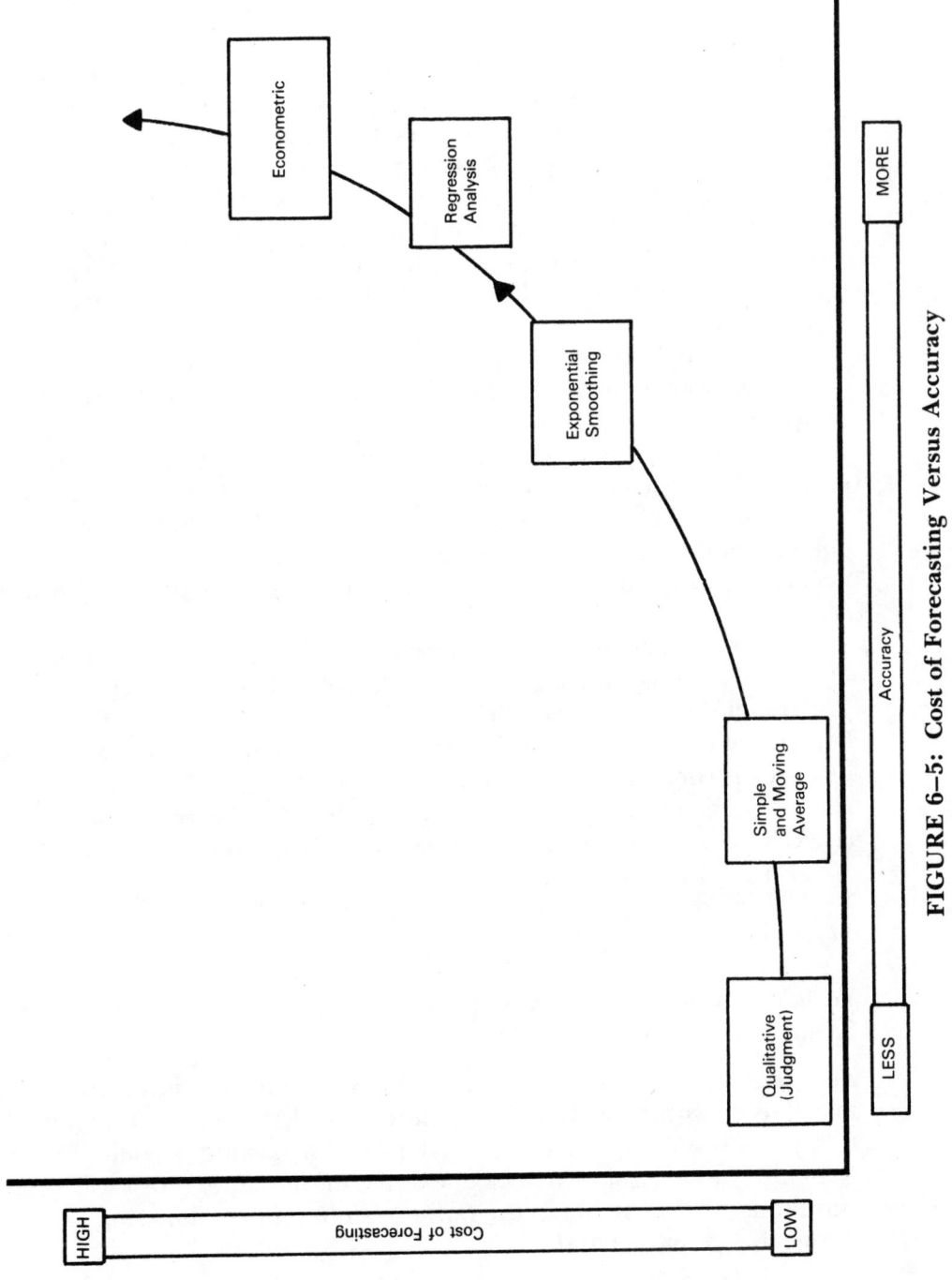

FIGURE 6–5: Cost of Forecasting Versus Accuracy

123

AN EXAMPLE OF A COMPUTERIZED
FORECASTING SYSTEM

A statistical forecasting computer model is ideally suited for carefully identifying the trend, seasonality, and average or base demand factors. It should be capable of using assistance provided by management. However, management should be able to best identify cyclic effects and strategic influences and promotions, with some assistance being provided by the computer.

In order to comprehend what can be accomplished through the use of a computerized forecasting system augmented with manual reviews, the following list of features and reports from the PLANNER system should be useful.[2]

PLANNER has the ability to meet the forecasting needs of manufacturing and distribution companies. This forecasting system maintains explicit total company sales forecasts for individual finished items and service (or repair) parts. These forecasts and related materials management parameters (for example, safety stock and reorder point) are used in the production planning, master scheduling, and procurement activities. Warehouse location (distribution point) forecasts are also maintained. Warehouse forecasts and related materials management parameters are used to plan and control distribution activities.

The system assists in the production planning, master production scheduling, and materials management activities of a manufacturing company. This is accomplished by maintaining accurate demand forecasts for both warehouses and the total company. It can be subdivided into two major areas. The first area is concerned with annual seasonal analysis, which results in seasonality parameters for use in forecasting. The second area periodically recalculates forecasts based on customer demand. Materials management parameters are also recalculated.

Features

Variable reporting frequency   The forecasting system allows for two reporting frequencies, monthly and 13 times per year.

Advanced statistical forecasting methodology   The statistical forecasting technique used within PLANNER is known as "Experiential Roughing." This technique is among the class of adaptive forecasting models. Experiential Roughing has been shown to be one of the most accurate forecasting methods because it remains stable in the face of random fluctuation, but still reacts to a true change in demand.

User forecast override   The system provides the user with complete manual forecast override capabilities. The annual forecast may be adjusted or a specific period forecast (monthly or four-week interval) may be controlled. A historical record of forecast overrides is maintained for reference purposes.

Monitor forecast model   To monitor the effectiveness of user overrides, a monitor computer control model annual forecast is maintained. The monitor model is not subject to user control. Each period the performance of the user-controlled or operational model is compared to the monitor model. Exceptions are highlighted for user management review.

Forecast error measurement   This part of the system tracks forecast performance by measuring the forecast error. This measurement is used to adjust the sensitivity of the Experiential Roughing model, to report exceptions to the user, and to calculate safety stock requirements.

Materials management parameters calculation   Two basic materials management parameters are calculated: safety stock and reorder point. The safety stock calculation is based upon historical forecast error and the level of customer service desired. The reorder point is the sum of the demand over the lead time plus safety stock. These parameters are necessary to use the "time-phased order point" master scheduling technique.

Multiple warehouses   The system can maintain a demand forecast for several warehouses and an overall "system" forecast. These warehouse forecasts are very useful in finished goods distribution planning. The "system" forecast is generally used in preparing the master schedule for a centralized production facility.

Group seasonality   The system analyzes seasonality patterns of individual items and seasonal groups. The group seasonality approach is helpful in identifying seasonality patterns that are accurate and useful for forecasting. The group seasonality feature permits seasonal forecasts for items with little or no history.

Automatic file maintenance   At the start of each period update cycle, the forecast master file is synchronized with the inventory item master/balance files so that basic item maintenance need not be entered twice. The system provides a list of all items added and deleted during the synchronization.

Mass maintenance   To assist the user in maintaining forecast parameters, a mass maintenance capability exists. This function applies maintenance of 16 different fields to items that meet a user-defined selection criteria. The selection criteria specified is based on any combination of four key identification fields.

Flexible reporting   The key forecast report can be printed in two different sequences and the appropriate level of detail may be specified by the user. Seasonal parameters can be presented in graphic format to aid in pattern analysis.

System internal controls   The system monitors processing results and sequence of processing through the system control file. This feature allows the system to alert the user to improper processing procedures and to prevent loss of key data. Effective dating of all major reports can be accomplished through the system control file.

Training Sequence

The system provides a complete training sequence for training the users in an isolated environment on all facets of the system.

Reports

All of these features are utilized to prepare four major reports:

- Forecasts and Exception—forecasts in units for individual items and forecast performance data.
- Forecast Summary—aggregate forecasts in units and extended standard costs for each product group or item value class.
- Inventory Parameter Summary—summary of the extended standard cost value associated with the calculated inventory parameters.
- Item and Class Profiles—shows the group seasonal profiles and related statistics for each volume subgroup within seasonal group; is also printed in graphical form for visual evaluation of seasonality patterns. Refer to Figure 6–6 as an example of this report.

HOW TO ENTER "DEMAND" IN THE FORECAST

"Demand" is what the customer wants. Forecasts utilize order data as: (1) bookings (by entry date), (2) shipments (by promise date), or (3) demand (by customer request date). "Shipment" data represent a measure of how many units were shipped, not necessarily what was the original customer demand. "Orders received data" may closely reflect what the demand was, depending upon how orders are accepted and the amount of cancellations (if any) prior to the order being shipped.

Orders received data may be collected by at least two methods. One method is to summarize orders during a particular time period, for example, a month; the "orders booked" during the period are without regard to requested delivery date. Another method is to summarize the orders by "requested shipment date." In this method the orders by requested shipment date for a particular period may have been booked during the current period or during one or more prior time periods. The use of both shipment and

EFFECTIVE DATE 1/03/

| PROFILE CODE 005 | CLS DESCRIPTION DIFFERENT BREAKS | ITEMS USED | 5 CLS MODELS 050000 | ITM RATIO 1.5 | VOL. RANGE 501-9999999 |
| VOLUME CODE 2 | ITEM PRINT Y | ITEMS 5 ITEMS ACPT. | 5 FILTER LEVEL .05 | CLS RATIO 1.1 | AVE. ANN VOL. 18031 |

CLASS MAD COEFFICIENTS

1	2	3	4	5	6	7	8	9	10	11	12	13
.021	.026	.022	.030	.031	.025	.023	.022	.020	.020	.016	.024	.000

CLASS SEASONAL COEFFICIENTS

1	2	3	4	5	6	7	8	9	10	11	12	13
.065	.102	.072	.130	.139	.090	.081	.073	.058	.065	.039	.085	.002

ITEM SEASONAL COEFFICIENTS

ITEM NUMBER	LOC	MODELS	YR.	LST YR. VOLUME	MAD NS	PROMOTION HISTORY	RATIO ITM	CLS	REC PC	1	2	3	4	5	6	7	8	9	10	11	12	13
2361	SYS	040000	1	6282	286	000000000000	0.0	1.4	Y	.026	.062	.110	.191	.137	.039	.110	.023	.103	.029	.059	.110	.001
0398	SYS	050000	2	48901	2176	000000000000	2.3	1.9	Y	.077	.100	.068	.138	.159	.071	.061	.072	.039	.074	.035	.106	.000
6171	SYS	070000	2	9163	549	000000000000	1.8	1.8	Y	.019	.064	.099	.146	.117	.092	.209	.053	.021	.075	.029	.065	.010
9601	SYS	020600	2	3454	182	000000000000	2.5	1.8	Y	.124	.150	.081	.111	.061	.145	.083	.053	.039	.018	.057	.065	.012
4816	SYS	020600	2	22355	652	000000000000	2.5	1.6	Y	.062	.121	.060	.088	.115	.134	.063	.104	.107	.059	.047	.040	.000

FIGURE 6–6: Item and Class Profiles

orders received indicators, as is sometimes done, may represent the best approach.

THREE POPULAR STATISTICAL METHODS: HOW TO SELECT THE BEST ONE FOR YOUR COMPANY

The task of selecting the best statistical forecasting technique for a company is not an easy one. Some of the key factors to consider are: (1) amount of calculations, (2) amount of information that must be stored from period to period, and (3) the necessity for electronic data processing equipment to perform the calculations (such as time versus cost).

Moving average and exponential smoothing methods produce far more reliable forecasts than the simple average. However, both of these methods could create some inventory control difficulties. As shown in Figure 6–6, in each month the forecast is below the actual sales. This is known as *bias* in the forecast. With this biased forecast, the amount of finished product produced will usually be less than needed and stock-outs are more likely to occur. Other more complex methods such as Double Exponential Smoothing adjust the forecast to changing conditions and reduce the amount of bias.

ENTERING NONSTATISTICAL DATA: THE EFFECTIVENESS OF MULTILEVEL AND COMBINATION FORECASTS

In numerous environments, the most effective forecasts are integrated, combining judgmental methods, time series and, perhaps, curve-fitting (economic) methods. Sometimes this is called entering nonstatistical data into the calculated forecast. It is the inputting of sales management information, along with the historical forecast, an economic forecast and trend analysis for subjective but highly experienced judgment. This procedure is illustrated in Figure 6–8 as tied into the corporate planning pyramid.

HOW TO OBTAIN MORE ACCURATE RESULTS: INTERPRET, THEN MODIFY

Instead of continuously refining the forecasting techniques, time often can be spent more valuably reviewing and revising the forecast and responding to forecast error input. Frequently, field personnel, which includes purchasing, marketing, and manufacturing representatives, are aware of circumstances that can affect sales volume in the near future. For example, customers may

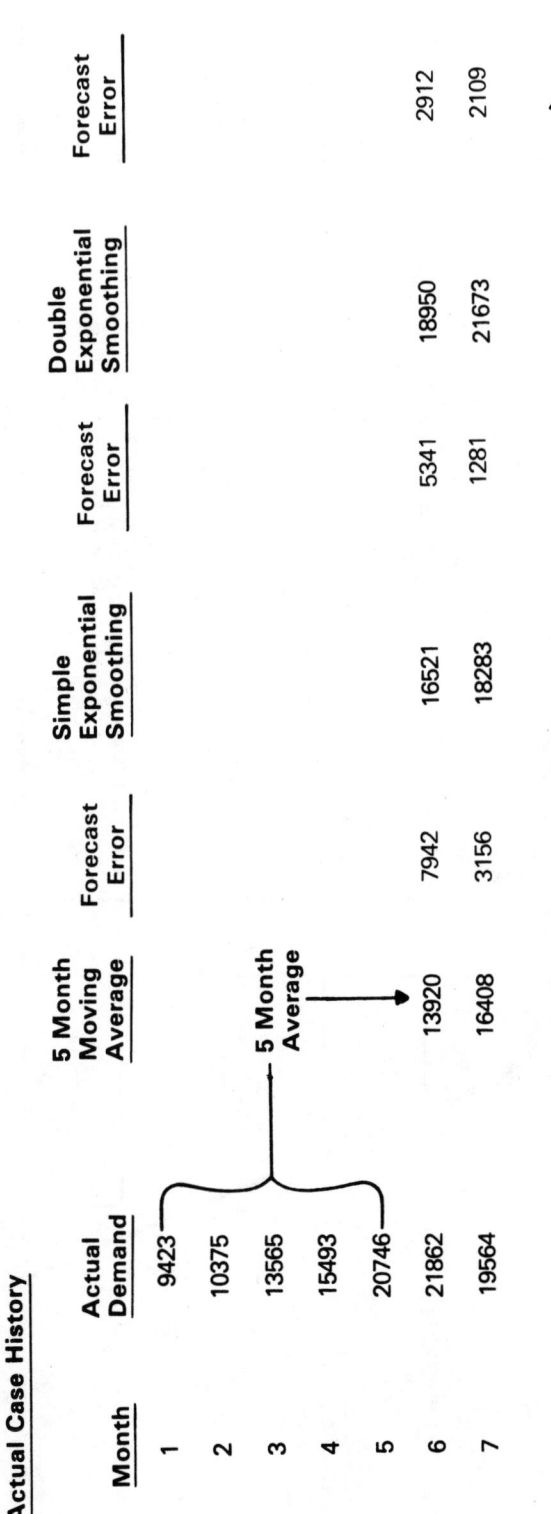

FIGURE 6–7: Comparison of Three Forecast Techniques

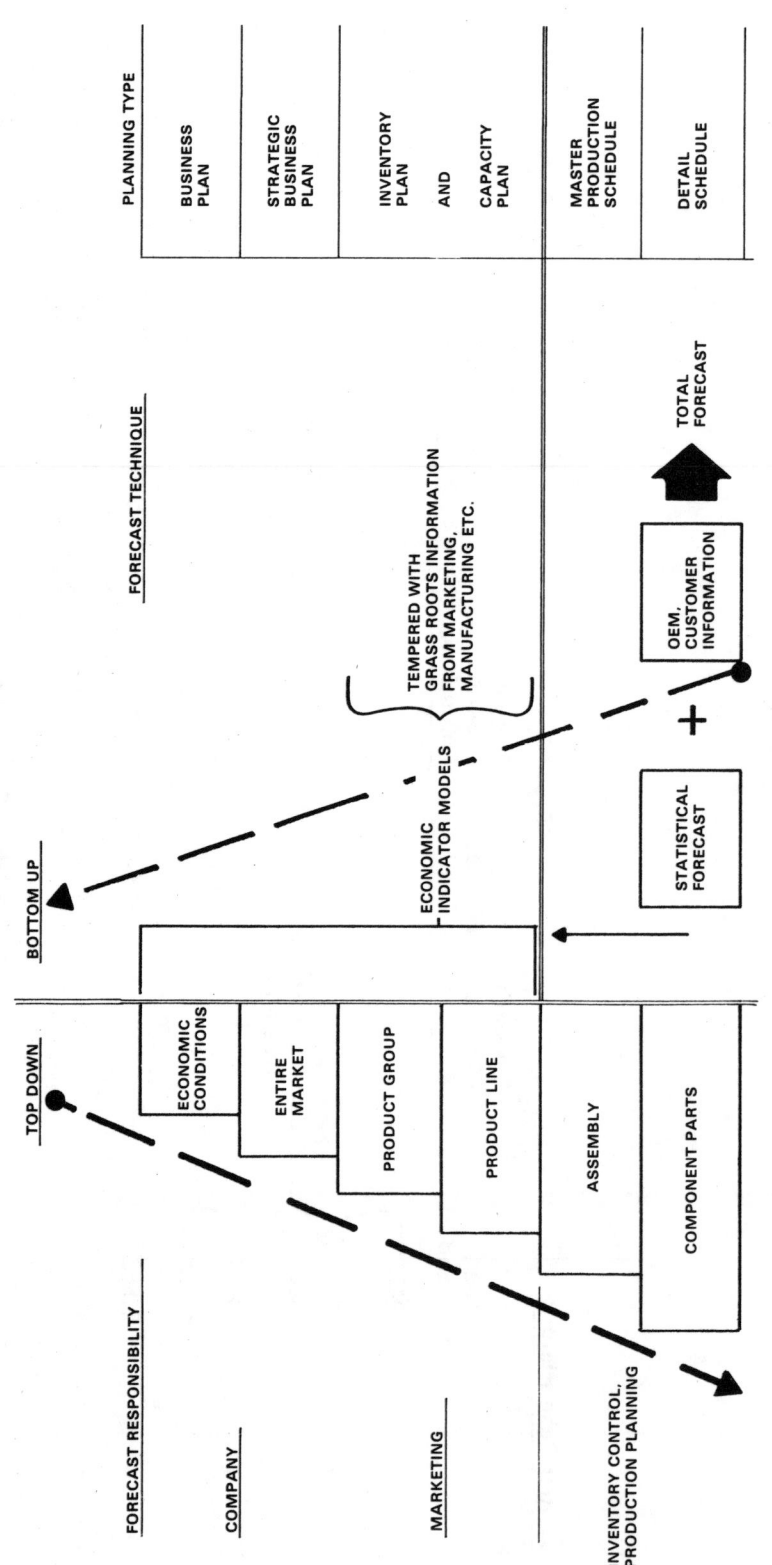

FIGURE 6–8: Combination of Forecasts

130

experience unanticipated breakdowns or possibly have scheduled overhauls of major facilities. Such downtime can lead to the cancellation or delay of orders that are based upon the statistical forecast. It is also possible that vendor lead times can become significantly extended. The receipt of such information provides the basis for overriding the system forecast. Such user intervention is necessary to obtain a forecast that is meaningful. Figure 6–9 illustrates the judgmental and statistical sequence, while Figure 6–10 is the Review Report Worksheet.

A QUALITATIVE QUARTERLY FORECAST PROCEDURE

In many manufacturing environments, a judgmental method can be quite valuable. One such procedure is described below:

1. **Scope.** This standard practice pertains to the method of establishing a quarterly forecast that will be utilized as the primary input into the production plan. This forecast is to be made for all finished assembly part numbers and any replacement parts for which a forecast is deemed necessary.

2. **Purpose.** The purpose of this standard practice is to provide the major tool for production planning by which the creation of an assembly shop order will be based. The overall intent is to have the forecast updated as often as necessary for each part or assembly on the forecast. Experience indicates that this updating will probably be necessary on a quarterly basis for at least one-third of the items on the forecast.

3. **Procedure.** The forecast worksheet is the form to be used to provide this forecast. This form is to be completed by the tenth of each month for each assembly or part number that has had a substantial deviation from the previously established forecast.

   a. The sales manager is responsible to provide the basic forecast to the Inventory Control Department on a quarterly basis. The input for this forecast will initially be based on the bookings that are anticipated from the customers for each model number. Until several months of history have been developed, the input to the forecast will be based on the shipments expected and not upon the bookings anticipated.

   b. The Sales Department is to provide the initial forecast by model number and this information is to be posted to the master schedule. The forecast is to be a projection for the current month and the next two months for a total 90-day projection.

POSITION	Sales Engineer	District Manager	Product Sales Manager	General Sales Manager	Vice President Mfg.	P&IC Manager
DUTIES	Obtain basic information by sales district / Include options and variables / Note any trends and potential new customers	Consolidate district forecast / Detail by model plus variables and options	Recommend and assist in preparation of forecast	Determine forecast / Publish after approval	Approve forecast	Check forecast
TYPE OF DATA	Units	Units and Dollars	Units and Dollars	Units and Dollars	Units and Dollars	Units
TYPE AND AMOUNT OF MODIFYING	None	None	None	Yes - by Percent	Yes - by History	Yes - by Judgment
PAPER FORM	Memo	List	Memo	Form	Form	Form
FREQUENCY	Quarterly / Monthly if appropriate	Quarterly / Monthly if appropriate	Quarterly / Monthly if appropriate	Quarterly	Quarterly	Monthly

(Between General Sales Manager and Vice President Mfg. columns: **CALCULATE STATISTICAL FORECAST**)

FLOW OF DATA →

FIGURE 6–9: Information Sequence for a Qualitative Review of a Statistical Forecast

PART IDENTIFICATION

Commodity Code No.	Product Line	Assembly No.	Part Number	ABC Class	Part Description
12	CEPTmobile	16719	1671	A	Frame-Welded

HISTORICAL INFORMATION

Avg. Mo. Usage (shipments)			THIS YEAR (YTD) (March)			
3yr. Avg.	2 yr. Avg.	Last Year	Average Monthly Bookings	No. of Customers	No. Of Orders	No. Of Stockouts
423	805	863	243	16	163	17

CURRENT INFORMATION

Reorder Point	Safety Stock	Reorder Quantity/EOQ	
81	18	123	
Forecast Error	Trend Factor	Group Seasonality	Alpha
26%	None	None	0.1

FORECAST BY MONTH

J	F	M	A	M	J	J	A	S	O	N	D
1	2	3	4	5	6	7	8	9	10	11	12

COMPUTER CALCULATIONS

—	—	—	81	109	62	83	79	87	93	97	—

TO BE PREPARED: MANUAL FORECAST

FIGURE 6–10: Forecast History Report and Worksheet

c. The Production Planning Department is responsible to accumulate the actual bookings by model number and to post this on an "as-received" basis to the planning board. The document to update the planning regarding new orders is the new orders summary list.

d. At the conclusion of each quarter, the Production Control Department is responsible for reviewing the planning and determining the percent of final assembly numbers whose bookings have deviated from the forecast by more than 20 percent for these items, a new three-month forecast is to be calculated and provided to Production Control by the Sales Department.

HOW FORECASTS INFLUENCE
THE CONTROL OF SAFETY STOCK

If we were able to predict the customer requirements with a high degree of accuracy, there would be no need for safety stock. But since all forecasts are wrong (at least a little), then we use extra material that is called safety stock as a cushion against unexpected (not accurately forecasted) customer needs. The extent of safety stock is also related to customer service goals, as explained in Chapter 2.

Forecasts are a mechanism to control inventory, with safety stock requirements very sensitive to forecast error, while working stock requirements are less sensitive. To control the safety stock, account must be taken of the demand characteristics, usually expressed as the forecast error of the item under consideration. This error is the inherent variability in the sales (never precisely known, always estimated), the degree of unreliability in the seasonality (never precisely known, always estimated), and the fallibility of the whole forecasting mechanism (never precisely known, always estimated). The best relatively simple way to set safety stock (and hence protect against stock-outs) is to use the MAD as the control.

THE FORECAST INPUT TO MASTER
SCHEDULE

The output of the forecasting system is the input to the master scheduling system. This output of a detailed forecast for a specific product is illustrated in Figure 6–11, which is a combination master schedule for January through April (based on actual customer orders in the plant) and a forecast for the May through December period (prepared on a judgmental basis) using the previously described quarterly forecasting procedures.

CHAPTER REFERENCES

1. J. C. Chambers, S. K. Mullick, and D. D. Smith, *An Executive's Guide to Forecasting*, (New York: J. Wiley & Sons, 1974). Copyright © 1974 by J. Wiley & Sons. Reprinted by permission of John Wiley & Sons, Inc.

2. "The PLANNER System for Statistical Forecasting," Ernst & Whinney, Chicago, IL, 1981.

CATEGORY \ MONTH	1 JAN	2 FEB	3 MAR	4 APR	5 MAY	6 JUN	7 JUL	8 AUG	9 SEPT	10 OCT	11 NOV	12 DEC	TOTAL
PRODUCT — CEPTMOBILE STANDARD MODEL: EXPRESSED IN ASSEMBLY MODELS													
DATE PREPARED — DECEMBER 31													
MASTER SCHEDULE • MATERIAL AVAILABLE • TOOLING REQUIRED • MATERIAL ON ORDER													
TOTAL BOOKINGS													
FORECAST • MAJOR CUSTOMERS — — — — — • OTHER CUSTOMERS													
TOTAL FORECAST													
GRAND TOTAL													

FIGURE 6–11: Combination Master Schedule and Forecast

Taking the Count: How to Obtain More Efficient Records Through the Cyclical and Annual Physical Inventory

7

CHAPTER HIGHLIGHTS

There is a close correlation between the accuracy of a company's physical inventory and the effectiveness of controlling inventory over the balance of the year. There is no one secret to taking a good physical inventory. This chapter details the procedures that must be planned and executed well in advance in order to have a true physical count of the goods within a company.

You'll find

- tips on how to motivate staff for taking a physical inventory count
- five choices of inventory counting methods—and why the least desirable choice is still the preferred one for most companies
- a six-step process for cycle counting
- when using the statistical sampling method is most helpful
- 31 ways to improve your annual physical inventory planning

You'll also learn how to minimize errors by consolidating inventory documents and what are acceptable error rates.

TAKING INVENTORY: WHY BOTHER?

A typical annual physical inventory in a larger company requires the involvement of 80 salary and 500 hourly employees totaling 13,920 hours during three days. A sizable investment is made both in time and money. The ideal team size is one captain for each twelve counting persons. The ratio of auditors, both company and outside accountants, to inventory counters, should be one to thirty people. Thus, an inventory is expensive to take, often costing one dollar for every $200 that has to be counted. Careful planning is necessary. Cycle counting, that is, counting selected items each day (or week), still requires about the same total expense, although it has the advantage of not interrupting production.

Since no one likes to take inventory and it costs so much to count the goods, why bother with counting the material? Because of two equally important reasons:

1. The company has to validate that the dollar asset on the balance sheet called "Inventory Investment" is fairly stated.

2. The company needs to have accurate inventory balance-on-hand records to achieve successful customer-order delivery.

HOW TO MOTIVATE STAFF FOR
THE PHYSICAL INVENTORY COUNT

- Create an organization for taking the physical that clearly defines "who is boss" in the chain of command (see Figure 7–1 for an example). It should be noted that an accounting person is never the boss; the financial people become fully responsible only when the count is completed, although they have an important role to approve the inventory program as it is developed.

- Train employees well in advance of the "big day," including use of visual aids to explain inventory documents and procedures.

- Get top management involved in the actual counting and checking. Not only may they be surprised by how much they learn, but it also will help break down communicating and understanding barriers.

- Have spare crews ready if counting gets behind schedule.

- Provide small "thank you" motivational items such as donuts, coffee, music, and so forth to the inventory personnel.

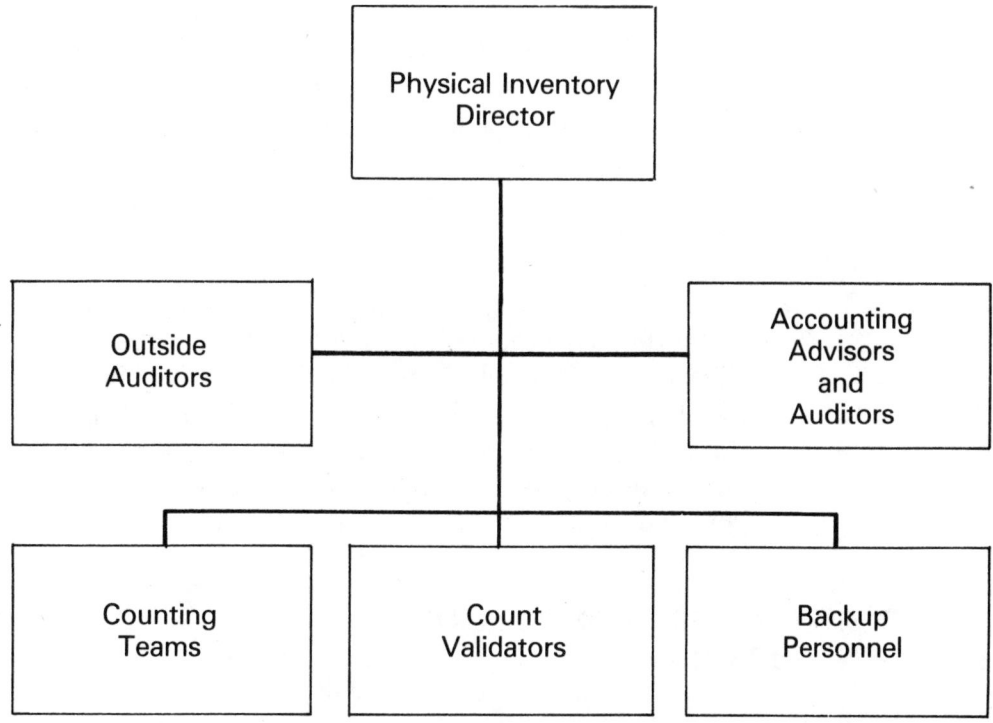

FIGURE 7–1: Physical Inventory Organization

FIVE POSSIBLE INVENTORY COUNTING
METHODS FROM WHICH TO CHOOSE

A company does not have to conduct an annual physical inventory; provided it can assure its accountants that it can accurately validate this asset by other means. To eliminate the annual counting, the perpetual records, which list the quantity in inventory, must be quite accurate. For inventory, accuracy that means, on an item-by-item basis, the perpetual balances and the actual amount in the storage area must be within 5 percent of each other. The actual choices of inventory counting methods in a sequence of most to least desirable are:

1. Expense items as received so the company has no "official" inventory, although this can cause other control, financial, and information problems. Less than 1 percent of the companies use this method, which is not in accordance with Generally Accepted Accounting Principles.

2. Maintain highly accurate perpetual records so one can take a list of quantities on hand, price them, and obtain the dollar value. Only about 1

percent of the inventory systems are this accurate. In this procedure, the auditors can satisfy themselves as to the accuracy of the inventory by testing the perpetual records, rather than observing a full physical.

3. Set up a statistical sampling method that, by monitoring cycle counting error rates, permits an annual dollar valuation based on the determined error of the perpetual to actual records. About 5 percent of the companies use this method.

4. Establish cycle counting procedures that help identify the causes of error, make the record balances more accurate and, eventually, should lead to use of the statistical sampling method described in number three. Today 15 percent of the companies have good cycle-counting procedures.

5. Conduct the annual physical inventory count. While the least desirable, this method is performed by an estimated 79 percent of companies and enables a once-a-year reconciliation of perpetual, actual, and accounting book balances.

THE PREINVENTORY COMPUTERIZED PLANNING REPORT

If a company has had unsatisfactory physical inventories in terms of missed items, inaccurate counts, and so forth, it usually requires three years (three tries) to achieve good annual physical inventory or six months (twenty-six tries) to set up a successful weekly cycle counting procedure.

Thus, the problems identified during one physical should be used to make the next one better. Figure 7–2 is the Preinventory Planning Report; it lists by location the time required, personnel used, discrepancies and problems discovered during the course of the last inventory, and provides a schedule by which to do better the next time.

Since the types of items can be counted with widely different means—bearings, light bulbs, horses, money, hardware, portable tools, capital equipment, furniture, iron ore in a mountain, and so forth—planning will differ depending on the commodity groups and storage method.

TECHNIQUES FOR FASTER AND MORE PRECISE COUNTING

In the good old days we counted each item by hand, sometimes spending more money to count the item than it was worth. Today several techniques are available that allow for quicker and more accurate counting. The initial evolutionary step was in the use of mark-counting pens, then mechanical scales, followed by the development of electronic scales—some so accurate a

LAST PHYSICAL AND YTD RESULTS

Type	Items Counted	No. Tags Used	Total Quantity	Total $ Value
Purchased Components				

	COUNTING ERROR RATES		BOOK TO PHYSICAL ADJUSTMENTS	
	% Item	% Tags	% $	Net %	Absolute %

Location Storeroom B				

Commodity Group(s) 33 and 34	Time Required to Count (Total Hrs)		No. of YTD Transactions	

THIS YEAR'S SCHEDULE

Day(s)	Names of Personnel Assigned	
	Captain(s) _____	
_____	Counters _____	
Time: Hours _____	Checkers _____	
Start _____		
Finish _____	Auditors _____	
No. of Persons Required _____	Back up _____	

FIGURE 7–2: Pre-Physical Inventory Planning Report

feather can be weighed. Then voice input to tape recording devices were introduced—tapes that can be "listened to" by keypunch operators or even by computers. More recently, the product itself is being marked with bar codes, magnetic stripes, or optical character recognition number and names. These codes and other similar methods (illustrated in Figure 7–3) allow inventory to be taken while driving a forklift truck down a warehouse aisle, with a hand-held microprocessor-based portable data terminal, with a bar code laser reader, or with an optical mark reader.[1] The latest development uses radio frequency identification which "reads" electronically stored data from an "identification tag" on the item.

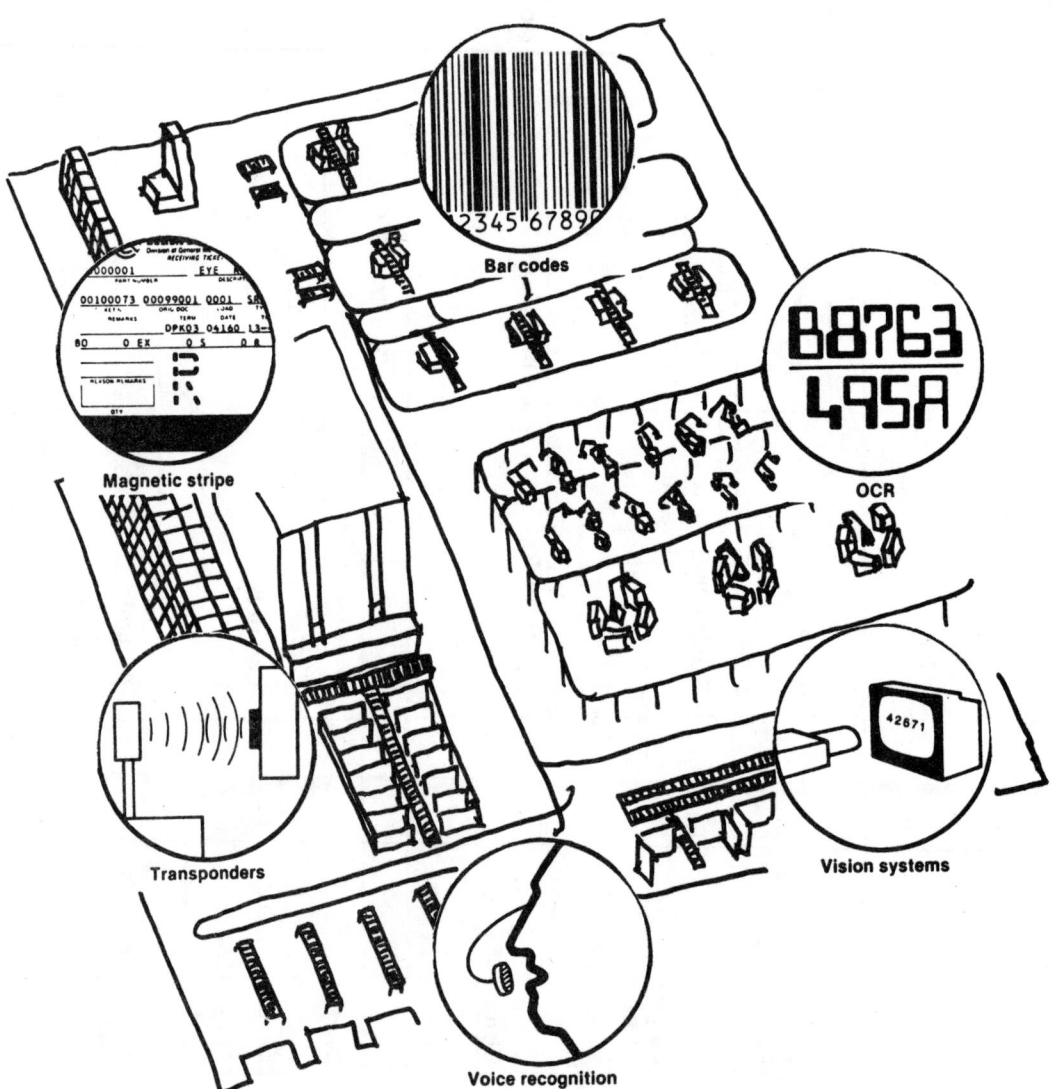

FIGURE 7–3: Electronic and Voice Character Recognition

You do not even have to do your own counting; outside services are available that will perform the task for your company!

Hand vs. Scale Counting

The R.G. CEPT Company approached the dilemma of inventory counting by using a mixture of techniques. Depending on the part size, they used

- hand counting for parts that are large, few in number, difficult to move, heavy
- scale counting for parts that weigh .01 oz. to 40 lbs., numerous items, in containers of uniform weight
- estimating for inexpensive items, such as fasteners.

A well-trained person counting and a calibrated scale both have about the same error rate—½ of 1 percent.

CYCLE COUNTING: A SIX-STEP PROCESS

The value of cycle counting is twofold: (1) a company is able to identify errors through transaction analysis in their inventory management system, then taking corrective action while gaining insight into problems, and (2) inventory record balances can be updated without having to lose production time due to plant shutdown for the physical counting. Cycle counting is not cheap—the cost about equals the direct labor cost of the complete annual physical inventory. However, the perpetual records are consistently more accurate throughout the year and the other costs and problems associated with plant and warehouse shutdowns are reduced.

The steps to cycle count are

1. *Select the items to be counted*, with the frequency based on inventory class; for example, "A" items once every week, "B" items every month, and "C" items twice a year.
2. *Take the actual count* using manual, mechanical, and/or electronic means as appropriate, making certain all locations for the same part have been included.
3. *Reconcile the actual count to the perpetual record* using plus or minus discrepancy control limits based on 1 percent for "A," 3 percent for "B," and 5 percent for "C" items, after first checking that all issue and receipt documents have been considered.
4. *Recount any discrepancies* that exceed the differential control limits.

5. *Analyze transactions to detect cause of errors*, such as part number or quantity transposition, lost receivers, or "midnight" requisitions; then plug the procedure gap!

6. *Report any adjustments made to the Accounting Department*, so that the inventory control record balance is the same as the accounting book balance.

One of the decisions necessary in cycle counting is how often to count an item. The best method, for many companies, utilizes a combination of the number of issues of an item, the frequency of receipt of additional material (either manufactured or purchased) and the A, B, or C inventory classification. This procedure recognizes that the more times an item is handled, the more chance for an error, plus the fact the amount of inventory is lowest prior to the time additional material is received. Thus, all "A" items could be cycle counted upon the next receipt after any combination of five issues and receipts, "B" items after ten such transactions, and "C" items after twenty stock movements. During the last three months of the year, any items not previously counted should be cycle checked. The actual counting can be done by specifically trained personnel, working before the first shift, at night, or even over the weekend.

An important aspect of cycle counting is enhancing the procedure for those items that are error-prone. Figure 7–4 is a computerized analytical report, organized for manual annotation of error cause in the far right column.

WHEN TO USE THE STATISTICAL SAMPLING METHOD FOR MONITORING INVENTORY RECORDS

In certain instances auditors will accept a year-end sample of the perpetual records, but they have to be assured these records are highly accurate and are monitored during a year. This procedure adopts a philosophy of monitoring the error in the records by taking monthly statistical samples. The sample estimates the difference between the total perpetual record value and the actual value of the inventory. This estimated difference is monitored over time. If it remains in an acceptable range, no action is needed. If it becomes too large, the sample size can be expanded or 100 percent inventories, in problem areas, can be taken to correct the records. At year-end, the auditors need to observe only a test sample inventory and review the statistics in order to adjust the book value, if necessary.

A statistical sampling system is more practical where the perpetual inventory records are maintained on a computer. Besides the actual counting, the system has three elements:

1. A computer program performs the sample selection using the perpetual inventory file, stratifies the inventory, and selects parts to be sample counted in categories called "strata."

Inventory Type Purchased Components   Stores Location Area 7

Period Covered January - March

Commodity Group Code No. 13   **Commodity Group Name** Axle Assembly

Part A - Item Detail

Part No.	Description	Inv. Class	U/M	Unit Cost	Record Quantity	Actual Count	Qty. Variance	$Variance	Probable Error Cause

Part B - Summary Totals of Errors

Net Units	Net Percent	Absolute Units	Absolute Percent

Net $	Net $ Percent	Absolute $	Absolute $ Percent

FIGURE 7–4: Cycle Count Detail and Analysis Report

2. Reconciliation procedures are followed to adjust the records as they exist during the exact time of the count. Reconciliation can be difficult, since the paper transaction may be either before or after actual receipt or shipment. However, this is crucial to having accurate sample data and is a significant portion of the cost of sampling.

3. Analysis of the sample inventory data and calculation of the estimated error are performed by a computer program.

Two other features can be included in this method to increase its usefulness. Although executives are primarily concerned with the net difference between the records and the actual inventory, all differences are costly. Overstated records risk possible stock-outs and understated records cause working capital to be tied up unnecessarily in inventory. A total (absolute error) is computed by the program in addition to the net error. The absolute error is valuable to the inventory manager in measuring performance, as discussed in Chapter 1.

Under certain circumstances, samples can be modified or biased to increase their corrective effect by including a disproportionately high number of items with errors. Proper statistical analysis can remove this bias so that both estimation and correction objectives can be achieved simultaneously.

31 WAYS TO IMPROVE YOUR ANNUAL PHYSICAL INVENTORY PLANNING

1. Announce the inventory date in a memorandum four months in advance and stress that all persons must participate. Then send a reminder memorandum four weeks before the actual date.

2. Make attendance at the inventory mandatory for both salaried and hourly employees. If it is necessary to count on a Sunday, explain carefully the importance to all employees.

3. Have each inventory captain assigned to a specific area and prepare a timetable as to when work is expected to be finished.

4. Ask each captain to select their own counters whenever possible. If possible, have the counters work in the area where they are most familiar with the parts.

5. Work-in-process inventory is the most difficult (and slowest) to count, so prepare well in advance for the shop.

6. Conduct training sessions in advance, explaining the value and actual procedures of a good inventory, since an untrained person has about a 2 percent count error rate. Hold an additional class for inventory captains.

7. Identify the part numbers before actual counting, since this is one key to success.

8. Carefully mark "Do Not Inventory" and segregate, if possible, all material that should not be counted such as consigned materials or items received after a designated cutoff time.

9. Circle the part number on shop papers in a bright color before the inventory if there is any chance of confusion.

10. Stack up or otherwise neatly arrange as many items as possible to encourage accurate and speedy counting.

11. Another key ingredient is a well-designed inventory list for cycle counting or the annual physical that can be completed with a minimum number of errors. Figure 7–5 is one example of such a computer list, which must be numbered for control purposes.

12. Prior to the inventory, have several housekeeping tours with the financial and manufacturing managers to assist in the cleanup for the inventory.

13. Put the material in clean containers as much as possible prior to the inventory.

14. Clean up the shop well in advance of the inventory and assign duties for area cleanups to specific individuals.

15. Run an extra copy of the shop order document overprinted for "inventory only." Use it to identify material in process by placing the paper with the material.

16. Remove any scrap, old signs, paper, and so on from the shop prior to inventory.

17. When a complicated assembly has to be inventoried, have a copy of the bill of material available to be used as a parts checklist.

Physical Inventory Date June 30   **Inventory List No.** 0074

Material Storage Area North Stores   **Assigned Foreman** M. Hammer

Line No.	Bin/Rack Location	Part Description	Part No.	Correct No.?	Unit Measure	Quantity Counted	Checked By
0074-1	A-1	Axle	2361		ea.		
0074-2	A-2	Wheel	0398		ea.		
0074-3	A-2	Battery	1092		ea.		
0074-4	A-3	Canopy	0011		ea.		
0074-5	A-4	Bumper	5549		ea.		
0074-5	A-4	Bench Seat	3146		ea.		

FIGURE 7–5: Computer Numbered Inventory List

18. Identify the parts at least ten days in advance of the inventory.

19. Precount various areas where there is a slow turnover of material and then seal these areas when completed.

20. Post large inventory area number location signs to eliminate confusion.

21. Stop issuing raw material and component parts to production prior to the inventory.

22. Close the Shipping and Receiving Department at midnight the day before the inventory, and notify your customers and suppliers of this plan well in advance.

23. Carefully segregate each area within the building, even drawing chalk marks on the floor if necessary, to identify the boundaries between adjacent areas.

24. Pass out inventory tags and lists in numerical sequence by area, and keep a close record of what documents numbers are issued to which captain.

25. Use a one-person counting "crew." This is much faster than a two-person crew, still accurate, and much less wasted time is spent chatting.

26. Make sure the part number is written completely on the inventory tag or list.

27. Be sure the unit of measure identification, if other than "each", is very clearly specified such as pounds, dozen, feet, etc.

28. Counting errors vary depending on the distance by which items are stored from the floor—the error runs about 2 to 3 percent for material stored in low shelves, 1 percent if three to six feet high (everyone likes to count easily reached parts), and 5 to 12 percent if stored where one has to reach up or use a ladder.

29. Audit each area separately and release a section only when approval is given by the auditors. Don't hurry this step, even if running late.

30. Never, never permit movement of material during the inventory unless you can accept the 10 to 20 percent error rate.

31. Counting accuracy decreases on the last day and when working overtime with an error rate of from 5 to 10 percent. Rather than rush, lock up a room or separate area and finish the count the next morning.

TEN MAJOR TOPICS TO INCLUDE IN YOUR INVENTORY INSTRUCTIONS

Irrespective of the type of physical inventory used—perpetual record list, stratified sample, cycle count, annual physical or a blend of techniques—a set of carefully worded instructions is desirable. The contents of this document should include these ten topics, and the suggested sub–topics. Appendix B contains an example of a complete set of physical inventory instructions.

List of major sections and contents

I. *Scheduled dates and times*

Date and exact hours
Overtime possibility/compensation

II. *Assignments by specific areas*

Inventory director
Corporate observers
Controllers
Counters
Checkers
Outside auditors

III. *Material to be inventoried*

Returnable containers
Tooling and material on consignment off-site
Items not to be inventoried

IV. *Preinventory preparation*

Shop cleanup
Notification of shutdown
Shipments and receipts cut off
Scrap removal

V. *General instructions*

Inventory headquarters
Inventory priority/sequence by area
Master inventory list
Progress reports of completion by area
Answers to questions during inventory
Time reporting by area

VI. *Specific instructions*

Special material counting procedures
Master routing or bill of material files
Restrictions of material movement during inventory
Scale use instructions and calibration
Unidentified material handling and tagging
Last-minute issues (requisitions)
Emergency shipments or receipts during inventory
Emergency counting crews

VII. *Inventory list, tag use, and control*

   Types of inventory tags, cards, and lists
   Printed inventory tags/lists
   Unit of measures
   Issuing of inventory documents

VIII. *Counting and tag writing*

   Procedure, count extension, separating, sorting, and filing
   Examples of properly filled-out documents
   Bulk counting, packaged goods counting
   Partially filled container counting
   Method to count same part in two different areas
   Last completed operation determination
   Partially assembled units
   Making tallies or calculations on back of tag
   Weight of inventory containers (tare)
   Use of decimals
   Obsolete and slow-moving items
   Action to change tag if wrong count or description is found
   Recounting request procedure
   Voiding inventory documents

IX. *Processing of documents*

   Comparison of A and B class item counts to perpetual records
   Posting of count to inventory control records

X. *Cleanup, report, and planning for next year*

Three points of note: First, a brief set of instructions—which can be put in the pocket of the inventory personnel—is most valuable; refer to Figure 7–6 for one example. Second, many persons do not write clearly, so continue to stress the need for legibility using check blocks whenever possible. Third, inventory job description of the primary inventory positions serve to clarify duties; these also can be abbreviated.

CONSOLIDATING INVENTORY DOCUMENTS TO MINIMIZE ERRORS

The overall goal is to make the inventory documents in as clear a design as possible to minimize errors. Remember that all of the thousands of items counted subsequently get screened for completeness, consolidated with other identical items, then cost extended in accounting; all by a combination of computerized and manual methods.

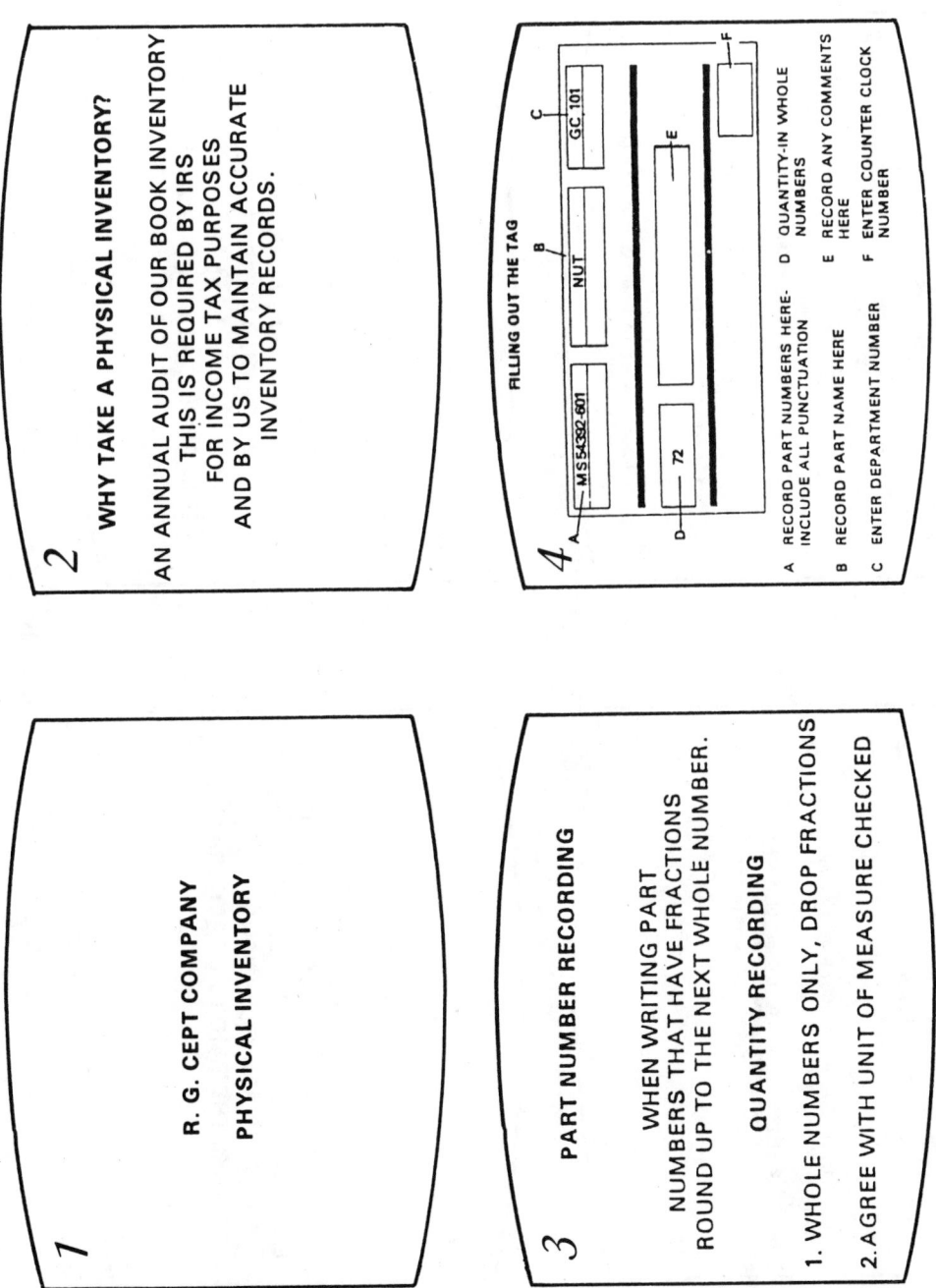

1

R. G. CEPT COMPANY

PHYSICAL INVENTORY

2

WHY TAKE A PHYSICAL INVENTORY?

AN ANNUAL AUDIT OF OUR BOOK INVENTORY
THIS IS REQUIRED BY IRS
FOR INCOME TAX PURPOSES
AND BY US TO MAINTAIN ACCURATE
INVENTORY RECORDS.

3

PART NUMBER RECORDING

WHEN WRITING PART
NUMBERS THAT HAVE FRACTIONS
ROUND UP TO THE NEXT WHOLE NUMBER.

QUANTITY RECORDING

1. WHOLE NUMBERS ONLY, DROP FRACTIONS

2. AGREE WITH UNIT OF MEASURE CHECKED

4

FILLING OUT THE TAG

MS 54392-601   NUT   GC 101

72

A   RECORD PART NUMBERS HERE-
INCLUDE ALL PUNCTUATION

B   RECORD PART NAME HERE

C   ENTER DEPARTMENT NUMBER

D   QUANTITY-IN WHOLE
NUMBERS

E   RECORD ANY COMMENTS
HERE

F   ENTER COUNTER CLOCK
NUMBER

FIGURE 7–6: Brief Inventory Instruction Booklet

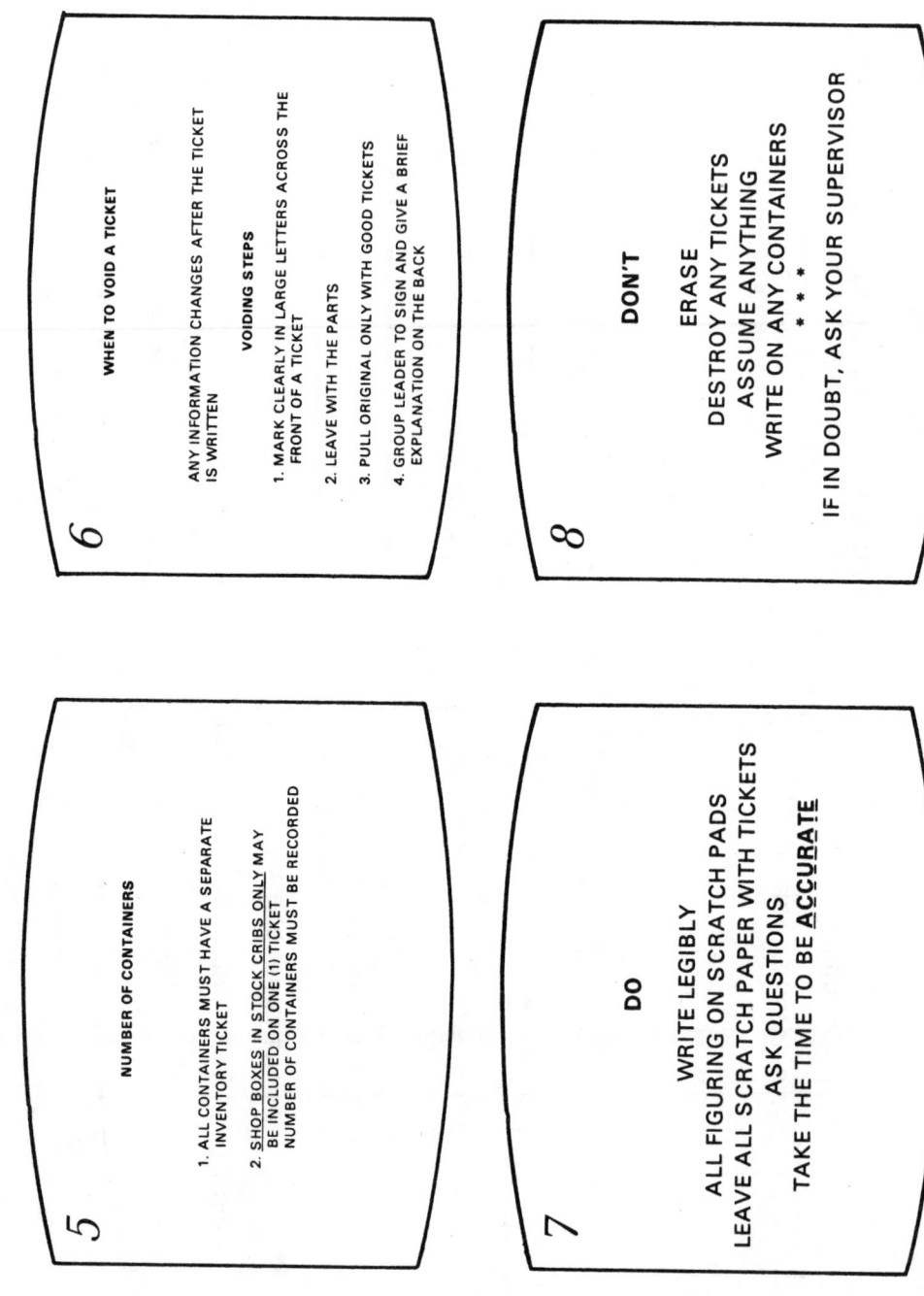

5

NUMBER OF CONTAINERS

1. ALL CONTAINERS MUST HAVE A SEPARATE INVENTORY TICKET

2. SHOP BOXES IN STOCK CRIBS ONLY MAY BE INCLUDED ON ONE (1) TICKET NUMBER OF CONTAINERS MUST BE RECORDED

6

WHEN TO VOID A TICKET

ANY INFORMATION CHANGES AFTER THE TICKET IS WRITTEN

VOIDING STEPS

1. MARK CLEARLY IN LARGE LETTERS ACROSS THE FRONT OF A TICKET

2. LEAVE WITH THE PARTS

3. PULL ORIGINAL ONLY WITH GOOD TICKETS

4. GROUP LEADER TO SIGN AND GIVE A BRIEF EXPLANATION ON THE BACK

7

DO

WRITE LEGIBLY
ALL FIGURING ON SCRATCH PADS
LEAVE ALL SCRATCH PAPER WITH TICKETS
ASK QUESTIONS
TAKE THE TIME TO BE **ACCURATE**

8

DON'T

ERASE
DESTROY ANY TICKETS
ASSUME ANYTHING
WRITE ON ANY CONTAINERS
* * *
IF IN DOUBT, ASK YOUR SUPERVISOR

FIGURE 7–6: Brief Inventory Instruction Booklet (cont'd)

For most computer-assisted physical inventories, the following documents are necessary:

Title	Description
Manual inventory tag	For items not on the computer list
Unidentified material tag	In a bright color to facilitate identification
Returnable containers list	To mark items not to be counted
Tag and list number control sheet	A mandatory record of numbers used—and not used
Area time control and release	The basic control of time and progress
Computer inventory lists	In storage location or part number sequence

Then certain supplies are necessary:

Title	Description
Masking tape or white chalk	To mark off certain areas
Wire or string	Often must tie a tag or list to something
Clipboards	Helps toward legible writing
Keys	In case doors or desks may be locked
"Golf type" red, blue, and green pencils	No erasers, different colors for counters, checkers, and auditors
Waterproof plastic containers	For outside material, since it may rain or snow
Ten-foot tape ruler	To spot-check dimensions

ACTUAL COUNT VS. PERPETUAL INVENTORY RECORD: A GUIDE TO ACCEPTABLE ERROR RATES

The first few hours of a physical inventory set the "tone" for the entire task. Thus, you should make special efforts—such as loud talking when a count error is discovered—to help stress the company means business and expects a "good" inventory. Since it is most difficult to recount material once the plant is back into production, the actual count should be compared with the perpetual inventory record balance before any areas are released. In order to

Table 7-1: Guide to 3 Percent Variance Allowance of Inventory Counts

COUNT	NUMBER OF PARTS VARIANCE ALLOWED	COUNT	NUMBER OF PARTS VARIANCE ALLOWED
1–49	1	184–216	6
50–83	2	217–249	7
84–116	3	250–283	8
117–149	4	284–317	9
150–183	5	318–349	10

Above 349, multiply "Number of Parts" times 3 percent to get "Variance Allowed."

facilitate this step, CRTs should be placed in the inventory headquarters so that a perpetual inventory record versus actual comparison can be made. As a guide, use the error rates shown in Table 7–1, remembering the various allowances ignore the plus or minus (above or below) the perpetual record:

GETTING ALONG WITH THE AUDITORS: KEY AREAS TO SPOT-CHECK FOR ACCURACY

Believe it or not, you and the auditors have the same goal—a successful inventory counting program that accomplishes the same objectives, and reflection of actual amount in the storage areas on both the inventory control record and the accounting books. Auditors look for

Count accuracy	Cutoff documents
Erasers on tags or lists	Unit of measure accuracy
Document number control	Reconciliation methods
Hidden inventory	Rust and dust on material
Part number correctness	Item description
Slow-moving parts	Obsolete items
Material at vendors	Area completion progress
Scale calibration	Tote pan weight uniformity
Outside processed parts	Count versus record differences
Count value extension	Lost tags or lists
Container tare weight	Duplicate part numbers

The accountants are responsible for

1. Spot-checking accuracy of list or tag contents.
2. Testing cutoff documents.
3. Pricing each item on the tags and extending the dollar amount.
4. Summarizing by type inventory.
5. Matching the counted dollar amount to the accounting book dollar inventory value.
6. Asking for recount if difference exceeds allowance.
7. Accepting the inventory and changing as necessary the book value.

When all is said and done, your accountants and external auditors issue their physical inventory results summary memorandum. This report lists things that are observed in the physical inventory, including

- Dates and hours observing counting
- Experience level of counters
- Experience level of checkers
- Adequate supervision
- Area completion
  Time and date
  Organization and housekeeping
  Indentification of boxes and parts
  Accuracy of locator records
- Test counts
  Total made by area; percent of total tags
  Number and percent wrong on quantity and description
  - From test counts
  - After final processing
  Number and percent with minor errors on tags
  Approximate percent of counts recorded for further testing
  Any poor counting crews
- Cutoff
  Last and first shipments/receipts before and after inventory noting document dates and numbers
  List of contents on railroad cards or freight trucks in back of plant
  Goods received or shipped without special number control
  Return goods in the Receiving Department
- Obsolete/slow-moving inventory examples observed
- "Do Not Inventory" material
  Approval signs on goods

Check (spot) adequacy of reason
Consigned material

- Material out of plant for rework

- Any entire areas not counted
How accounted for; if perpetual record, checked by sampling floor to
    records and vice versa
Percent of total checked and error percent

- Tag and list control
Number of lost tags/lists
Date clearly written
Design/description clear
Part number correct
Method of issuing and controlling
Size of number series issued
List of unused tag numbers
Enough tags available

- Inventory instructions
Meetings to discuss instructions
Adequacy and completeness
Clarity
Sections not followed
Improvements possible next year

- Counting scales
Enough available
Instructions on how to use made clear
Calibration checked by scale number

- Completion of inventory
Release procedure followed
No production started without authorization
No materials moved during inventory

- Final tour of areas
Nothing missed
Nothing moved

- Final opinion
Does this Inventory represent the goods fairly?

NOW LET'S USE THE RESULTS

All of this work will be for nothing if we do not make use of the inventory counting effort—so initially summarize the results in several ways answering such questions as a typical post-physical analysis, shown below. Then, in the next chapter we will discuss procedures to perform a detailed analytical study.

	Typical Numbers
■ What is the net dollar physical to book percentage adjustment?	1%
■ What is the absolute total dollar record to actual difference percentage?	17%
■ How much of the inventory represents more than one year's supply on hand?	23%
■ What percent of the perpetual records significantly differ from book?	19%
■ How many inventory tags or lists were lost?	2

The analysis can go further. Figure 7–7 is a Physical Inventory Data Collection Worksheet. The information recorded can assist in making these various analyses concerning the inventory investment.

CHAPTER REFERENCE

1. "Automatic Identification," *Modern Materials Handling*, Copyright September 6, 1983 by Cahners Publishing Company, Division of Reed Holdings, Inc.

Part Number (7986 A)	Part Description (axle)	Unit of Measure (each)	Physical Count Quantity (69)	Book Balance Quantity (73)	Reason for Difference Code (3)	Inventory ABC Class (A)	Annual Usage (763)	Usual Reorder Quantity (62)	Usual Safety Stock (31)	Unit Cost ($0.78)

Inventory Date _____

Area/Storage Location _____

Commodity Description _____

Page No. _____

Type Inventory: _____

Commodity Code No. _____

FIGURE 7–7: Physical Inventory Data Collection Worksheet

How to Achieve Document Accuracy: Guidelines for Measuring Tolerance Levels and Monitoring Transactions

8

CHAPTER HIGHLIGHTS

This chapter describes the more important measures of inventory management, demonstrates the impact of inaccurate records on inventory investment, and then suggests several ways to achieve more accurate transactions.
Specifically, you'll find

- six major inventory control documents and how accurate they need to be
- why absolute error is the true measure of a perpetual inventory system
- ground rules for establishing an effective bill of material system
- how to achieve accuracy on the receiving docks
- why Kanban cards are a successful solution to the work-in-process problem
- how automatic identification systems show promise for more speedy and precise inventory recording

SIX MAJOR INVENTORY CONTROL DOCUMENTS AND THEIR MINIMUM ACCURACY LEVELS

The emphasis in recent times on close monitoring of inventory investment places considerable stress on the accuracy of the part number and then for the six major inventory control documents.

Part numbers are unique identifiers, should be as short as possible, and nonsignificant, composed of no more than eight numerical digits. Their accuracy should be 100 percent.

The documents include:

1. A *perpetual inventory record* is the primary information document in the inventory system; depending on the type of inventory control method, the record to actual accuracy should be at least 90 percent.

2. A *bill of material* or product structure is a list of the part numbers and respective quantities that make up a parent item, including component parts, raw materials, and so forth. Its accuracy should be 98 percent.

3. A *routing* or operation sheet is a road map showing how a manufactured part travels through the plant, listing the operations for a part and identifying the amount of labor/machine time required for each operation. Its overall accuracy should be 95 percent.

4. A *blueprint* is a visual drawing to help in the manufacture of an item. This drawing, its specification accuracy, and any subsequent engineering change data should be 95 percent.

5. *Receiving or completion reports*, for purchased or manufactured parts, are the quantity entry documents into the storage or point of use areas. These reports should have an accuracy of 97 percent.

6. *Time and piece count reports* are the primary way to record production progress. The accuracy of the time and piece counts should be 96 percent.

As a rule of thumb, the overall minimum accuracy of all documents should be 90 percent, and the data timing done within 24 hours.

HOW TO ESTABLISH AN INTERNAL PART NUMBERING SYSTEM

A big problem facing the automation of an inventory system is establishing an internal part numbering system. A part number does not:

- Describe the part.
- Classify the part.

- Suggest its size.
- Indicate the material from which it is made.
- Suggest the product it goes into.
- Indicate where it is stored.
- Tell if it is purchased or fabricated (it could be either).
- Indicate how much it costs.
- Indicate its similarity to other parts.
- Suggest any of its physical or chemical properties.
- Duplicate the customer's number for that part.

The purpose of a part number is to identify—not to describe. Product classification and coding schemes do this and do it much better, and they can be changed without affecting the part identity.

Limit Numerical Characters to Minimize Errors

A pioneering work on numbering systems[1] concluded that—given the choice—a person should use a sequential, nonsignificant number system limited to six numerical characters if at all possible, and no more than eight. Any schemes larger than eight have high probability of transposition or other data entry errors. For example, when using numerical (N) and/or alphabetical (A) characters in various part designations, the following errors can occur as a result of daily transaction writing and posting:

TYPE PART IDENTIFIER	PROBABLE DAILY USE ERROR
8 Characters	
NNNNNNNN	36%
NNNNAAAA	45%
AAAAAAAA	53%
10 Characters	
NNNNNNNNNN	43%
NNNNNAAAAA	53%
AAAAAAAAAA	61%

The advantages of nonsignificant numbers are

- Same part will always be identified by same number.
- Different parts will never be identified with same number.
- Assignment of numbers is independent of classifications.

- Identification is made with fewest number of digits.
- One system is used for all parts—manufactured or purchased.
- There is no "running out" of numbers—no preallocated digits.
- They are easily understood and serve the whole company.
- Common use of components is encouraged—not inhibited.
- They force creation of necessary and convenient classifications.
- Retrievals by user classifications is facilitated.

In fact, it is suggested you start with a five-position numeric part identifier "10000" and if late expansion is necessary, go to "010000."

Check Digits for Increasing Transaction Accuracy

The purpose of a check digit—which is used on your personal checks—is to add a last (suffix) number to the base part number. When reading the recorded number, the computer automatically recalculates the check digit number to validate the base number. For one check digit system, called "Modulus 10," each of the base number's position is multiplied times a weight. When added up the last number becomes the check digit. For the correct number 349726 and transposed number 347926, the calculations are:

CORRECT NUMBER				*TRANSCRIPTION ERROR*			
349726				*347926*			
Position and Weight		*Number*	*Total*	*Position and Weight*		*Number*	*Total*
1	×	3	3	1	×	3	3
2	×	4	8	2	×	4	8
3	×	9	27	3	×	7	21
4	×	7	28	4	×	9	36
5	×	2	10	5	×	2	10
			76 GO!				78 NO GO!

In a computerized inventory management system, when using check digits, each part number would include a one-position numeric suffix. While the check digit is unobtrusively hidden, it serves to help increase transaction accuracy.

HOW TO ESTABLISH ACCEPTABLE TOLERANCE LIMITS FOR YOUR INVENTORY SYSTEM

In any given inventory transaction, one of three conditions will exist: (1) the perpetual record balance and the actual quantity in the storeroom will be the same; (2) the perpetual will be greater than the actual, or (3) the perpetual will be less than the actual.

Certain acceptable quantity tolerance limits should be established; these are shown in Table 8–1 for both ROP and MRP inventory systems. In each case, the example is based on an actual count in the stores area of 100 items. Allowing for these tolerances, only a few items should exceed the ranges.

Table 8-1: Acceptable Quantity Tolerance Limits for ROP and MRP Inventory Systems

Inventory Class	*ROP*		*MRP*	
	Tolerance	*Range*	*Tolerance*	*Range*
A	±2%	98–102	±1%	99–101
B	±4%	96–104	±2%	98–102
C	±10%	90–110	±5%	95–105
OVERALL	±5%	95–105	±3%	97–103

As a rule of thumb, a successful cycle count program is one in which 95 percent of the item record balances fall within these tolerances. While the overall dollar net error can be up to ±2 percent, the absolute quantity difference cannot exceed 10 percent. Any book to actual differences—in excess of these tolerances—are called "significant errors." For the last R.G. CEPT physical inventory, the comparison of the actual physical count when compared to the perpetual inventory record revealed the following, shown by type of inventory:

	Raw Material %	*Parts %*	*Total %*
Acceptable			
Same count	28%	44%	40%
Minor error (less than 5%)	32	23	27
SUBTOTAL	60	67	67
Significant error (more than 5%)			
Count more than record	20	11	12
Count less than record	20	22	21
SUBTOTAL	40%	33%	33%
GRAND TOTAL	100%	100%	100%

ABSOLUTE ERROR—
THE DIFFERENCE COUNTS IN INVENTORY
CONTROL EFFECTIVENESS

Although the common measure of inventory control effectiveness is the "net" difference between perpetual book and actual physical count, it is the "absolute" error that really counts. This is the true measure of a perpetual inventory system. While the "net" dollar differences usually run from 0.1 percent to 2 percent of the total dollar value, the "absolute" quantity error in the same system often is at least 22 percent and can be as high as 58 percent.

The annual physical inventory results, as reported by the Accounting Department in terms of the net dollar difference, can be very misleading. In fact, it almost always hides a multiplicity of errors. This annual exercise, while necessary to determine the dollar value of the asset called inventory, can serve very limited purposes for effective inventory management unless the absolute error is also calculated.

The R.G. CEPT Company had a book inventory value (on a FIFO basis) on its financial records at $3,107,018. The annual physical inventory was taken. Each item of raw material and parts on hand as well as finished goods was counted, the unit cost obtained, the two numbers multiplied together, and an item dollar value calculated. Then all the item dollar values were added up and the total inventory worth was determined. The annual physical inventory was worth $3,069,734 and books were off by only 1.2 percent or $37,284 (perpetual book value of $3,107,018 minus actual physical count value of $3,069,734).

The overage (more inventory on hand than on the books—total "plus") was valued at $305,367, and the shortage (less inventory on hand than on the books—total "minus") was worth $342,651, for the overall net shortage difference of $37,284 (1.2 percent). When summarized on an absolute or total error basis, the overages and shortages as a percent of the total book value showed an absolute error of 20.8 percent, as shown in the following table.

Type Differences	Value of Differences	Percent of Total Book Value
Overages	$305,367	9.8%
Shortages	342,651	11.0%
TOTAL	$648,018	20.8%

THE BILL OF MATERIAL DOCUMENT: 16 PROCEDURAL GROUND RULES TO FOLLOW

The bill of material should only be as complicated as necessary to permit accurate inventory transactions. If you can get by with a single level bill of material (sometimes called a parts list), then by all means use this more simple form.

A company may have several bills of material for the same product to serve various departmental needs. However, all should be constructed from the same computer data base. Figure 8–1 is the CEPTmobile computer-pre-

```
R.C. CEPT COMPANY          E&W PLASTICS ADVISOR              DATE 3/31/
PROGRAM# OF1318   INDENTED BILL OF MATERIALS LISTING         PAGE     1
```

BILL OF MATERIAL ITEM	OPERATION NBR	DESCRIPTION	OPERATION DESCRIPTION	QUANTITY USED PER EACH	MACH/ WORK CTR.	QUANTITY PER HOUR	NBR OF OPERATORS	LEAD TIME (WKS)
CEPT-STD	01	STD CEPTMOBILE	CONSTRUCT FRAME	1.0000 EA	01	5.00	1.00	01
* 147	01	FRAME-WELDED	WELD FRAME	1.0000 EA	10	10.00	1.00	01
** 9999		STEEL-		56.0000 LB				
** 9994		NUTS & BOLTS-		20.0000 EA				
* 0401	01	HOOD-STEEL	FORM HOOD	1.0000 EA	20	4.00	1.00	01
** 9999		STEEL		13.0000 LB				
* 0402	01	SIDE-STEEL	FORM SIDE	2.0000 EA	20	5.00	1.00	01
** 9999		STEEL-		18.0000 LB				
* 0911		GRILL-ALUMINUM		1.0000 EA				
CEPT-STD	02	STD CEPTMOBILE	ASSEMBLE AXLE		02	3.0	1.00	01
* 2361	01	AXLE	BUILD AXLE	2.0000 EA	10	10.00	1.00	01
** 9999		STEEL-		86.0000 LO				
** 9994		NUTS & BOLTS-		40.0000 EA				
* 0398		WHEEL-FRONT-		1.0000 EA				
* 7614		WHEEL-BACK-		2.0000 EA				
* 6171	01	HUB CAPS-ALUMINUM	FORM HUB CAP	3.0000 EA	30	8.00	1.0	01
* 9999		STEEL-		45.0000 LB				
* 9601		BRAKES-DRUM-		3.0000 EA				

FIGURE 8–1: Computer Produced Bill of Material

"Explosion"/As used (top down) Listings:

- Single Level

A
B
C   (2 Per)

C
D
E   (4 Per)

- Indented

```
A
  B
  C  (2 Per)
    D
    E  (4 Per)
```

- Summarized

A
B
C   (2 Per)
D   (2 Per)
E   (8 Per)

"Implosion"/Where-used (bottom up) Listings:

- Single Level

E
C

C
A

- Indented

```
E
  C
    A
```

- Summarized

E
A   (8 Per)
C   (4 Per)

FIGURE 8–2: Six Standard Bill of Material Formats

pared bill of material, listing the assembly, subassembly, component part number, and the quantity required of each item. Using these data, three different bills of material for the same product could exist: (1) as designed by engineering, (2) as assembled by manufacturing, and (3) as material is issued by inventory control.

It is this last bill of material document that must be the most accurate in order to have a successful inventory. For example, if part 0169 (support), which requires four for the subassembly, is listed as "three," than any subsequent explosion to produce 10 assemblies will show a demand of 30, not the required 40.

In establishing a bill of material, certain procedural ground rules should be followed:

1. The bill of material can be entered at any level, linked upward or downward, and designed for modular production. Figure 8–2 shows various possible bill of material formats.

2. The document can be used as a parts list to pull items from the storeroom.

3. The raw material part number, material specifications, material name, and vendor number can be annotated on the bill of material (in brackets).

4. Procedures should permit the use of phantom part numbers (an item usually not manufactured and put into the stockroom) and also indicate which are assemblies.

5. The bill should be organized in the appropriate sequence of the assembly (only in reverse).

6. The levels of the bill may be indicated visually by indenting. The top level will be designated the "0" level.

7. There should be a limited number of pages utilizing a consecutive type bill of material. One space should be skipped between each subassembly.

8. The use of this document should be well explained via training programs and a brief procedural writeup.

9. The bill must permit the lowest unit cost accounting.

10. The bill should indicate which parts are stock and which are nonstock for potential service replacement use.

11. The bill data base must be maintained accurately by the Engineering Department.

12. The bill should be updated via the engineering change notice (ECN) procedure. In case of dispute, an ECN/Bill of Material committee meeting should be held to resolve the problem.

```
R.G. CEPT COMPANY               WHERE USED REPORT              DATE 3/31/
PROGRAM# OF1318                                                PAGE   3
```

PART NUMBER OR MATL NO.	DESCRIPTION	USED IN PART NO.	DESCRIPTION	QUANTITY USED	PER UM
7814	ALUMINUM ROD	0011	CANOPY	2.00	E
		0169	SUPPORTS	1.00	E
		1397	SIDE CURTAINS	2.00	E
7260	DRIVER CONTROLS	CEPT-STD	STD CEPTMOBILE	1.00	E
8723	PLASTIC GUARD	1394	DROP WINDSHIELD	4.00	E
		5549	BUMPER ALUMINUM	8.00	E
9994	NUTS & BOLTS	0113	DRIVE SHAFT	60.00	E
		0286	INDUCTION MOTOR	80.00	E
		0987	INDUCTION CUSTOM	60.00	E
		1671	FRAME-WELDING	20.00	E
		1683	GEAR SHIFTS	10.00	E
		2361	AXLE	20.00	E
		3334	TRANSMISSION	20.00	E
		5549	BUMPER ALUMINUM	20.00	E
		7118	STEERING TILLER	10.00	E
9999	STEEL	0113	DRIVE SHAFT	34.00	E
		0401	HOOD-STEEL	13.00	E
		0402	SIDE-STEEL	9.00	E
		0986	INDUCTION MOTOR	92.00	E

FIGURE 8–3: Computer Produced Where Used Report

13. The bill should permit certain "add to" bills of material for accessories, modification, and special needs on a "matrix" type form for these variable items.

14. There should be provisions for the inventory classification, product code, and commodity code.

15. The bill should use the part number as a blueprint number, adding to it the blueprint alphabetical size designation.

16. Permit where used cross reference analysis to determine which assemblies utilize the same component part (see Figure 8–3).

ROUTING SHEETS:
KEEPING TRACK OF HOW A PART IS PRODUCED

Whatever name is given to this document (routings, route sheets, process documents), its purpose is to define the means by which a part is produced; this is in contrast to a bill of material, which details what a product contains and how an item is assembled. A routing has two important contents but differing accuracy needs. It is imperative that all steps in the operation sequence be accurately listed; therefore, 100 percent accuracy is necessary. However, the operation times have to be only fairly accurate (within 10 percent plus or minus). From an inventory management perspective, the inventory controller must be kept appraised of the latest routing information, as shown in Figure 8–4.

ENGINEERING CHANGE NOTICE (ECN)

Engineering changes are the bane of the inventory controller's life. There are hundreds of them, which impact: first, the value of parts in inventory which must be reworked, and second, accurate information to the routing and/or bill of material regarding the change details. For good control, all parts on routings and bill of materials should be annotated with the latest change date and number. In addition, in considering a part change, the inventory controller should have an opportunity to "use up" the parts before the change is implemented.

ACCURACY ON THE RECEIVING DOCK:
QUALIFYING THE VENDOR'S PACKING SLIP QUANTITY

Your vendors will differ widely in their ability to count accurately the material shipped to you as evidenced by the quantity on their packing slip placed on the cartons. Studies indicate[2] that vendors can count accurately, provided the quantity is less than 100 units (pounds, dozens, cartons, and so forth). For these smaller amounts you can safely use the vendor's packing slip quantity. However, if the quantity is more than 100 units, then counting errors can occur in over half of the receipts. Thus, you should make receiving counts based on the inventory class and dollar value of the material. Figure 8–5 provides a series of counting decision rules based on the above characteristics. You should also be guided by history with the vendor. Certain suppliers are surprisingly accurate; others are not and all of their receipts should be counted—at least until they improve.

PROGRAM RGC 34	ROUTING SUMMARY		As Of 03/03/xx			Page 64
Part No.	Description	Sequence	Department	Qty. Req.	Std. Hrs./100	Prim. Mach.
6171	Hub Caps-Aluminum	010	063-Purchasing	1 ea. Forging	—	—
		020	011-Receiving Inspection	1 ea. Forging	3.333	—
		030	018-Rough Drill	1 ea. Forging	5.00	664
		040	036-Finish Drill		7.50	107
		050	039-Sand Blast		2.30	608
		060	054-Paint		6.45	—

FIGURE 8–4: Manufacturing Routing

RECEIVING DEPARTMENT DECISION TREE					
Decision Point	**Consideration for Decision**				
1. Shipment Quantity	Less than 100	More than 100			
2. Shipment Value	Less than $500	More than $500			
3. Action to Take	Do not Count Use Packing Slip Quantity	Continue on Below			
4. Containers		1	2 to 50		Above 50
5. Inventory Class			A	B	C
6. Initial Counting Action, Open specified containers and check		All Items	All Containers	Every 2nd Container	Every 5th Container / 10% of the Containers
7. Error Rate Requiring Additional Counting		--	--	3%	7% / 3%

FIGURE 8–5: Receiving Department Action Guide

WORK-IN-PROCESS CONTROLS

Just as work-in-process items are the most difficult to count in a physical inventory, the problem is this inventory is also the toughest to control. Much of the difficulties are a result of two or more shop orders being split or combined, abnormal rate of rejections with subsequent rework, conversion of material from pounds of raw material to units after the first operation, and similar parts being identified as another part. For example, one product line work-in-process record to actual count comparison showed:

Pieces Difference	No. of Items	Percent Difference	Accumulated %
±0	83	13%	13%
+1 to 50	174		
−1 to 50	171	56%	69%
+51 to 100	31		
−51 to 100	35	11%	80%
+101 to 200	19		
−101 to 200	28	8%	88%
+201 to 7,650	33		
−201 to 7,650	44	12%	100%
TOTAL	618	100%	

Kanban Cards:
Both a Control and a Checkpoint System

One successful solution to the work-in-process problem is to use a shop floor card control system called Kanban (Japanese for sign board), which acts as a checkpoint control system. It is a paperless system,[3] using dedicated containers and recycling traveling requisitions/cards, which is quite different from the old, manual shop packet system. Kanban is a "pull" type of reorder system in that the authority to produce or supply comes from forthcoming operations. While work centers and vendors may plan their work based on computer produced schedules, they execute based on Kanbans, which are completely manual.

There are two types of Kanban cards. The Production Kanban authorizes the manufacturing of a container of material that contains a specific quantity. The Withdrawal Kanban authorizes the withdrawal and movement of that container. The number of pieces in a container (such as a tote pan) never varies for a given part number. When production rates change, containers

CALCULATION OF NUMBER OF
OUTSTANDING KANBAN CARDS

$$\left.\begin{array}{l} \text{NUMBER OF} \\ \text{KANBAN} \\ \text{CARDS} \end{array}\right\} = \frac{D\ (WT\ +\ PT)\ (1\ +\ PV)}{Q}$$

WHERE:

D = Average daily quantity demand for the month
WT = Waiting time in minutes
PT = Processing time for one container in minutes
PV = Policy variable - determined by management-
     up to 10% of day's demand
Q = Container quantity - limited to 10% of daily demand

FIGURE 8–6: Kanban Formula

will be added or deleted from the system. The formula used to determine the number of containers (and associated Kanban cards) is shown in Figure 8–6. It is a simple variation of the standard reorder point formula. The idea of safety stock is introduced here (called "policy variable"), but it is usually limited to 10 percent of the single day's demand. While this calculation is the theoretical number of Kanban/containers required, in practice efforts are made to reduce the number in circulation to keep inventories to a minimum. The main points of Kanban include:

- The concept to receive material and build small quantities very frequently.
- One move card and one production card per part number.
- When one work center empties a material container, its Kanban card is taken to the preceding work center as authorization for more parts.
- When a lot is produced, the production card is removed and left as authorization to produce more assemblies.
- Use of the same material card to be sent to vendors.
- A Kanban "lot size" as the container quantity capacity, usually a small lot size.
- It works best in high volume repetitive production environment, with frozen level schedules.

BAR CODES: THE GROWING DEMAND FOR
AUTOMATIC IDENTIFICATION SYSTEMS

The use of automatic identification systems, such as bar codes as graphic representations of characters of information, promise to assist greatly in achieving speedy and accurate inventory recording. The use of these neat little black stripes (and white ones too, though the human eye cannot read these as well) is expanding from the grocery supermarket to the world of manufacturing.

A bar code is easily read by scanning devices, decoded by computers, and then utilized by management. The advantage is a speed that far surpasses human counters, keypunch operators, and, with a degree of accuracy, far surpasses manual efforts. Not only is the possibility of human error greatly lessened, but since the counter does not have to write data by hand, key punching is eliminated, as are transposition and legibility problems. Some say bar codes are for a computer as the Braille alphabet is for the blind.

What a Bar Code Consists of

Several different bar code languages called "symbologies" are used, but the principle is the same for each. Each code is made up of computer binary digits and groups of black (and often white) bars which make up numbers and digits. For instance,

Number	Code	Number	Code
1	0011001	6	1010000
2	0010011	7	1000100
3	0111101	8	1001000
4	0100011	9	1110100
5	0110001	10	1110010

- Numbers 1 through 5 begin with a white space ("0" to the computer), are followed by a bar ("1" to the computer) and a second space, and end with a second bar.
- Numbers 6 thru 0 begin with a bar, are followed by a white space and a second bar, and end with a second space.
- Each bar (both black and white) can have one of four thicknesses; thus, the number 1 consists of a double width white space, a double width bar, another double width space, and a single width bar.

The Universal Product Code

This code (as shown in Figure 8–7) is the set of thick and thin black bars and white spaces printed on supermarket items now sold in the United States. Six of them, to the left of the "center guard pattern," are each represented by a light space, a dark bar, a second space, and a second bar. The other six, to the right of the center-guard pattern, are each represented by a bar, a space, a bar, and a space. The arrangement enables the computer bar code reader at a grocery checkout counter to determine whether the code has been scanned backward by the sensor at the counter (in that case, the computer inverts the data). The 12 digits have various meanings. The first decoded digit, which also appears in "human-readable form" at the left of the pattern of bars, is called the number-system character. A zero signifies a standard supermarket item. The next five decoded digits (number 12345 in the Figure 8–7 example) identify the manufacturer of the item. The five digits after that (67890) identify the item itself. The last digit is a check that serves to confirm the other

FIGURE 8–7: Universal Product Code

11 encoded digits have been scanned and decoded correctly. The four corner markings define an area that should be blank around the set of bars to facilitate error-free scan reading.

How to Interpret the Bar Code

Reading the bar code is simple (provided you have the proper equipment). A scanning device shines a light across the bars. This device contains a light source, an optical system, a photosensor that reacts to the reflected light and transmits analog signals to the decoder, and a computer interface; cassette tape, or memory. Since black bars absorb the light and white ones reflect the light back, the scanner translates pattern of dark and light into electrical impulses. A decoder then translates these impulses into binary digits that can be interpreted by the computer. In the example of the Universal Product Code, the thin bar is a binary "1" while the thickest bar are four binary "1s." The key is the scanning device, either simple portable wands that look like large ball point pens or sophisticated fixed position scanners that utilize low intensity lasers and scan across the bars up to 800 times a second.

The decoder does not read absolute bar widths; hence, a constant, fixed stroke rate is not necessary. Instead, the decoder senses the difference between the high- and low-level impulses to determine when one bar ends and another begins. Then it compares the "time-width" of each bar with the previous bar to determine relative widths. Since wide bars are two, three, or four times the width of the narrowest bar, an accurate relative comparison is made.

Consider These Present Uses for Bar Codes

- Using to inventory logs floating in a river
- Locating electronic circuit board orders in a factory
- Cycle-counting material in a storeroom
- Recording department location and arrival time of inventory employee counters
- Keeping track of inventory cartons on warehouse conveyors
- Instructing inventory employees where to count next

Caution: A bar code tracking system can cost considerable money, so care must be exercised when selecting a bar code, since in manufacturing, unlike the grocery industry, there is as yet no universal code. Some of today's codes are numeric only—these do not utilize an alpha character set. Certain codes are self-checking to minimize errors. Special printers are necessary with stringent standards for quality, accuracy, and uniformity. Label quality is impor-

Designed and printed by Doreen Gold, Euclid Bar Code & Labeling Systems

FIGURE 8–8: Bar Code and Optical Character Recognition (OCR) Label

tant. Sharp-edged bars with good contrast against the label background are important. Black bars on a white surface are most common, but various colors can be used provided there is good contrast. Expensive magnetic inks (like those used on your personal checks) are not required. To facilitate reading, most bar code labels also print a human readable number, as well as optical character recognition (OCR). Figure 8–8 is a combination vendor part number label which can be placed on the outside of each carton.[4]

A 19-STEP ACTION PLAN FOR ESTABLISHING AN INVENTORY ACCURACY PROGRAM

A major task is to provide for a continuing effort to obtain and then maintain accuracy, such as the medium-size company's 19-step action plan shown on page 178. These steps can be taken to help control the inventory and have more accurate records. One especially useful technique is a "Document Control Center" (step 4 and Figure 8–9) wherein all inventory transaction documents such as receivers, requisitions, and the like, flow through one central office where document accuracy can be easily monitored.

	TIMING		Responsibility
	Start	*Finish*	*Responsibility*
1. Establish an Inventory Control Steering Committee	March	March	President
2. Publish an inventory control policy and investment targets	March	March	President
3. Post a sign that reads, "We can achieve accuracy by carefully counting"	March	March	Inventory Manager
4. Establish a Document Control Center	April	May	Inventory Supervisor
5. Revise A, B, and C inventory classifications	April	May	Inventory Controller
6. Have Foreman validate labor tickets for quanities	May	Continuous	General Foreman
7. Tighten cut-off dates and times	May	Continuous	Receiving Foreman
8. Establish one inventory transaction system for all departments	May	June	Inventory Manager
9. Initiate cycle counting procedures	June	Continuous	Inventory Manager
10. Obtain accurate receiving counts	June	Continuous	Receiving Foreman
11. Update weight count instructions	June	September	Inventory Supervisor
12. Reconcile cycle count book to inventory balances monthly	July	Continuous	Inventory Controller
13. Update Bill of Material/Route Sheet Accuracy	August	October	Chief Engineer
14. Review open purchase order report for completed orders	August	Continuous	Purchasing Agent
15. Measure excessive "charge out" of inventory	August	November	Financial Manager
16. Post scrap pieces as reported to inventory records	Sept.	Continuous	Inventory Controller
17. Correct scrap tickets if erroneous	Sept.	Continuous	Quality Control Supervisor
18. Approve material substitutions and standardization	Oct.	Continuous	Chief Engineer
19. Institute a requisition system	Nov.	Continuous	Inventory Manager

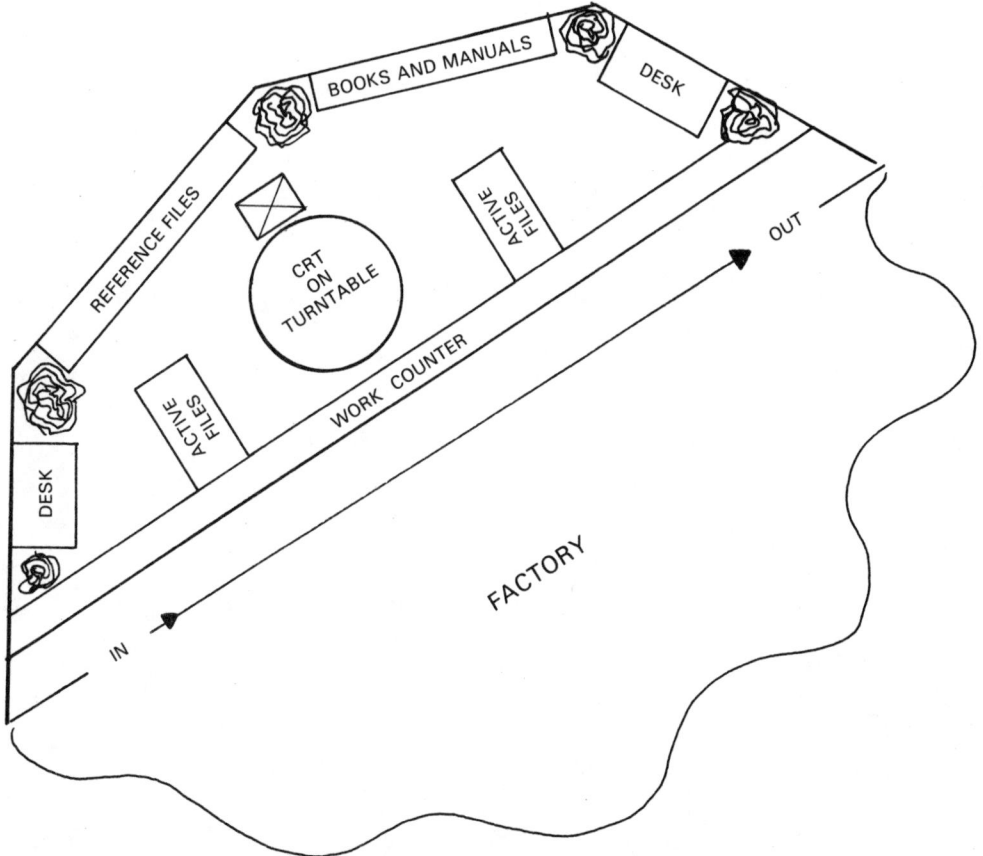

FIGURE 8–9: Inventory Management Document Control Center

CHAPTER REFERENCES

1. J. G. H. Carlson, "Item Identification and Classification in Management Operating Systems," *Production and Inventory Management*, American Production and Inventory Control Society, Falls Church, VA, 2nd quarter, 1971.

2. B. C. Domeck, "Analysis of Receiving Accuracy," private study, Ernst & Whinney, Cleveland, Ohio, 1980.

3. Reprinted with permission from *P&IM Review*, September 1981. Copyright 1981 by T.D.A. Publications, Inc., Hollywood, FL.

4. Designed and printed by Doreen Gold, Euclid Bar Code & Labeling Systems, 1985.

Training Inventory Personnel

9

CHAPTER HIGHLIGHTS

Inventory is created, reduced, maintained, and controlled at lower levels in the organization by inventory controllers, stockroom clerks, material handlers, and by the manufacturing hourly employees.

This chapter tells how to train inventory personnel, with emphasis on clearly stating the inventory policies, creating procedures that describe in simple terminology the methods to be used, establishing investment targets, and monitoring the results—all within a climate for people to meet the established goals.

You'll find simple steps for preparing job descriptions, including a detailed description of the requirements for a corporate inventory coordinator.

A step-by-step procedure of input-output transaction control in your computer is included, as are control rules for using a CRT terminal.

The last section covers a series of methods for developing an inventory training program.

FOUR BASIC INVENTORY POSITIONS

A wide range of talents are necessary to achieve the goal of good customer service at minimum inventory investment. The primary inventory positions are

- Corporate inventory coordinator/executive
- Inventory manager
- Inventory controller
- Inventory stock handler

Figure 9–1 provides a summary list of the key aspects of each of these major position's responsibilities; note the stress on transaction completeness and accuracy. This information should be utilized to develop these few major inventory job descriptions.

HOW TO PREPARE INVENTORY JOB DESCRIPTIONS IN FOUR STEPS

It may be possible that your company does not have job descriptions tailored to each employee's unique position responsibilities. Should this be the situation, it is easy to establish simplified one-page job descriptions in four steps using the form illustrated in Figure 9–2.

Primary Responsibility	Inventory			
	Executive	Manager	Controller	Handler
1. Create Inventory Policy	✓			
2. Determine Service Level	✓			
3. Write Inventory Procedures		✓		
4. Train Inventory Personnel		✓		
5. Review Inventory Status Report			✓	
6. Prepare Replenishment Orders			✓	
7. Check Amount of Parts Received				✓
8. Fill Requisitions Accurately				✓
9. Deliver Material to Production				✓
10. Enter Transaction into CRT			✓	
11. Expedite Material Needs			✓	
12. Check Transaction Completeness & Accuracy			✓	
13. Maintain Clean, Labeled Storeroom				✓
14. Review for Unusual Part Specifications			✓	
15. Report Unusual Demands & Low Stock Levels				✓
16. Determine Month's Supply on Hand		✓		
17. Determine Forecast Error		✓		
18. Prepare Slow Moving & Obsolete Lists			✓	
19. Perform Cycle Counts				✓
20. Appraise Employee Performance		✓		
21. Monitor Inventory Levels		✓		
22. Review Inventory Investment Results	✓			

FIGURE 9–1: Inventory Responsibility by Position

EMPLOYEE JOB DUTY WORKSHEET

NAME OF EMPLOYEE_____
DEPARTMENT_____
SUPERVISOR _____
JOB TITLE_____
SUPERVISES_____

PRIMARY DUTIES - What is done almost every day.

1. _____

2. _____

3. _____

4. _____

5. _____

SECONDARY DUTIES - What is done occasionally or
                   as backup for someone else.

1. _____

2. _____

3. _____

4. _____

MEASURES OF PERFORMANCE

1. _____

2. _____

3. _____

APPROVED   BY:_____ DATE_____

FIGURE 9–2: Employee Job Duty Worksheet

1. Both individual employee and supervisor independently complete this form, with each person describing the position responsibilities as he or she sees them.

2. The supervisor reviews both input forms and resolves all differences with the employee.

3. The superior of the supervisor, and if possible the personnel manager, approves the document.

4. Copies are made and given to all persons involved.

POSITION SPECIFICATIONS FOR CORPORATE INVENTORY COORDINATOR

In a large company with numerous divisions, a corporate inventory coordinator will oversee the use of the inventory investment. However, in a smaller company, a senior executive (sometimes the president) will fulfill these duties. The following description is typical of the detail necessary for an effective corporate inventory coordinator position explanation.

Position Functions and Responsibilities

This position has responsibility for planning inventory investment, overseeing corporate inventory control, and monitoring adherence to established targets. The position's specific functions include the development, implementation, and monitoring of policies and procedures for forecasting and inventory planning. Significant direct participation in these activities is required.

Organizational Relationship: Internal and External Contacts

- *Internal:* The inventory coordinator reports to the corporate vice-president of materials. This person maintains coordinating contacts with plant and functional managers throughout the company to coordinate and control the above functions appropriately.

- *External:* The inventory coordinator is required to maintain contacts with outside inventory experts and will occasionally interface on behalf of the company with industry representatives and other outside individuals, as appropriate.

Five Measures of Performance Levels

The following are considered indicators of performance by the coordinator.

1. Effectiveness in planning and meeting inventory commitments.
2. Achievement of efficiencies in inventory due to improvements in planning and scheduling methodology.
3. Maintenance of adequate yet efficient inventory levels.
4. Achievement of cost improvement in the control of materials.
5. Contribution to interdepartmental coordination and team effort to accomplish company objectives and improve company profit.

Position Qualifications

Five or more years of experience in a manufacturing environment is a minimal requirement. A college degree is desirable. Experience in inventory, production control, and with equipment or processes similar to those of your company would also be helpful.

Two essential characteristics of a corporate inventory coordinator are an even temperament and the ability to work with people with varying backgrounds and educations. Creativity, open-mindedness, and decision-making ability are other important characteristics.

KEY PROCEDURES TO BE READ BY CLERICAL PERSONNEL

Copies of standard procedures, such as the following partial list, should be given to all inventory personnel:

No.	Title
101	Reorder point control
102	ABC classification system
103	Ordering "A," "B," and "C" items
104	Inventory control parameters
105	Stock levels
106	Clerical duties CRT transaction
107	Clerical duties cycle counting
108	Traveling requisition system
109	Accountability for parts
110	Labor/move ticket
111	Scrap and obsolete material reporting
Etc.	

Key Documents to Utilize

Document Description	Purpose
"A" and "B" inventory record	Inventory control
Traveling requisition	Requisitions to purchasing
Shop order completion report	Production order completions
Shop order	Orders to production
Labor/move ticket	Specific operation movement
Scrap ticket	Loss of material
Master schedule	Production plan
Bill of material	Components of an assembly
Routing	Manufacturing sequence
Blueprint	Production description
Receiving Report	Quantity received

INPUT/OUTPUT TRANSACTION CONTROL: A STEP-BY-STEP PROCEDURE FOR INVENTORY PERSONNEL

Since inventory on hand is like money in the bank, the various transactions should be treated like your own checking account—money (inventory) is put in, money (inventory) is taken out, and every so often service charges (interest) and inventory adjustments have to be made.

The first step in computerized inventory is to describe the various CRT "posting rules," as shown in Table 9–1, which explain the actual commands (from an application menu) and the computer "posting" (or entry).

Impact of Transactions

The type of inventory transactions to be entered through a terminal are numerous. Figure 9–3 provides the type and the volume of CRT transactions input each day, for the $15 million R.G. CEPT Sales Company. This information is necessary for any EDP software/hardware decisions.

Table 9–1: CRT Posting Rules

MENU SECTION NO.	TITLE	EXPLANATION OF PURPOSE
1.	Description	List alphabetic description of item.
2.	Weight	Show weight of the item, expressed as "unit" weight or per "so many" items.
3.	Where Used Model, Quantity	Indicate the higher level models this item is used on and the number of items per model.
4.	ROP (Reorder Point)	Obtain the stock level from procedure calculation when a replenishment order is needed.
5.	Steel, Component, Castings, Final Assembly	List the applicable term.
6.	Lead Time (Weeks)	List the normal time required (in weeks) to replenish this item.
7.	Annual Usage	Input or show the number of units to be used (issued) based on the forecast for the current year.
8.	Stores Location	Indicate the bin, floor, and/or location the item is stored.
9.	History Usage	Show the usage for the past three years by year.
10.	SS (Safety Stock)	Indicate the quantity of items kept within the ROP as safety stock.
11.	ROQ (Reorder Quantity)	Note the number of parts which should be reordered, based on calculations. When reordering, always add to the ROQ the number of units the balance has fallen below the ROP.
12.	Date Transaction	List the month and day, such as "3–15." Show only the year when (a) the end of the calendar year, or (b) when a physical inventory is taken.
13.	No. (Number)	Indicated the shop order, purchase order, model, credit or debit memo number.
14.	Rec. (Received)	Show the quantity of items received into inventory from a purchase or shop order.

Table 9–1: CRT Posting Rules (cont'd)

MENU SECTION NO.	TITLE	EXPLANATION OF PURPOSE
15.	Allocated	Note the quantity of items allocated (or reserved) for a specific order number.
16.	Accum. YTD (Accumulated Year-to-Date)	Add the quantity found in item 15 to the previous quantity in this section (No. 16) to get the accumulated items used (reserved) since the beginning of the year (YTD).
17.	Order Quantity	Show the number of parts on a replenishment order.
18.	On Order Balance	Keep as an accumulated quantity on all open replenishment orders.
19.	Inv. Bal. (Inventory Balance)	Indicate the number of items available for future orders (demands). When posting a quantity in item 15, subtract the same quantity from the previous balance in No. 19.
20.	Part Number or Specification	List the numerical designation of the item, occasionally with some alphabetic characters.
21.	Control No.	Put the six digit, numeric part identification in this space.
22.	Pattern No.	For forgings or castings, show the die or pattern number.
23.	Unit Standard Cost	List the current unit cost input by accounting.
24.	B/M or Dwg No. (Bill of Material or Drawing Number)	Note the actual bill of material or blueprint drawing number.
25.	Item Out Flag	In this section, position the flag (indicator) when a negative balance appears in column 19.
26.	Inv. Cl. (Inventory Class)	Show the A, B, or C inventory classification.
27.	Mfg./Pur. (Manufactured or Purchased)	Indicate if the item is manufactured or purchased.
28.	Product Class	List actual class designation.

DATA FILE	Size of Record	X	Number of Allowed Records	=	Total Information
Item Master	128		200		25,600
Bill of Material	512		100		51,200
Routing	128		75		9,600
Tooling	32		30		960
Shop Order					
Header	128		40		5,120
Component	64		100		6,400
Operation	32		80		2,560
Notes	96		50		4,800
Customer Order					
Header	64		500		32,000
Detail	32		1000		32,000
Purchase Order					
Header	64		600		38,400
Detail	96		1800		172,800
Customer Master	64		350		22,400
Vendor Master	96		175		16,800
SUBTOTAL					415,840
Future Expansion					1,000,000
TOTAL REQUIREMENTS					1,415,840

FIGURE 9–3: CRT Transaction File Requirements

CONTROL RULES WITH A CRT TERMINAL: SELECTED EXPLANATORY INSTRUCTIONS

Another method to clarify inventory transactions is to write selected explanatory instructions in the form of CRT use rules.

Controlled Versus Noncontrolled Areas

A "controlled" designation signifies that the material balance-on-hand quantities are known for each storage area. All storage areas at this plant have been designated as either controlled or noncontrolled inventory areas. In general, all production stores areas are noncontrolled and all others are controlled.

Receipts of Purchased or Shop Order Material

1. All material sent to a controlled area must have its paper work so marked.
2. This includes receiving reports and shop order completion notices.
3. All "A" items regardless of stores location are controlled.

Issues (Disbursements) of Controlled Material

1. Requisitions will be required for all "A" items, regardless of stores locations.
2. Requisitions will be required for all "B" and "C" items from controlled locations.
3. Issues of "B" and "C" items from noncontrolled (production) areas will not require a requisition.
4. Each requisition must clearly indicate quantity, part number, and date. "All" is not considered a quantity.

Miscellaneous

1. *Deliveries and stores location:* Be sure to note exact location on appropriate papers.
2. *Returned material:* Note on paper the "delivered to" location.
3. *Credit:* Note on form the "delivered to" location.
4. *Defective material:* (a) If scrapped from shop order in process, note this on paperwork; (b) if pulled from controlled stores, a requisition is necessary.

5. *Shippers:* A copy of all shippers must be sent to inventory control.

6. *List of stores locations:* Must clearly indicate area as controlled or noncontrolled.

7. *Shop order change notices:* Must be utilized by shop controllers when appropriate. Special attention must be given to (a) first operation quantity; that is, plus or minus 10 percent different from order quantity and (b) any changes of sufficient amount during course of production.

8. *Reorder points and quantities:* Will be recalculated at least every six months.

THE INVENTORY TRAINING PROGRAM: A MULTIFACETED SEMINAR COVERING FOUR PHASES

It is necessary to use a series of training methods in order to develop a cadre of well-trained inventory personnel. This training approaches each of the four primary inventory positions: corporate controller executive, inventory manager, inventory controller, and stock handler.

The ingredients to be used in this program are multifaceted, consisting of the

Inventory Policy Statement

Inventory Procedures Manual

Inventory Reference Library

Cathode Ray Tube Menu Screen Formats

Executive, Managerial, and Technical Seminar

On-the-Job Training Program

Self-Appraisal Review

The seminar topics should be extensive and arrayed to inform members of each of the four positions. Figure 9–4 shows an outline of a four-part, six-hour seminar that covers these topics, giving enough detail for each person's responsibility level, e.g., (1) overview and policies, (2) general procedures, (3) specific techniques, and (4) specialized training. A more detailed, three-day inventory seminar should include these topics:

I. Strategic Inventory Planning

II. Information Necessary for Inventory Control

III. Inventory Management Organizations

IV. Forecasting and Understanding Demand

V. ABC Inventory Classification Procedure

VI. Item Commodity Coding and the Master Record

PHASE AND PURPOSE	TYPICAL CONTENTS	AUDIENCE				LENGTH	TYPE TRAINING & VISUAL AIDS
		Executives	Inventory Manager	Inventory Controller	Stock Handler		
I - Overview & Policies	A Purpose and goals of department B Importance of all participation C Use of chain of command D Management and self-measures	X	X	X	X	60 minutes	Lecture with 35 mm. slides
II - General Procedures	A Organization of inventory manual B General duties of each job C Serving the requisitioners D Planning one's daily work	–	X	X	X	60 minutes	Lecture and Overhead Slides
III - Specific Techniques	A The CRT work cycle B Using inventory reports C Expediting methods D Importance of computer input accuracy	–	–	X	X	120 minutes	Lecture and Group Discussion with Overhead Slides
IV - Specialized Training	A Types of inventory measures B Use of cycle counting C Methods to analyze inventory D Computerized inventory control	–	–	X	–	120 minutes	Lecture and Role Playing

FIGURE 9–4: Inventory Seminar Outline

192

VII. Two Major Inventory Systems: ROP and MRP

VIII. Reorder Point (ROP) Systems

IX. Determining Lot Size and Safety Stock

X. Material Requirements Planning (MRP) Systems

XI. Step by Step Through MRP

XII. Five Levels of MRP II

XIII. MRP for Tool Control, Restaurants, and Hospitals

XIV. Simulating Inventory Levels

XV. Serving the Customer Needs

XVI. Vendor Capacity Planning for Just-in-Time

XVII. Choosing the Correct System

XVIII. Inventory Documents

XIX. Accounting for the Inventory

SHOP INVENTORY TRAINING FOR A FAST AND BRIEF PRESENTATION

The second major training effort should be directed to the manufacturing shop personnel. This program—due to audience time constraints and interests—should be a fast-paced, somewhat terse presentation. The "reminder style" outline of such an inventory program includes the following.

SHOP PERSONNEL INVENTORY TRAINING PROGRAM LESSON PLAN

Section	Topics	Time	Training Aid
A	**INTRODUCTION** Purpose of this program Responsibility of chain of command Brief discussion of reason for inventory Importance of employee participation in physical setup and systems	5 minutes	None
B	**EFFECT OF A MISTAKE** Example of error causes and effect of a wrong balance Inventory records, lost production, purchase order not required and expediting Two major failures; poor records and counts	10 minutes	Flip Chart

SHOP PERSONNEL INVENTORY TRAINING PROGRAM LESSON PLAN
(cont'd)

Section	Topics	Time	Training Aid
C	**PEOPLE IMPORTANCE**		
	Paper work chain of command	10 minutes	Flip Chart
	The critical document: requisition		
	Signature requirements		
	Authorized persons in storeroom (even stop vice-presidents)		
	Counting receipts, both from vendor and manufacturing		
	Keeping door closed or locked		
D	**PHYSICAL ARRANGEMENT**		
	Value of clean, orderly storeroom	10 minutes	Large Locator Card
	Location of goods accuracy		
	Primary and secondary locations		
	Part identification		
	Piece and weight counts		
E	**SYSTEM CHECKPOINT**		
	Control checks and balances	10 minutes	Large Requisition
	What computer does with the requisition		
	Monthly cutoff points and why		
	Cycle counting and why necessary		
	Accuracy points; correct count by item and percent		
	ABC class review to highlight problem items		
	"Common sense test"—ask if looks wrong		
F	**ACTUAL PROCEDURE**		
	Step-by-step "walkthrough" of brief written procedure	15 minutes	Mini-procedure
	Kinds of problems to watch for: wrong quantity, part number, location, order number, etc.		
	Clear writing to help key punching		
	"Rush" requisitions that bypass normal procedure		
G	**GROUP SUGGESTIONS, QUESTIONS, AND ANSWERS**	30 minutes	None
	TOTAL TIME	90 minutes	

THE STATISTICAL INVENTORY GAME: A TRAINING TOOL PERFORMED ON A COMPUTER

A fun way to show the methods—and dilemmas—of managing inventories is to use the statistical inventory game.[1] Since this game is performed on a CRT, it helps persons become acquainted with a computer. However, it also can be used on a manual basis. This training tool includes the following.

Overview and Objectives of the Game

Managing inventories of finished goods, in-process parts, and raw material can be a significant task in business and industry. Thousands—and even tens of thousands—of items (stockkeeping units) are involved; the cost of money is high; other costs (labor, storage, and so forth) are rapidly increasing; competition has increased; and the problems have generally become more complex.

A statistical inventory game is used to illustrate the complexities of inventory management and to compare individual results achieved by the participants with those obtainable by computer calculated and statistical methods. However, these mathematical methods are a supplement to (not a replacement for) managerial judgment.

In this game, a highly simplified problem is presented, namely, that of managing the inventory of two electrical appliances (electric stoves and portable broilers). You—acting as the finished goods inventory manager—will be given the sales histories of the two products and other basic information. Future demands for the two products will be selected randomly in order to make the simulation, or game, more realistic. Using the CRT Inventory Screen for electric stoves—there is a similar screen for portable broilers—(Figure 9 –5), you are to keep a running record of sales, inventories, orders placed (on the shop), orders received, and stockouts (i.e., back orders) for each of the two products. You are to place orders for the products to satisfy sales requirements. The objective is to minimize the sum of inventory costs, reorder (and setup) costs, and shortage (i.e., out-of-stock) costs.

Of course, real-life problems are much more complex, and many additional significant factors are involved. There are many more products; manufacturing lead times (here assumed to be exactly three weeks) will vary by item; adjustments, returns, product damage, and errors will be involved; and so forth. Nevertheless, this inventory game will prove to be valuable in illustrating the complexities of inventory management and the need for (and benefits from) scientific decision rules.

While the game refers to manufactured items, it applies equally to purchased items. In the latter case, the "reorder and setup" cost relates to the

Week	ELECTRIC RANGE						PORTABLE BROILER						
	Initial Inventory	Receipts	Available Inventory, This Period	Sales, This Period	BALANCE Inventory	BALANCE Back Order	Ordered	Initial Inventory	Receipts	Available Inventory, This Period	Sales, This Period	BALANCE Inventory	BALANCE Back Order	Ordered
0														
1														
2														
3														
4														
5														
6														
7														
8														
9														
10														
11														
12														
13														
14														
15														
16														
17														
18														
19														
20														
21														
22														
23														
24														
25														
26														
27														
28														
29														
30														
31														

FIGURE 9–5: Inventory Game CRT Screen

196

average cost associated with preparing purchase specifications, asking for and evaluating quotations, receiving the products, posting the inventory records, paying the invoice, etc. Also, the manufacturing lead time simply becomes the purchasing (vendor) lead time.

The Rules of the Game

1. Orders may be placed for each product at the end of any week.
2. Orders will be available for inventories (or for sales) only at the end of a manufacturing lead time, that is, three weeks later. This means, for example, that an order placed during week "0" will be delivered and available to satisfy sales at the beginning of week "4."
3. If a stock-out occurs, the demands accumulate and must be satisfied from stock received later (that is, unfilled demands are back-ordered).
4. Unit sales figures for the last ten weeks are shown below.

Electric Stoves		Portable Broilers	
18	23	14	9
11	9	12	13
1	15	11	8
21	5	5	23
10	7	14	11
TOTAL	120	TOTAL	120
Average 12		Average 12	

Future sales are expected to have a similar pattern. Past experience shows sales have no trend and are nonseasonal. Therefore, the sequence of the above figures is not important.

Sales will be determined randomly by the computer or manually by chance from each of four thrown dice, which represent a week's demand for the corresponding product.

5. Present warehouse capacity is such that a maximum service level of 98 percent could be maintained.
6. At the beginning of the game, there are 80 units in the Electric Stove inventory and 60 units in the Portable Broiler inventory.
7. The relevant costs are

	Electric Stove	Portable Broiler
Variable cost per unit	$260	$52
Reorder and setup costs . . . . . . (This is an average total cost of ordering and machine setup.)	$200	$50
Annual inventory carrying cost rate	20%	20%
Stock-out cost per unit per week . . .	$ 60	$10

8. At the end of the simulation, you will determine the average inventory, the number of orders placed in the factory, and the number of stock-outs (unit stock-out weeks). With these data, you will then compute the total cost of your inventory control program using the Results Calculation form furnished in Figure 9–6. The total cost serves as a measure of the system performance. Here is an example of total costs:

Ref. No.	COST SUMMARY	ELECTRIC STOVES	PORTABLE BOILERS
	HIGHEST INVENTORY	87	85
	LOWEST INVENTORY)0	4	0
1	AVERAGE	52.51	37.88
2	GAME WEEKS	40	40
3	COST/UNIT/WEEK	$1.00	$0.20
$1 \times 2 \times 3$	TOTAL CARRYING COST (A)	$2,101	$303
	NUMBER OF ORDERS	5 × $200	4 × $50
	TOTAL ORDERING COST (B)	$1,000 $200	$200
	STOCKOUT WEEKS	0 × $60	1 × $10
	TOTAL STOCKOUT COST (C)	$0	$10
	TOTAL COST PER ITEM	$3,101	$513
		A + B + C	
	GRAND TOTAL COST	$3,614	

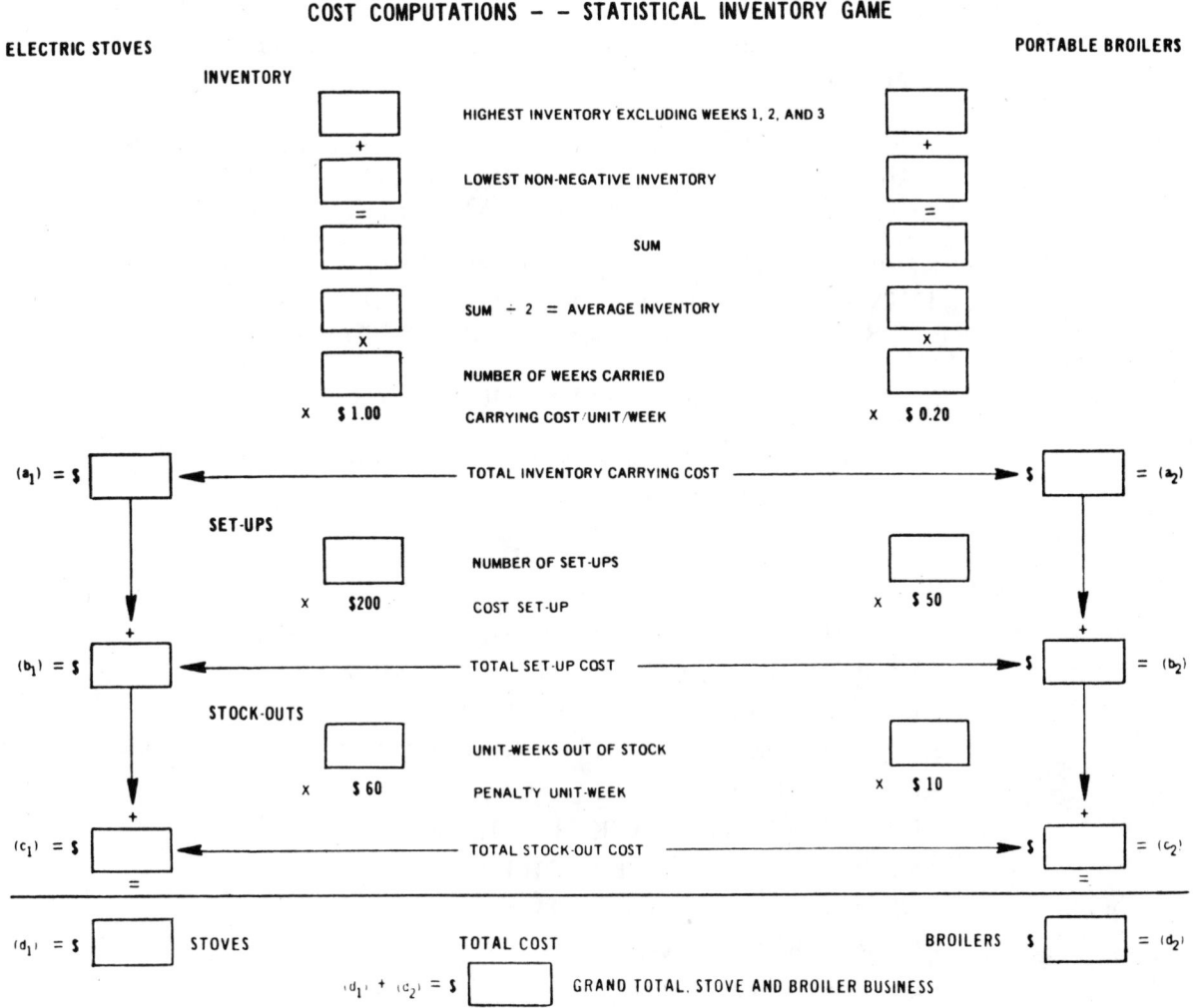

FIGURE 9–6: Inventory Game Results Calculation Form

On to the game. Here's to fun, information, and CRT familiarization by following these instructions, designed for your computer using LOTUS 1–2–3 Macros.

YOU MAY REFER TO THE MASTER MENU AT ANY TIME BY PRESSING THE "ALT" KEY AND "M" AT THE SAME TIME. TO GET BACK INTO THE GAME SIMPLY PRESS "ALT" AND "S".

KEEP IN MIND THE OBJECTIVES OF THE GAME AT ALL TIMES. THINGS TO CONSIDER THROUGHOUT INCLUDE:
)RELATIVE COSTS TO BUY, CARRY AND HAVE STOCKOUTS

)THE LEAD TIME TO BUY YOUR STOCK

)THE MINIMIZING OF TOTAL COST FOR
        BOTH PRODUCTS!!!!!!!!!

MASTER MENU

ALT A: TO GET TO THE SALES GENERATION FILE.
ALT B: TO GET YOU BACK TO THE GAME FILE.
ALT E: POST ELECTRIC RANGES SALES.
ALT F: TO GET TO THE FINANCIAL SUMMARY.
ALT I: GIVE THE INSTRUCTIONS.
ALT M: TAKES YOU BACK TO THIS MENU.
ALT P: POST PORTABLE BROILERS SALES.
ALT Q: QUIT OR END THE GAME.
ALT R: RESTART GAME.
ALT S: STARTS THE GAME.
ALT Z: GOTO THE INTRODUCTION SCREEN.

CHAPTER REFERENCE

1. B. O. Marshall and M. J. Netzorg, modified by T. R. Corman, "Statistical Inventory Game," Ernst & Whinney, 1969.

Calculating Specific Inventory Targets and a 12-Step Reduction Program for Meeting Your Goals

10

CHAPTER HIGHLIGHTS

This chapter explores what's involved in targeting specific inventory turnovers and how to calculate the estimated impact on profits.

You'll discover why it's important to compare your inventory investment to other companies and industries, as well as by product market strategy.

The three most common methods for determining proper inventory levels are discussed and analyzed.

The five inventory groups for calculating proper investment targets are broken down according to desirable, permissible, and nondesirable levels. This allows special inventories to be maintained.

How to reduce your inventory to your calculated level is also discussed, including a 12-step program that reduces your investment without decreasing your customer service level.

Inventory Class	How Determined (Annual Part Issues)	Last Year's Issues	Turnover Desired	Inventory Target	Actual	Excess
A	$5000 and Above	$4,745,936	4X	$1,186,484	$1,398,156	$211,672
B	$1200 - $5499	1,405,864	3X	468,621	776,753	308,132
C	Below $1200	827,518	2X	413,759	932,158	518,399
	TOTALS	$6,979,318	3X	$2,068,864	$3,107,067	$1,038,203

FIGURE 10–1: Quick Calculation of Inventory Targets

One of the worst mistakes an executive can do is to arbitrarily set a specific inventory turnover as a target—without first calculating the proper level based on the company's service level objectives. But Figure 10–1 can be used to make a quick calculation of inventory targets.

INVENTORY RECORD ACCURACY ANALYSIS: AN OVERALL ASSESSMENT

One way to get an overall idea of the impact of inventory value and inaccuracy is to utilize the following bits of data collected during and at the completion of the annual physical inventory. In doing any inventory calculations, use the FIFO, not year-end LIFO, inventory value.

Data Worksheet

Data Code	Explanation	Typical Data	Your Company
	INVENTORY VALUE		
A	Inventory investment (before physical inventory)	$3,107,018	
B	Book to physical net adjustment (last time taken)	($37,284)	
	RECORD ACCURACY[a]		
C	Perpetual book and actual storeroom balances quantities are *within 10 percent* of each other	67%	
D	Perpetual book balances exceed *actual stock by more* than 10 percent	21%	
E	Actual stock quantities exceed *perpetual book balance* by *more* than 10 percent	12%	
	Total of C, D, and E	100%	100%

TURNOVER

F	Actual overall annual inventory turnover	2.246	
G	Desired overall annual inventory turnover[b]	3.218	

CARRYING COSTS

H	Company's current bank loan interest rate	10.0%	
I	Material handling, storage, insurance costs, and so forth	10.7%	
J	Total Inventory Carrying Costs	20.7%	

PURCHASES

K	Annual Purchases—Production materials	$6,979,316	
L	Annual Purchases—Miscellaneous items	$1,369,637	
M	Total Purchases	$8,348,953	

TAX AND PROFITS

N	Present Company Federal Income Tax Rate	42%	
O	Company profits last year	$ 615,000	

[a] Random sample permissible to obtain percentages
[b] Obtain from company executives

Then use the data obtained in the first step to estimate the impact on increasing company profits through better inventory control. This is accomplished using this calculation worksheet.

HOW TO ESTIMATE THE IMPACT ON PROFITS THROUGH IMPROVED INVENTORY CONTROL

Step 1: Begin by posting the data obtained from the Data Collection Worksheet.

1. Inventory investment (before physical inventory adjustments)

    $3,107,018
    (Data Code A)

2. Physical inventory adjustment (plus or minus)

    ($37,284)
    (Data B)

3. Subtotal (add or subtract lines 1 and 2)

    $3,069,734

4. Target inventory level

$$\frac{2.246}{\text{(Data F)}} \div \frac{3.218}{\text{(Data G)}} = .6979 \times \frac{\$3,107,018}{\text{(Data A)}} = \quad \$2,168,388$$

5. Subtotal (subtract line 4 from 3) to obtain "Excessive Inventory"

    $901,346

Step 2: Determine the cost of inaccurate inventory records and excessive inventory.

6. Inventory carrying costs

$$\underset{\substack{\text{(From Line 5)}}}{\$901,346} \times \dfrac{20.7\%}{\substack{\text{Carrying} \\ \text{Cost} \\ \text{(Data J)}}} = \dfrac{\$186,579}{\text{(Annual Carrying Costs)}}$$

7. Purchasing excessive costs

$$\dfrac{\$6,979,316}{\substack{\text{Annual} \\ \text{Purchases} \\ \text{(Data K)}}} \times \dfrac{21\%}{\substack{\text{Rush} \\ \text{Purchases} \\ \text{(Data D)}}} = \$1,465,656 \times \dfrac{10\%}{\substack{\text{Extra Cost} \\ \text{of Rush} \\ \text{Purchases}}} = \dfrac{\$146,566}{\substack{\text{(Excess} \\ \text{Purchasing} \\ \text{Costs)}}}$$

8. **Annual cost of excess inventory and rush purchases** (Add lines 6 and 7) Total

$$\dfrac{\$333,145}{\text{(Total Excessive Annual Costs)}}$$

Step 3: Finally calculate the additional profit potential if you obtain accurate inventory record balances and lower inventory to the target.

9. Additional dollar profits possible

$$\dfrac{\$333,145}{\substack{\text{(Total Excessive} \\ \text{Annual Costs)}}} \times \left[100\% - \dfrac{42\%}{\substack{\text{Income Tax Rate} \\ \text{(Data N)}}} \right] = \dfrac{\$193,224}{\text{(Additional Profits)}}$$

10. Percent profit increase possible

$$\dfrac{\$193,224}{\substack{\text{Dollar Additional} \\ \text{Profits Possible} \\ \text{(Line 9)}}} \div \dfrac{\$615,000}{\substack{\text{Company Profits} \\ \text{Last Year} \\ \text{(Data 0)}}} = \dfrac{31.4\%}{\text{(Percent Increase)}}$$

HOW YOUR COMPANY COMPARES WITH OTHERS

Considerable insight into the inventory investment of other companies can be obtained from various statistical sources. The following list shows readily available sources of information relative to inventory, usually by Standard Industrial Classification (SIC).

A. Historic Statistical Studies

1. **Robert Morris & Associates**

   a. This reference is useful in describing three very important statistics. The statistics are

      i. Inventory as a percentage of total assets

      ii. Cost of goods sold/inventory

      iii. Inventory turnover in days

    b. The cost of goods sold (CGS)/inventory ratio measures the number of times during the year inventory is turned over. High turnover can indicate either good liquidity, such as, effective management while low liquidity can mean the opposite. The ratio is calculated by taking end-of-year figures and thereby ignoring seasonality, and so forth. The turnover in days is calculated by dividing 365 by the CGS/Inventory statistic. These statistics are broken down first by a four-digit SIC code and then by total asset size up to $100 million. In general, this is a comprehensive listing of inventory statistics by SIC code.

  2.   Dun & Bradstreet: Key Business Ratios

    a. This reference has three relevant statistics compiled for a selected group of four-digit SIC codes. The reference gives some statistics for upper, medium, and lower range of responses. These are

      i. Net Sales to Inventory

      ii. Inventory to Net Working Capital

      iii. Current Debt to Inventory

B. Aggregate Inventory Data

1. There are various sources that contain aggregate inventory data either for all manufacturers or other classification such as hospitals, banks, and so forth. These sources include useful overall information and can be helpful in determining trends in general.

    a. Survey of Current Business, U.S. Department of Commerce

    b. U.S. Statistical Abstract

    b. National Industrial Conference Board Economic Almanac

    d. U.S. Industrial Outlook, U.S. Department of Commerce

C. Trade Publications

1. The most useful reference materials, in addition to the references above, which are usually located at the local public library, are the various trade publications.

2. These publications, ranging from heavy industrial equipment merchandising to soft goods and supermarket retailing, often have industry inventory statistics and related industry figures.

3. Three trade publications of particular interest are the magazines *Production & Inventory Management Review*, *Purchasing World*, and *Purchasing*.

These magazines show inventory information and lead times on various products and commodities.

D. U.S. Department of Commerce Overall Census Materials

1. The most recent census contains some relevant information by SIC code and is broken down using the two-digit SIC codes. However, in terms of specific inventory information, there were only two sources of usable information found:

   a. Census of Wholesale Trade
      This reference does contain merchandise inventory by type of operation, such as SIC 50, 51 up to the four-digit SIC code in each category.

   b. Annual Survey of Manufacturers
      This reference is perhaps the most comprehensive up-to-date reference available to determine the value of manufacturing inventories by SIC codes (Numbers 20-39).

Industry	SIC No.	Description	Inventory as % of Assets	Cost of Goods Sold to Inv. Ratio
Manufacturing	27	Printing & Publishing	15	13
	30	Rubber & Misc. Plastics Products	24	7
	32	Stone, Clay, & Glass Products	20	10
	34	Fabricated Metal Products	26	7
	35	Machinery, Except Electrical	28	5
	38	Instruments & Related Products	29	3
		Average of 20 Manufacturing SICs	27	9
Retail	52	Building Materials & Garden Supplies	44	5
	54	Food Stores	28	16
	55	Auto Dealers & Service Stations	56	8
	56	Apparel & Accessory Stores	58	3
	58	Eating & Drinking Places	7	28
		Average of 8 Retail SICs	41	9
Wholesale	50	Durable Goods	3	7
	51	Non-Durable Goods	2	16
Agriculture	01	Agricultural Production-Crops	17	8
	02	Agricultural Production-Livestock	36	5
Construction	15	General Building Contractors	15	N/A
	16	Heavy Construction Contractors	3	N/A
Services	73	Business Services	5	N/A
	75	Auto Repair, Services & Garages	17	N/A
	79	Amusement & Recreational Services	5	N/A

FIGURE 10–2: Inventory Statistics for Selected Industries

HOW INVENTORY INVESTMENT IN YOUR INDUSTRY COMPARES TO OTHERS

As detailed in Figure 10–2, the inventory investment can vary widely by industry.[1] This example gives some representative statistics for 20 different industries represented by SIC codes. The data provided are the averages for each industry and RMA cautions that the studies be regarded only as a general guideline and not as an absolute industry norm. This is due to the categorization of companies by their primary Standard Industrial Classification (SIC) number only, and different methods of inventory financial reporting by companies within the same industry. For these reasons, RMA recommends that the figures be used only as general guidelines. For your own industry, annual reports of competitors (if published) and trade association information may be useful.

COMPARISON BY PRODUCT MARKET STRATEGY

Inventory investment can be based on the product market strategy[2]:

	Raw Material and Parts	Work in Process	Finished Goods	Spare Parts
Low cost—make to stock	Low	Low	Med.	Low
Narrow product line—make to stock	Low	Low	Med.	Med.
Wide product lines—make to stock	Med./High	Med.	Med.	High
Rapid customer response with customized product	High	Low	None	Low
Level production for seasonal demand	Low	Low	High/Low	High/Low
Rapid delivery of spare parts	Low	Low	—	High

Inventory investment for work-in-process usually varies the most. It often is directly related to the length of the manufacturing cycle (such as the number of operations and time necessary to fabricate the product). An important consideration for finished goods and some raw material is the customer service level desired. If the sales order entry processing cycle is unusually long, then additional inventory is required.

HOW TO SIMULATE THE PROPER INVENTORY INVESTMENT: FIVE VARIABLES TO CONSIDER

There are five variables to be considered when trying to simulate or calculate the proper inventory level:

1. ability to forecast customer needs, as represented by the forecast error
2. desire to give prompt delivery service, as represented by planned in-stock service level
3. accuracy of inventory perpetual records compared to actual balance on hand, as represented by percent of parts that deviate
4. amount of "vertical" integration of the product line, as represented by the amount of manufactured versus purchased parts
5. completeness of manufacturing documents; as represented by accuracy of bill of materials, route sheets, and so on

Figure 10–3 is the inventory computer simulation for the R.G. CEPT Company based on three different sales levels, all developed as part of the inventory plan using a strategic business plan.

"STOCK IN" SERVICE LEVEL

Sales Level	MAD: Service Level	1.0 84%	1.5 93%	3.0 99.9%
$10,000,000		$1,954,000	$2,071,000	$2,442,000
$15,000,000		$2,931,000	$3,107,000	$3,663,750
$20,000,000		$3,908,000	$4,142,000	$4,885,000

FIGURE 10–3: Inventory Computer Simulation

THREE METHODS FOR DETERMINING THE PROPER INVENTORY LEVEL FOR YOUR COMPANY

The purpose of establishing an inventory investment standard is to set a level to prevent the buildup of extra inventory that, at some point, would become excessive and eventually obsolete material.

Day's Usage Method

The calculation worksheet shown in Table 10–1 should be completed by the materials manager and submitted to the vice-president of Manufacturing for approval. The recent historical and/or forecasted "dollar usage per day" should be obtained by taking the total inventory issues in dollars last year and dividing by the number of work days. Insert this number next to the appropriate "type inventory." By using the desired "days supply" column, an extension is made to determine the "standard in dollars." The "actual dollar inventory" should then be posted and the "deviation" from the "standard in dollars" determined.

Forecasted Sales Method

Although the second procedure is more judgmental, you can establish target levels by ascertaining the amount of inventory desired by Sales to meet anticipated customer orders. To use this method, take the historical sales last year, establish months' supply targets, and calculate dollar inventory by various categories. The following example lists inventory target levels for a CEPTmobile distributor.

Historical Annual Sales

1,200 Stock CEPTmobile

520 Custom-Ordered CEPTmobile

600 Used CEPTmobile

300 Rental CEPTmobile

$33,000 Parts Sales

Stock CEPTmobile Inventory

1 month supply or 100 on hand at $1,995 each   = $199,500

Custom-Ordered CEPTmobile

1 week supply or 10 on hand at $3,150 each   = $ 31,500

Used CEPTmobile from Trade-Ins

2 months' supply or 100 at $1,000 each   = $100,000

Table 10-1: Calculation Worksheet

Type Inventory	Dollar Usage per Day	×	Days Supply	=	Standard in Dollars	Actual Dollar Inventory	Std. to Actual Deviation Less	Std. to Actual Deviation More
Raw Material								
Local Suppliers	$ 1,760		30		$ 52,800	$ 41,673	$ 11,127	
Distant Vendors	4,150		70		290,500	402,693		$112,103
Purchase Components	2,180		60		130,800	196,532		65,732
Work-in-Process—Parts	1,870		30		56,100	187,961		131,861
Manufactured Components	4,700		45		211,500	399,711		188,211
Work-in-Process—Assembly	9,600		60		576,000	781,003		205,003
Finished Assemblies	16,100		30		483,000	716,943		233,943
Replacement Parts	4,360		90		392,400	181,296	211,104	
TOTAL	$44,720		49		$2,193,100	$2,907,812	$222,231	$936,943
							Net	$714,712
							Absolute	$1,159,174

Rental CEPTmobile

  300 on rental or available for rent at $1,995   = $598,000

Parts Sales

  4 months' supply on hand $ 11,000

    TOTAL TARGET INVENTORY $940,500

Calculation Method

The preceding two methods can be easily utilized. However, it often is desirable to perform a more complete target determination. This procedure is described below.

At any given point for the items in stock, some will be at maximum amount (for example the reorder quantity of 6,000 items, plus safety stock of 600 for total of 6,600), some at the reorder point (1,800), some at the safety stock level (600) and, of course, all sorts of other levels. The average quantity on hand for an item can be determined by dividing the reorder quantity by 2 and adding to it the safety stock quantity. If we reordered 6,000 sheets of paper, the average quantity on hand would be 3,600 (6,000 divided by 2 plus 600 safety stock). If we determine the average quantity on hand plus the safety stock quantity and multiply this amount times the unit cost for each item on hand, we then can determine the dollar inventory target standard for all items kept in the stockroom merely by adding each item's average quantity on hand. This determination can be done by the various inventory groups—raw material, product line, storage location, and so forth.

Most organizations have to maintain additional inventories for the special needs of their customers. This material can be for sales promotions, unusual emergency requirements, prebuilding for seasonal goods, hedges for possible strikes, reserves for special customers, and so forth. Even the most perfect inventory control systems end up with surplus (slow moving items), as well as obsolete material due to changing customer or even design engineering needs.

To calculate the proper inventory investment's standard level, you should consider the five groups of inventory shown in Figure 10–4. One of these groups is the "desired" inventory, two more are "permissible," and the last two are the "not desired." Group 2 is under the control of Manufacturing or Operations, while Group 3 is the responsibility of the Sales or Special Users Department. Thus, with permission from management, special inventories can be maintained over and above the normal inventory item balances in Group 1.

THE FIVE INVENTORY GROUPS

Group No.

> **PLANNED**

> (Desired)

1   • Normal Inventory Items

> **EXCEPTION**

> (Permissible)

2   • Manufacturing Preference: Long Runs,
          Vendor Rework, Emergency Items, New Products,
          Strike Hedge

3   • Sales Preference: Stocking Plans, Favored
          Company, Promotion, Credit Holds, Etc.

> (Not Desired)

4   • Surplus: Excess of Current Needs

5   • Obsolete and Phased Out Material

FIGURE 10–4: Five Inventory Groups

FIVE INVENTORY GROUPS FOR DETERMINING PROPER INVESTMENT TARGETS

With the previous discussion in mind, let's establish the inventory standard for the R.G. CEPT Company.

Group 1: Normal, Planned Inventory (Desired)

To calculate the inventory for this group, you obtain the reorder quantity and safety stock for each of the departments allowed to maintain inventory. Each reorder quantity is divided by 2 to get the average on hand amount.

The planned safety stock is added to this amount to get a unit total, which is multiplied by the unit cost to obtain the dollar value. Then, all dollar values are added up by department to get departmental and grand totals for Group 1.

Group 2: Manufacturing Preference Items (Permissible)

Some departments in the company are permitted by management to maintain certain items where no stock-out can be permitted. The projected dollar value of these items should be obtained and listed by each storing department.

Group 3: Sales Department Preferences (Permissible)

In any organization, some departments require what we called "preference" items. The actual dollar value of these permitted items upon sales and management approval, such as special finished goods for a favorite customer, should be listed on the worksheet.

Group 4: Surplus Inventory (Not Desired)

There is no perfect inventory system; in any organization surplus or excess material will develop through the normal chain of events. Surplus inventory is defined as good, usable inventory for which you have too much on hand. The maximum amount of inventory on hand, for any item, should be the reorder quantity plus the safety stock. Thus, surplus inventory is that amount on hand that exceeds the reorder quantity plus safety stock dollar value—so list the actual dollar value by department and total of all surplus material.

Group 5: Obsolete Inventory (Not Desired)

This last group includes items no longer required due to changes in supplies used and/or equipment required. In this group—also by department—you should list the actual (book or original) value of all obsolete material by department and in total.

In summation: The inventory standard target is the total of groups 1, 2, and 3. Groups 4 and 5, by being identified, can eventually be disposed of through exchanges, substitution, scrapping, and so forth.

Figure 10–5 illustrates both typical inventory targets and actual investment for the R.G. CEPT Company. The total actual inventory of $3,107,018 (at FIFO) represents a turnover of 2.2 times, since the annual inventory usage was $6,979,316 worth of material. However, if the investment was decreased to the target of $2,168,470, turnover increases to a more respectable 3.2 times.

WORK-IN-PROCESS INVENTORY TARGET

This calculation (which is necessary for most manufacturing companies) can be made by determining two statistics: (1) the value of the average daily usage (called day's supply), and (2) the average manufacturing actual cycle time in days. The work-in-process target is then calculated by the method in Figure 10–6. Use Figure 10–7 as a worksheet for the your company's inventory calculation.

R. G. CEPT COMPANY
INVENTORY TARGETS

NORMAL PLANNED (DESIRED)		EXCEPTION INVENTORIES					
		(PERMISSIBLE)			(NOT DESIRED)		
GROUP 1		2	3		4	5	
Type Inventory	Average	Mfg. Preference	Customer Preference	Total Target	Surplus	Obsolete	Grand Total
Raw Material	$481,616	$41,600	$0	$523,216	$221,064	$47,683	791,963
Purchase Components	775,530	61,100	0	836,630	214,336	47,145	1,098,111
Work in Process	462,037	0	0	462,037	110,325	19,642	592,004
Finished Goods	126,087	50,000	170,500	346,587	78,611	199,742	624,940
Total	$1,845,270	$152,700	$170,500	$2,168,470	$624,336	$314,212	$3,107,018
Calculation	a +	b +	c =	d +	e +	f =	g

FIGURE 10–5: Inventory Targets for the R.G. CEPT Company

WORK IN PROCESS MATERIAL TARGET CALCULATION

1. Divide annual value of raw material and purchased component issues by the number of work days in a year to get "average daily usage" of these materials. For example:

$$\frac{\$6,978,733}{240} = \$29,078$$

2. Determine the average production "cycle time" (sometimes called the "manufacturing lead time"). We'll use 9 days in this example.

3. Multiply the average daily usage times the average cycle time to obtain the work in process inventory target.

$$\$29,078 \times 9 = \$261,702$$

FIGURE 10–6: Calculating Work-in-Process Investment

HOW TO CALCULATE EXCESS AND OBSOLETE INVENTORY

The question often raised is how to establish the "classical" procedure to calculate obsolete inventory. You should not have the Finance Department responsible for the determination of the proper obsolete inventory reserve for the following three reasons:

1. It removes the responsibility for obsolete inventory from Manufacturing, where it belongs.
2. It lessens the responsibility of Marketing to provide a forecast or historical customer demand for each item expected to be ordered in the future.
3. It eliminates the independent "check and balance" review, which is a prime duty of the Finance Department.

The following details the proper method to select the items and make the obsolescence calculation. The preferred procedure to determine the obsolete inventory reserve is depicted in Figure 10–8. Since any obsolete calculation is very sensitive to (and dependent upon) a correct forecast, this procedure

	NORMAL PLANNED (DESIRED) GROUP ①	EXCEPTION INVENTORIES (PERMISSIBLE) ② ③			(NOT DESIRED) ④ ⑤		
Type Inventory	Average	Mfg. Preference	Customer Preference	Total Target	Surplus	Obsolete	Grand Total
Raw Material							
Purchase Components							
Work in Process							
Finished Goods							
Total							
Calculation	a +	b +	c =	d +	e +	f =	g

FIGURE 10–7: Inventory Target Worksheet

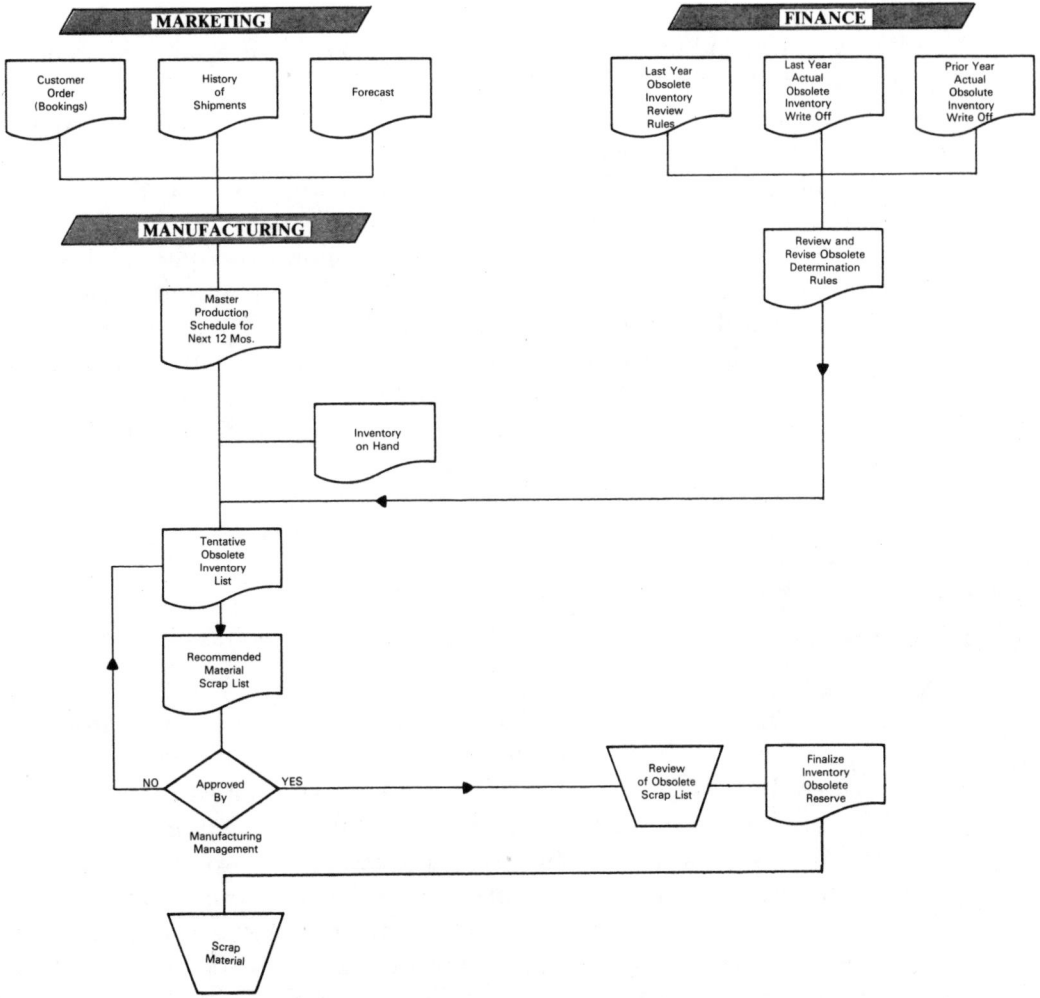

FIGURE 10–8: Excess and Obsolete Inventory Procedure

begins in Marketing. Projections for future customer demands (orders) come from a combination of

1. a forecast for assembly products
2. historical activity for spares
3. the existing open customer orders

This information is given to Manufacturing, which makes a gross requirement master schedule for the life of the inventory specified by Finance. Manufacturing compares the schedule needs versus the inventory on hand and makes a "Tentative Obsolete List." Since the obsolete item determination is dependent upon the forecast, a double-check should now be performed to ascertain if any item/product was inadvertently missed. The finalized, recommended list should then be given to Finance.

During this entire process, Finance can and should validate the procedure through selected checks. This independent review would include the study of the final recommendations from Manufacturing, giving Finance the ultimate decision of setting the dollar reserve. One last point for consideration: The type of inventory control system (Reorder Point or Material Requirements Planning) is of little significance in determining the obsolete inventory. This procedure will identify, by item, those that are slow moving (inventory in excess of demand) and those that are obsolete (no anticipated demand will occur in the future). In a MRP system—using computerized inventory techniques—it is possible to print out by item those that exceed one or more tests.

REDUCING INVENTORY TO THE CALCULATED LEVEL: A 12-STEP PROGRAM

The raw material, work in process, and finished goods inventories in most companies are excessive, usually at least 20 percent too high. There are two ways to reduce the inventory investment of the company to a more appropriate operating level. The first is a "crash" program, which almost never succeeds, since it does not consider the many aspects of the problem. The second is a carefully planned approach, normally taking from six to eighteen months, which reduces the inventory investment without any decrease in service level to the customer. The challenge is to reduce carefully the inventory investment using a 12-step program suggested (in storybook fashion) in Figure 10–9.

Initial Step: Create an Inventory Reduction Team

The initial setup is to establish the Inventory Reduction Team that will review all areas and activities affecting the factory and warehouse inventory levels. The team is not assigned any operating responsibility for the inventory control function, but is to serve as a strong assistance to the Production and Inventory Control Departments. The team objectives are to

1. Review and analyze specific inventory management problems.
2. Suggest immediate and obvious steps to balance and reduce inventories.
3. Assist in formulation of inventory management programs.
4. Develop necessary procedures to implement recommended changes.

1 Define Program Objectives	2 Select Reduction Team	3 List High Inventory Symptoms	4 Set Monthly Reduction Targets
5 Train Employees	6 Start Standardization Process	7 Write Policy and Procedures	8 Recognize Initial Success
9 Chart and Report Progress Monthly	10 Modify Program if Necessary	11 Develop Inventory Target Maintenance Plan	12 Present Final Report

FIGURE 10—9: 12-Step Inventory Reduction Program Story Board

5. Provide systems and procedures needed to carry out inventory policies as established by the Inventory Policy Committee.

6. Recommend changes for improvements to the Inventory Policy Committee.

7. Provide for accomplishment of corporate inventory objectives while improving the level of service to customers.

Although the ideal time to reduce inventory is during good economic conditions (it is much easier to use up the excess and write-off the obsolete inventory), most companies undertake inventory reduction programs during a poor business climate.

The efforts should be on both a broadly gauged (macro) basis and a specific item (micro) approach. Timing is short, intermediate, and longer range. Usually a substantial decrease can be achieved after three months of work followed by a relatively slow period—in terms of reduction—for the next three months (the first plateau). Good reductions are then achieved during the seventh to twelfth month (a second plateau) and then steady but smaller decreases until the optimum level is reached at about eighteen months after starting.

Short-Range Reductions

An example of the initial efforts that gain short-range reductions can be classified into three groups. The first are tasks that give tangible results, such as

1. Review shop order before final release.
2. Reschedule orders in process.
3. Cancel or reschedule slow-moving products.
4. Cancel or reschedule open purchase orders.
5. Fill branch requisitions from plant inventory.

The second group includes work that cannot be readily measured. These include

1. Hold up purchased materials for delivery.
2. Review steel and shop order coverage.
3. Return rejected material rapidly.
4. Audit inventory analyst's decision.
5. Return supply inventory from field warehouse to central warehouse.

In the third group, on-the-job training of employees should be increased, policies reviewed and emphasized, and supervision efforts magnified.

Intermediate-Range Reductions

Intermediate range results can be achieved by using these reduction techniques:

1. Buy at a smaller economic order quantity or at the EOQ—if you weren't before.
2. Reduce the protective, safety stock level.
3. Reschedule shop or purchase orders to later deliveries.
4. Telegram vendor to stop delivery for "X" days.
5. Substitute one type of raw material on hand for another.
6. Clean up the shop, scrapping or reworking old material.
7. Reject all overshipments on purchased items.
8. Police the overissues of material.
9. Buy more items on a short-range basis.
10. Reduce ordering costs.
11. Review high order points and high order quantities.
12. Use old stock first.
13. Use Just-in-Time quick delivery flow principle, telling suppliers the day and time to deliver.
14. Deliver by truck or air freight, not by railroad car.
15. Review all A items daily, B items weekly, and C items monthly for excess coverage.
16. Review all purchase orders valued above $300 weekly.
17. Cancel all unneeded shop and purchase orders.
18. Modify excess or obsolete parts into another part number.
19. Arbitrarily reduce lot sizes and requisitions by "X" percent.
20. Maintain list of items in all warehouses and move goods from one warehouse to supply another.
21. Accelerate the scrap processing program.
22. Speed up the receiving inspection process.
23. Rework rejected material rapidly.
24. Send a list to customers of certain items you wish to sell at special prices in a "preinventory clearance" sale.
25. Obtain material from vendors on a delayed invoice payment basis.
26. Use the run-out ratio to prioritize various items in process.
27. Use the critical ratio to provide last-minute priority for production sequence.
28. Break critical machine capacity bottlenecks.

Longer-Range Reductions

Longer term reduction can be achieved by several of these possible techniques:

1. Watch the number of months' supply of material by item number.
2. Sell unneeded steel and other material.
3. Release shop orders or requisitions just prior to production or purchasing.
4. Consolidate the number of inventory stores locations or warehouses or redesign layouts to eliminate multiple stores.
5. Set up inventory level charts by item classification.
6. Monitor the adherence to the target inventory level.
7. Redesign the inventory ledger cards for clarity and accuracy.
8. Standardize and/or simplify the product.
9. Eliminate certain products from the product line.
10. Reduce manufacturing and suppliers' lead time.
11. Set up stocking programs with suppliers.
12. Request suppliers to stock goods for quick delivery at a local warehouse.
13. Buy on a consignment basis.
14. Buy on a supplier "make and hold" basis.
15. Reduce the replenishment paper cycle time.
16. Get better forecasts.
17. Install a value analysis program.
18. Reduce safety stock at several bill of material levels.
19. Maintain materials at subassemblies, not final assemblies.
20. Minimize seasonal building of material.
21. Do not have complete plant shut down; vary vacations.
22. Simulate the capacity of the shop; release orders only to the limit.
23. Provide incentives to employees for successful low-cost, high turnover inventory control.
24. Set up a sample department for small orders.
25. Speed up the routing reproduction by having more standardized forms.
26. Use numerically controlled machines.
27. Have several assembly lines and move crews from one line to the next one, which has been set up previously.
28. Check the machine maintenance reports to ascertain production delay points.
29. Review the posting accuracy on ledger cards.

30. Cancel excess "float" on orders.

31. Use line balancing, milestones, or Gantt charts for control of in-process items.

32. Study purchasing statistics for poor vendor deliveries or quality.

33. Speed up sales order entry and engineering document processing time control.

34. Cease supplying old service parts; send customer blueprints instead so they can produce the parts themselves.

35. Set up more blanket orders.

36. Conduct group brainstorming meetings for idea selection.

37. Decrease time span between filling of order and replacement of stock sold.

38. Utilize where-used lists.

39. Control the inventory investment carefully on single customer use items.

For a Little Encouragement: The Results of Three Inventory Reduction Programs

Figure 10–10 shows a "Case in Point" of the results of three inventory reduction programs, indicating the duration, reduction dollars, and percentage plus the impact of increased turnover. In reviewing these case examples, be encouraged. Inventory can be carefully reduced, but to do so requires planning and effort.

CHAPTER REFERENCES

1. *Annual Statement Studies*, Robert Morris and Associates, Philadelphia, PA, 1985.

2. E. C. Huge, "Manufacturing Strategy, Part IV," *Purchasing World* (June 1982). Reprinted with permission from *Purchasing World* magazine, copyright June 1982, Huebner Publications, Inc.

Program	Inventory Type	Duration of Program - Months	Value of Inventory ($000)		Reduction Dollars	Percent	Turnover	
			Start	Finish			From	To
1.	Raw Material	12	$4,358	$3,050	$1,308	30.0%	2.4	3.4
2.	Raw Mat'l., WIP & FG	9	2,500	2,005	495	19.8%	2.8	3.5
3.a	Raw Matl.	24	2,022	1,518	504	24.9%		
b.	Work in Process	24	3,200	2,210	990	30.9%		
c.	Finished goods- for prod assembly	24	2,884	2,285	599	20.8%	2.4	3.0
d.	Finished goods- for service	24	2,561	1,669	892	34.8%		
e.	Branch plant- RM & WIP	24	6,931	5,942	989	14.3%		
	SUBTOTAL		17,598	13,624	3,974			
	GRAND TOTAL		$24,456	$18,679	$5,777	23.6%	2.5	3.3

FIGURE 10–10: Results of Three Inventory Reduction Programs

Vendor Capacity Planning and Other Purchasing Contract Techniques for Improving Deliveries and Reducing Costs

11

CHAPTER HIGHLIGHTS

The old days of issuing purchase orders, expediting like mad, then waiting for the material to come in are gone. Now, and in the future, a close vendor-customer relationship is necessary.

This chapter details the use of vendor capacity planning (VCP), an extension of material requirements planning and the just-in-time delivery concept. You'll discover why VCP contracts are especially useful for reducing lead times and controlling inadequate supplies.

The VCP technique in action and 13 steps for establishing VCP in your company are examined in detail. Also discussed are other purchasing contract methods such as systems contracts and subcontracting. In addition, cost considerations are included, such as price breaks (are you really saving money with them?) and standard parts versus special orders.

EIGHT PURCHASING ACTIONS TO HELP CONTROL INVENTORIES

The purchasing function can greatly assist in helping manage the inventory through the following actions:

1. Determine prices using a combination of techniques that protect both buyer and seller in volatile market and interest rate times.
2. Buy more from less suppliers after a long, careful selection process.
3. Establish Vendor Capacity Planning that includes long-term contracts using a forecast of production material requirements.
4. Set up blanket order stocking contract arrangements with vendors for operating supplies.
5. Schedule delivery of production materials using statistical process controls, and just-in-time/Kanban style releases.
6. Maintain tight order quantity control over subcontracted operations.
7. Analyze months' supply on hand immediately prior to ordering or expediting miscellaneous supplies.
8. Utilize an inventory and purchasing budget to obtain overall control of inventory investment. (This last action is explained in Chapter 14.)

HOW TO SELECT THE BEST PURCHASING CONTRACT TECHNIQUE FOR YOUR COMPANY'S NEEDS

Analyze Purchases and Categorize into Groups

Before selecting the better types of purchasing contract techniques to use, purchasing and inventory personnel should jointly analyze last year's purchases of both production and nonproduction items. This study should categorize purchased goods and materials into one of these general groups:

1. Raw materials
2. Purchased components
3. Subcontracted production services
4. Production supplies and services
5. Office supplies and services
6. Capital equipment
7. Utilities

If detailed data by these above groups are not available, then the company's annual list of accounts payable by vendor (usually available from Accounting), can be utilized to approximate the dollars by group. The R.G. CEPT Company's prior year purchases are shown in Figure 11–1, which shows the dollar purchases by commodity code. This information should be used for inventory management planning for this year.

Determine the Most Effective Contract per Group

The next step is to determine which is the most effective type of purchase contract to use for each group. A number of choices are available. The following lists the types of contracts with a brief explanation of the order terms.

- Blanket Order: A type of purchase order in which the same order number is used for a period of time. This order usually is subsequently amended by blanket order releases, mostly written but sometimes handled by telephone. It can be for a specific part or a similar commodity group. Four types exist:

  1. Standing Purchase Order: A type of blanket order that has a specific quantity specified for regular interval delivery, such as every month, week, and so forth.

  2. Fixed Order: Quantity is established on the original blanket purchase order but shipments are governed by material releases against the order. No shipments are authorized without a release.

  3. Open Order: Quantity is not established on the blanket orders though estimated annual usages are established. Raw material procurement, fabrication, and shipment are authorized by releases only.

  4. National Contract: A blanket purchase order that covers multiple releases by "ship to" locations within a corporation. It is sometimes called a corporate purchase agreement.

- Subcontract: For special outside processing by a vendor performing work which the buyer's company cannot do or lacks the capacity to do. This is one of the most difficult areas to control from an inventory standpoint.

- Systems Contracting: This type of contract usually covers a plant or a department's requirements for MRO (maintenance, repair, and operating) supplies and miscellaneous production parts. It provides for the supplier to carry inventory and to make regular off-the-shelf (J-I-T type) timely deliveries.

- List Order: This is a preprinted purchase order parts list that has provisions for flexible release quantities.

- Service/Maintenance Agreements: These are usually established for routine check on equipment and may include repair parts.

No.	Raw Materials (10-29)	Annual Value
11	Aluminum	$146,993
12	Canvas	517,413
13	Chemicals	64,843
14	Colorants	31,469
15	Forgings	203,116
16	Resin	407,634
17	Rubber	42,447
18	Steel Bars	193,716
19	Steel Sheets	1,235,914
20	Wire	23,747
21	Miscellaneous Raw Materials	310,169
	TOTAL	3,177,461

No.	Purchased Components (30-49)	Annual Value
31	Batteries	464,119
32	Brakes	106,484
33	Bumpers	197,631
34	Electric Motors, Control and Parts	363,951
35	Grills	361,774
36	Hoods and Sides, (Polyethylene)	549,262
37	Seats	299,003
38	Transmissions	884,632
39	Wheels and Hub Caps	303,444
40	Miscellaneous	109,766
	TOTAL	3,640,066

No.	Subcontracted Production Services (50-59)	Annual Value
51	Heat Treating	41,786
52	Plating	107,119
53	Miscellaneous	12,884
	TOTAL	161,789
	TOTAL MATERIALS	6,979,316

No.	Production Supplies and Services (60-69)	Annual Value
61	Dies, Molds and Tools	66,493
62	Equipment Rentals, Repair and Parts	26,147
63	Gasoline and Lubricants	13,148
64	Packing and Shipping Supplies	37,949
65	Paints	19,611
66	Plant Maintenance Supplies	5,619
67	Transportation Services	189,006
68	Miscellaneous Production Services	9,656
	TOTAL	367,629

No.	Office Suppliers and Services (70-79)	Annual Value
70	Building Maintenance	27,841
71	Office Equipment Rental	13,014
72	Paper and Forms	47,929
73	Miscellaneous Office Supplies	6,986
	TOTAL	95,770

No.	Capital Equipment (80-89)	Annual Value
80	Computer Hardware	33,500
81	Office	16,745
82	Plant	406,117
	TOTAL	456,362

No.	Utilities (90-99)	Annual Value
91	Electricity	152,161
92	Gas	226,003
93	Telephone	37,916
94	Water	33,796
	TOTAL	449,876
	GRAND TOTAL	$8,348,953

FIGURE 11–1: Analysis of Purchases

HOW THE JUST-IN-TIME DELIVERY
CONCEPT WORKS
WITH VENDOR CAPACITY PLANNING

This process utilizes vendor capacity planning (VCP), a logical extension of the computerized material requirements planning system and the Japanese inspired "just-in-time" delivery concept. VCP contracts are useful for longer lead time and more expensive parts. Because the purchaser is giving more firm, reliable commitments to the seller, considerably reduced lead time is possible. The schedule—released at the beginning of one month for the next month's vendor production—goes directly into the vendor's machine loading. In effect, it is a purchase order with very special scheduling efforts. Once the contract is established, very frequent deliveries (daily and sometimes hourly), minimize raw and work-in-process inventories.

Eight Benefits of the J-I-T Supply
and Scheduling Concept

The supply and scheduling concept of just-in-time, commonly called J-I-T, utilizes a close working business relationship between two company functions—shop floor control and purchasing—along with the vendors who provide the essential materials and parts. It should be noted that J-I-T is an improved version of the Short Internal Scheduling technique popular in the 1950s. When fully implemented, J-I-T has these characteristics:

- Few suppliers, most of which are sole source, usually located within 200 miles of the company
- Longer term contracts with these suppliers resulting in business relationships lasting for several years
- Steady production schedules with frequent but gradual changes, well-communicated increases or decreases
- Purchased materials received in standard sizes, well-marked cartons or even in supply bins sent directly to production areas and subsequently sent back to the vendor for refilling
- Design of parts, specifications, and quality closely coordinated by the company and vendor Engineering Departments
- Statistical process control charts furnished by the vendor which eliminates the need for receiving inspection by the buyer
- Delivered quantities represent only a few days' requirements and sometimes just a few hours
- Vendor invoice received for entire month's deliveries similar to a bank statement

REPLENISHMENT LEAD TIME

A. Using Conventional Purchasing

Paperwork Lead time ①	Manufacturing Time for Vendor ②	Transportation Lead Time ③	Receiving & Inspection ④

◄───────────── Total Replenishment Lead Time ─────────────►

B. Using Just-in-Time

①	②	③	Process Charts

ORDERING COST

A. Using Conventional Purchasing

Negotiation ①	Open Order Status Paperwork ②	Expediting ③	Transportation ④	Receiving ⑤	Receiving Inspection ⑥

◄───────────── Total Ordering Cost ─────────────►

B. Using Just-in-Time

①	②③	④	Process Charts

FIGURE 11–2: Reductions Possible Under Just-In-Time

How to Reduce Costs and Improve Lead Times

The just-in-time concept recognizes that purchasing is the starting point for the materials flow cycle. In order to enable suppliers to deliver materials frequently to your plant, four critical elements are necessary:

1. Reduced order quantities
2. Frequent and reliable delivery schedules

3. Reduced and highly reliable (e.g., consistent) lead time

4. Consistently high quality levels for purchased materials[1]

The underlying concept, when successfully implemented, reduces the supplier's workload for a specific period. The benefits of J-I-T of lower inventory costs occur to both buyer and seller as do improved business relationships. Figure 11–2 illustrates how the ordering cost and replenishment lead times drastically decrease in a J-I-T environment. In all of this J-I-T planning, you should keep in mind that this system is not one you just plug in—it takes months and even years to accomplish the vendor rapport.

HOW VENDOR CAPACITY PLANNING MEETS THE J-I-T CHALLENGE: FOUR ESSENTIAL INGREDIENTS

The challenge: Suppose your boss demands that you improve the company's ability to meet your customer delivery requirements, yet at the same time reduce your inventory. In fact, your boss wants 30 percent less inventory at 10 percent lower prices, with a 20 percent increase in customer on-time delivery. What do you do?

The solution: Vendor capacity planning (VCP). This task is raised even though your boss knows, as you do, that the long lead time for much of your important raw material makes it very difficult to forecast, causing you to keep heavy safety stock.

If you ever have the above challenge, rush to see your purchasing agent and suggest that vendor capacity planning contracts be established. Vendor capacity planning is a methodology that expands considerably on the time-tested blanket order techniques plus a purchase order with a schedule. These types of contracts, which are difficult to establish but well worth the effort, have four essential ingredients:

1. A vendor who is willing and able to let you buy and load his or her plant's capacity. (You load only that portion of the capacity that will meet your requirements.)

2. Carefully worded purchase orders with clarification of the details of the contract concerning price, design, and quantity flexibility.

3. Releases based on the master schedule and/or your material requirements planning system.

4. Weekly and daily just-in-time deliveries.

The VCP Purchase Order

You might say that this is "one step beyond" the traditional blanket order. This contract is the kind that either party can cancel within a certain period of time, such as advance notice of six months. The terminology of the vendor capacity planning purchase order should be similar to the following:

> This purchase order is written to establish a vendor capacity planning blanket order with the Montford Foundry Company. It is valid for the one year period beginning January 1, 19————. The forgings covered by this contract, along with their minimum monthly schedule and unit prices, are as listed below. Delivery will be FOB at our plant. We will issue forging releases giving Montford 30-day shop lead time for all finished requirements and 60-day lead time for raw material. We will also furnish you, at no obligation whatsoever to our company, a forecast of our anticipated requirements for the third, fourth, fifth, and sixth months in the future. Each month's release will average 96,000 pounds of forgings produced by your company, but individual monthly releases can vary plus or minus 20 percent on a month-to-month basis. You will reserve production capacity each month for approximately 96,000 pounds of forging. We will machine load appropriate work centers to the established levels using the standards that you have previously furnished us. You will deliver the forgings to our plant three times a week based on our delivery schedule.

The VCP Technique in Action

The supplier officially reserves an amount of capacity for your needs. Your input to him, in the form of purchase order releases, goes into the work-in-process "load." The output of this backlog or load is equal to the production capability reserved for you. When your business—as well as the vendor's—increases, you place more orders, and the supplier's "load" (capacity reserved for you) increases.

Vendor capacity planning solves the dilemma of inadequate supply by establishing a contractual communication between you and your main vendors. A comparison to a manufacturing system shows:

Manufacturing	*Purchasing*
Shop Capacity Planning	Vendor Capacity Planning
Shop Orders	Blanket Orders
Dispatch List	Expedite Reports
Parts List	One-Time Purchase Orders

13 STEPS IN ESTABLISHING VENDOR CAPACITY PLANNING

1. *Select candidates for VCP.* One rule of thumb is to find out which parts and vendors dominate your own production using an ABC analysis similar to Figure 5–9 in Chapter 5 as a guide. Single-source vendors, captive suppliers, and hard-to-find vendors are good starting points. Parts in high demand, subject to rejection for quality and raw materials that become critical parts, are also candidates.

   - Output—a list of potential parts and vendors for a VCP program.

2. *Obtain a forecast of requirements.* Be on the look out for at least six months, but preferably up to one year, to obtain a forecast of requirements. Rough estimates based on historical usage and/or a strategic market plan will suffice.

   - Output—forecast by month periods for each item.

3. *Collect detailed information about possible VCP vendors.* Even though you may have dealt with the vendors for many years, it is uncertain if you will have adequate data. Use a Vendor Capacity Planning Supplier Questionnaire (Figure 11–3) with special emphasis on vendor capacity information.

   - Output—completed VCP Supplier Questionnaire.

Name of Potential Vendor _____

Prepared By _____ As of _____

Annual Sales _____

Location of Plants _____

Number of Employees _____

Type of Union _____

Date of Last Strike _____

Number of Shifts Worked _____

Total Floor Space Available _____

Type of Buildings _____

Date Built _____

Type of Special Equipment _____

General Housekeeping Conditions _____

Quality Control Methods _____

Production Capacity for Our Company _____

Number of Machines Used for Our Production _____

Ability to Deliver Frequently to Our Plant _____

Use of Statistical Process Control _____

Receptiveness to VCP Contract _____

FIGURE 11–3: Vendor Capacity Planning Supplier Questionnaire

| Commodity Group _____ | Part No. _____ | Cutoff Date _____ |
| Quotation No. _____ | | Time Period _____ |

Vendor Name				
Date Quote List Sent				
Date Quote List Received				
Number of Items on Quote List				
Number of Items Quoted				
$ Spent Last Year with Vendor				
Vendor Location(s)				
Delivery Method(s)				
Lead Time				
Special Vendor Terms				
Total $ Amount of Quote				
Price Difference?				
Firm Prices?				
Past Delivery Performance				
Past Quality Performance				
Vendor Selected				

FIGURE 11–4: Comparative Quotation Matrix

4. *Interview potential VCP sales representatives.* Inquire about the vendor's interest and willingness for a VCP arrangement, credit ratings, freight costs, production facilities, frequent just-in-time delivery abilities, and even the vendor's management style.

   ■ Output—VCP vendor quotation list.

5. *Send out Request for Quotations (RFQ).* Stress this as a potential VCP contract. Ask for quantity price breaks and methods by which the vendor calculates capacity and measures the production process.

   ■ Output—Request for Quotations.

6. *Select the best vendor candidates.* Use a Comparative Quotation Matrix (Figure 11–4). Be certain to structure the capacity data carefully. Capacity can be expressed in units (for castings), square feet (sheet metal), pounds (forgings), gallons (paint), tons (steel), or though more complex to calculate, standard machine hours. The easiest measure, though sometimes misleading, is simply dollars per month.

   ■ Output—Comparative Quotation Matrix.

7. *Negotiate and select the VCP vendor.* Use time-honored, face-to-face discussions. Since the RFQ is not necessarily the best or final price, details must be determined through negotiation.

   ■ Output—summary of negotiated agreement.

8. *Send out a blanket-style purchase order.* Stress the vendor's production unit of capacity measure, quantity, item specifications, authorized raw material requirements, and setup/changeover costs. Specify the lead time required by vendor, but allow provisions for a certain percent of rush shipments. Set a method to update the capacity requirements continuously for the period covered.

   ■ Output—Purchase order.

9. *Obtain written acknowledgment of P.O.* Specify this mandatory requirement on the front of your purchase order.

   ■ Output—Vendor acknowledgment.

10. *Invite vendor's production people to meet your production and engineering staff.* This allows for a long-term relationship to develop.

    ■ Output—Reference list of people with position title.

11. *Issue purchase order schedule release.* This is usually released to the vendor monthly via buyer or schedulers, specifying item due dates, and adding any "one time" purchases using a handwritten monthly schedule (similar to Figure 11–5), production master schedule, or a computer-prepared MRP schedule.

    ■ Output—Monthly release and forecast.
         —Daily J-I-T delivery schedule.

VENDOR_____ PURCHASE ORDER NO._____ RELEASE NO._____

PART NO._____ LAST SHIPMENT CONSIDERED,_____DATE_____QUANTITY_____

SCHEDULE/ RELEASE DATE	FIRM, RAW MATERIAL ONLY, AND FORECAST QUANTITIES												
	Month	JAN	FEB	MAR	APR	MAY	JUNE	JULY	AUG	SEPT	OCT	NOV	DEC
	Firm												
	Raw Matl. Only												
	Forecast												
	Month	FEB	MAR	APR	MAY	JUNE	JULY	AUG	SEPT	OCT	NOV	DEC	JAN
	Firm												
	Raw Matl. Only												
	Forecast												
	Month	MAR	APR	MAY	JUNE	JULY	AUG	SEPT	OCT	NOV	DEC	JAN	FEB
	Firm												
	Raw Matl. Only												
	Forecast												
	Month	APR	MAY	JUNE	JULY	AUG	SEPT	OCT	NOV	DEC	JAN	FEB	MAR
	Firm												
	Raw Matl. Only												
	Forecast												
	Month	MAY	JUNE	JULY	AUG	SEPT	OCT	NOV	DEC	JAN	FEB	MAR	APR
	Firm												
	Raw Matl. Only												
	Forecast												
	Month	JUNE	JULY	AUG	SEPT	OCT	NOV	DEC	JAN	FEB	MAR	APR	MAY
	Firm												
	Raw Matl. Only												
	Forecast												
	Month	JULY	AUG	SEPT	OCT	NOV	DEC	JAN	FEB	MAR	APR	MAY	JUNE
	Firm												
	Month	DEC	JAN	FEB	MAR	APR	MAY	JUNE	JULY	AUG	SEPT	OCT	NOV
	Firm												
	Raw Matl. Only												
	Forecast												

FIGURE 11–5: Blanket Order Schedule and Release

12. *Monitor the vendor's performance.* This should be done against the capacity reserved for you. Watch delivery trends, monitor early shipments, and utilize several progress reports.

- Output—Aggregate inventory commitment.
  —Requirements using capacity measure.
  —Open stock status for expediting backlog by vendor.

13. *Plan for next year.* Look for new items for VCP, contract improvements, and ways to better vendor relations.

- Output—Materials and parts for potential VCP contracts next year.

CASE IN POINT: Schedule Forecast

The document provided in one VCP system is a copy of the master schedule, one for each vendor on the system. The master schedule should be converted into the agreed unit of capacity measure (step 5). In Figure 11–6, your MRP and Capacity Planning systems are used to machine load the vendor's production work centers.

CAPACITY PLANNING INFORMATION - As Of: March 3

Blanket Purchase Order No: 6986   Scheduler: DeMore
Unit of Capacity Measurement: Pounds of Polyethylene
Monthly Capacity Reserved: 3850 Pounds
Last Shipment Considered: February 27
Work Center: Molding

Vendor Is Authorized the Following for These Parts:

| | | Required on the First of these Months | | | | | |
| | | April Produce | | May Order Raw Material | | June Forecast Only | |
Pt. No.	Desc.	Pieces	Pounds	Pieces	Pounds	Pieces	Pounds
1401	Hood-Poly	86	1892	43	946	79	1738
1402	Side-Poly	172	1720	86	860	158	1580
Total	Capacity Load	—	3612	—	1806	—	3318
Unused	Capacity	—	238	—	2044	—	532

FIGURE 11–6: Vendor Capacity Planning Schedule

SYSTEMS CONTRACTS: THE BETTER CHOICE FOR LOWER NONPRODUCTION MATERIALS INVENTORY

While the better method of use for the important, longer lead time parts is VCP, less costly production items and nonproduction items can have a "lower inventory investment" procedure. For these materials, the "least total cost" often is a systems contract—one where you may pay 1 percent more for the material but save 3 percent overall since the vendor maintains your inventory at his or her plant. All you do is send releases via telephone or in writing.

This procedure begins with an analysis of the dollars spent by vendor for a recent time period—at least six months. What stock or repeatedly purchased items are not on VCP should be considered as candidates for systems contracts.

CONTROLLING SUBCONTRACTING: THREE PROBLEMS AND HOW TO OVERCOME THEM

If you think it difficult to set up vendor capacity planning and system contracts, then control of subcontracting will also be a challenge. Three basic problems exist when a company selects another enterprise to do outside processing/subcontracting, such as plating, heat treating, and machining. The first is the control of pieces; the quantity shipped and the quantity received seldom are the same. The second is a scrap allowance, while the third challenge is prompt return of the material. For a company that subcontracts a fair amount of production—say 20 percent for the R.G. CEPT Company—this could be $1 million a year. With an average of 24 production days at an outside processor, about $100,000 of work-in-process inventory is tied up at 21.7 percent carrying costs. The company must therefore spend $21,700 a year for this inventory.

Subcontracting and outside processing must be carefully controlled. The first step is to assign a lot number to every shipment made to vendors, making it mandatory that each vendor controls and returns the material coded by this lot designation. The second step is a CRT Subcontract Tracking Screen that follows all the activities, similar to that shown in Figure 11–7.

THOSE MISCELLANEOUS BUYS: SHORTCUT DOCUMENTS TO USE

In order to free purchasing buyers and clerks to concentrate on VCP, system contracts and subcontracts, shortcut documents like the following should be used:

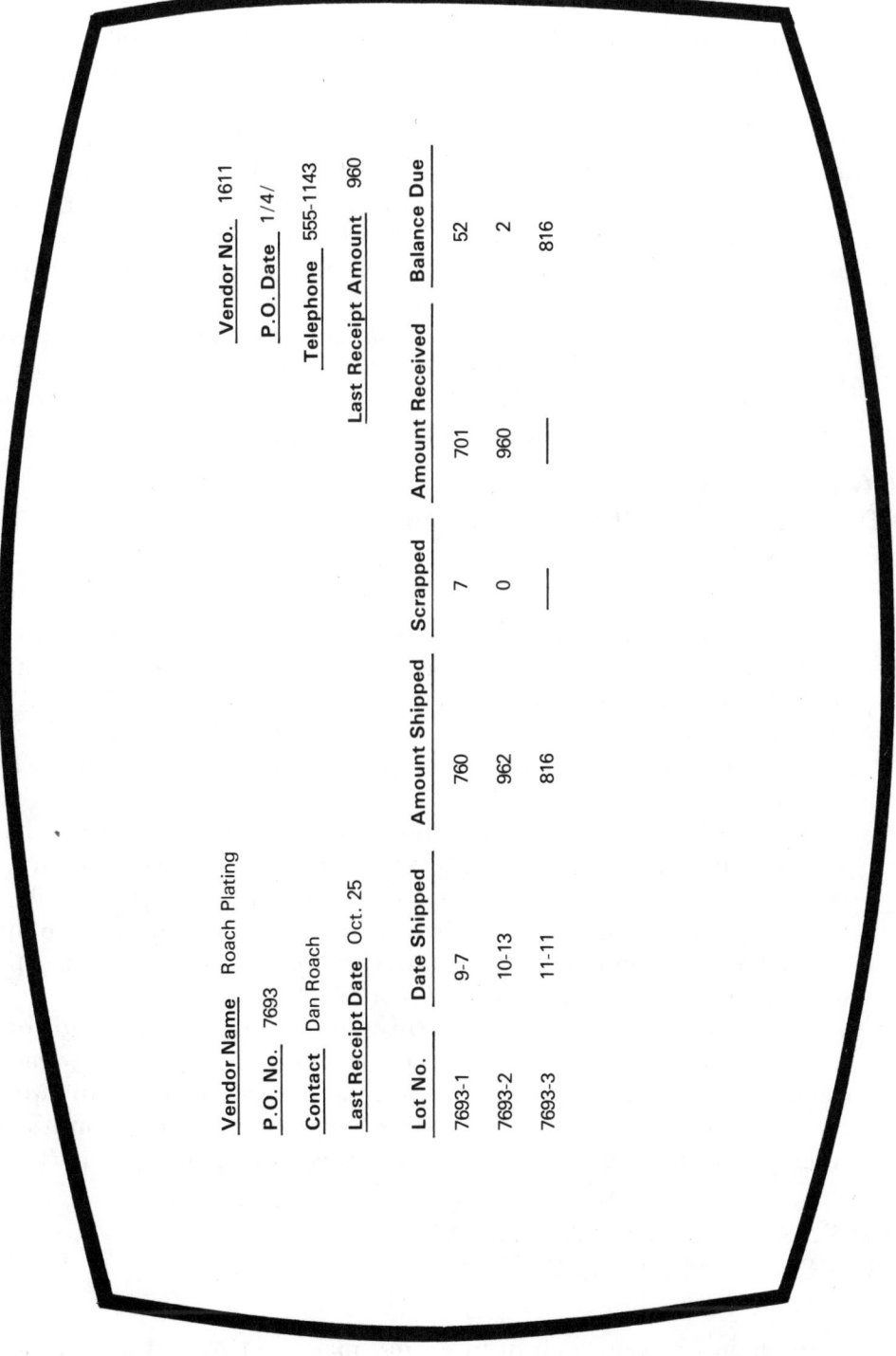

Vendor Name Roach Plating

P.O. No. 7693

Contact Dan Roach

Last Receipt Date Oct. 25

Vendor No. 1611

P.O. Date 1/4/

Telephone 555-1143

Last Receipt Amount 960

Lot No.	Date Shipped	Amount Shipped	Scrapped	Amount Received	Balance Due
7693-1	9-7	760	7	701	52
7693-2	10-13	962	0	960	2
7693-3	11-11	816	—	—	816

FIGURE 11–7: Subcontracting Vendor Tracking Screen

239

- Requisition/purchase order
- Check attached purchase order
- Self-invoice purchase order

- Verbal, telephone order
- Cash purchase pickup order
- Telephone log and order

Figure 11–8 shows a combination requisition and purchase order. This example even includes a vendor performance rating block in the lower left-hand corner. Buyers rate the vendor performance immediately upon completion of each order while their memory is fresh. Periodic summaries can be made and given to sales representatives during their next visit, and a copy can be mailed to the vendor's home office.

These shortcut procedures also save the company processing costs, especially on small value buys. Remember, it is almost impossible to save enough money on a $50 purchase to pay for the buyer's time. Therefore, place these orders quickly and concentrate on larger purchases.

HANDLING PRICE BREAKS: HOW TO DETERMINE IF YOU'RE LOSING OR SAVING MONEY

Suppose a salesperson drops by your office one day and offers to sell you 10,000 tail lights more than your usual purchase quantity at a "fantastic discount" of 8 percent off the normal price you pay. Is this a good deal for you? How can you determine whether you should take this "outstanding" offer? The answer can be determined simply by using the calculation worksheet in Figure 11–9.

You will note that this calculation determines how many months' supply you are buying and the carrying cost to keep this inventory. The carrying cost per month would be 1, 2, or 3 percent (12, 24, or 36 percent annually, divided by 12 months). By filling in the blanks, you can obtain quickly an answer as to whether you will lose or save money on this deal, by comparing the "total order carrying cost" against the "discount offered."

This comparison used 2 percent monthly carrying cost and found that the company would lose 2 percent if it accepted this "fantastic" deal. At a 36 percent annual carrying cost—3 percent a month—the company would have lost 7 percent on this possible deal. The "inventory" average month's historical usage can usually be obtained from the Inventory Control Department.

STANDARD PARTS VS. SPECIAL ORDERS: TEN AREAS FOR ANALYZING COST

A common concern, both in inventory management and in purchasing, involves minimizing inventory investment by ordering standard parts and materials in contrast to specially produced items. In many companies, due to the

REQUISITION, PURCHASE ORDER AND BLANKET ORDER RELEASE	Req'n. No. _____ Date _____

Dept.	Requested By	To Be Used For	Required By
Acc't. No.	Cost Center No.	Appro. No.	Deliver Att. of

SPECIAL INSTRUCTIONS _____   Approved By: _____

Quantity	Part No.	Description	Unit Price

Vendor Name and Address

_____

_____

_____

_____

TAXABLE☐   EXEMPT☐
Vendor No. _____

OUR PURCHASE ORDER NUMBER

Confirming To:_____ Date: _____

Terms and   FOB_____   Payment Disc. _____
Conditions   Other _____

Buyer Authorization: _____
(Must be signed to be valid)

FOR OUR USE ONLY
VENDOR PERFORMANCE ON THIS ORDER

QUALITY	PRICES & TERMS
☐ GOOD	☐ AS ON ORDER
☐ REJECTED	☐ DIFFERENT

DELIVERY

☐ AS REQUESTED
☐ LATE
☐ UNAUTH. SPLIT

ACTUAL LEAD
TIME _____ WEEKS

Vendor Please Note: Unless you provide us written expressed exception to the contents of this order, we will assume you agree and will pay your invoice accordingly. If this order is $500 or greater, mandatory acknowledgment is required.

FIGURE 11–8: Combination Requisition and Purchase Order

specifying of nonstandard items, the actual vendor selection is really made by the requisitioners. These requisitioners can be design engineers, computer department managers, marketing executives, and even clerical personnel. These persons actually "select the vendor" as they perform one of four actions when preparing a requisition or a bill of material:

1. specify a specific vendor
2. select an item or material furnished by only one vendor
3. designate an item not available "off the shelf"
4. design a special part to be custom made

$$\frac{10{,}000}{\text{Quantity Offered}} \;\div\; \underset{\text{(Divided)}}{} \;\; \underset{\text{(Equals)}}{2} \;=\; \frac{5{,}000}{\substack{\text{Average}\\\text{Quantity}\\\text{On Hand}}} \;\underset{\text{(Divided)}}{\div}\; \frac{1000}{\substack{\text{Average}\\\text{Month}\\\text{Historical}\\\text{Usage}}} \;\underset{\text{(Equals)}}{=}$$

$$\underset{\text{(Equals)}}{=} \; \frac{5}{\substack{\text{Month}\\\text{Supply}\\\text{Buying}}} \;\underset{\text{(Times)}}{\text{x}}\; \frac{2\%}{\substack{\text{Carrying}\\\text{cost}\\\text{Per}\\\text{Month}}} \;\underset{\text{(equals)}}{=}\; \frac{10\%}{\substack{\text{Total}\\\text{Order}\\\text{Carrying}\\\text{Cost}}} \;\underset{\text{(Minus)}}{-}\; \frac{8\%}{\substack{\text{Discount}\\\text{Offered}}} \;\underset{\text{(Equals)}}{=}\; \frac{2\%}{\substack{\text{Loss}\\\text{(or Savings)}\\\text{on This}\\\text{Deal}}}$$

Part Number and Description   Vendor

Prepared By: Date

FIGURE 11–9: Discount Value Calculation Worksheet

Whenever any one of these actions is taken, the requisitioner limits the amount of competitive buying that can be done and, as a result, increases the price paid for the purchased goods while also complicating the control of inventory.

Companies should arrange requisitions, inventory, and purchasing selection into ten categories for analytical purposes. Then the dollar amounts purchased can be placed into these categories as shown below:

Vendor Selection Category	Last Year's Purchases	Percentage
1. Least total cost based on annual commodity review	$ 338,533	9
2. Lowest price based on telephone competitive quotations	564,210	15
3. Lowest price based on written competitive quotations	526,594	14
4. Single qualified source specified by Engineering	714,666	19
5. Vendor specified by requisitioner	263,296	7
6. Propietary item: Only one possible vendor	188,070	5
7. Proven superior quality performance	413,753	11

8. Only vendor with acceptable delivery	488,981	13
9. Emergency purchase	112,841	3
10. Low value order; no special review	150,456	4
	$3,761,400	100

From a competitive viewpoint, the first three vendor selection categories are the "good news," since these selection reasons have a high probability of obtaining the best price and service. The last seven categories may not be the best buy because concerns other than price dominate the selection rationale.

Effective inventory and purchasing cost control management companies use what is called the Rationale for Buying Decision illustration in Figure 11–10. This form should be completed whenever a larger value order is placed (perhaps $500 and greater) and attached to the purchase order file copy. Then, prior to mailing the vendor's copy, the purchasing manager should check the vendor selection rationale, ascertaining that the proper choice was made. If the selection is dominated by one category (as were $714,666 of annual purchases in which the vendor was determined by Engineering in the preceding list), then a discussion should be held with this department manager to see if alternate parts (and/or sources) can be utilized. One caution in the use of this technique—price isn't the only consideration; the least total cost vendor considering quality, delivery, and service must be studied.

SENSIBLE EXPEDITING: THE LAST-MINUTE REQUIREMENTS REPORT

No inventory system is perfect—there is just no way to predict exactly the customers' delivery needs or anticipate their product design changes. Thus, prior to performing any expediting for inventory items, the expediter should look at the "Last-Minute Requirements Report." Figure 11–11 illustrates this document, which provides an up-to-date (via a real-time computer program) inventory status. By noting the expected or actual stock-out date, the expediter can tell the vendor more accurately the production timing requirements.

CHAPTER REFERENCE

1. C. K. Hahn, P. A. Pinto, and D. J. Bragg, "Just-in-Time Production and Purchasing," *Journal of Purchasing and Materials Management*, National Association of Purchasing Management (Fall 1983), pp. 2–10.

Vendor Name _____ Purchase Order No. _____

Item Description(s) _____ Part Number(s) _____

Commodity Group _____ Value of Order $ _____

VENDOR WAS SELECTED BASED ON:

_____ 1. Annual Commodity Review Based on Least Total Cost

_____ 2. Lowest Price Based on Telephone Competitive Quotations

_____ 3. Lowest Price Based on Written Competitive Quotations

_____ 4. Sole Qualified Source Specified by Engineering

_____ 5. Vendor Specified by Requisitioner

_____ 6. Proprietary Item; Only One Possible Vendor

_____ 7. Proven Superior Quality Performance

_____ 8. Only Vendor with Acceptable Delivery

_____ 9. Emergency Purchase

_____10. Low Value Order

_____11. Other Reason: Explain_____

_____

Additional Cost Paid Compared to Lowest Quote: $_____

Date _____Purchasing Agent _____

FIGURE 11–10: Rationale for Buying Decision

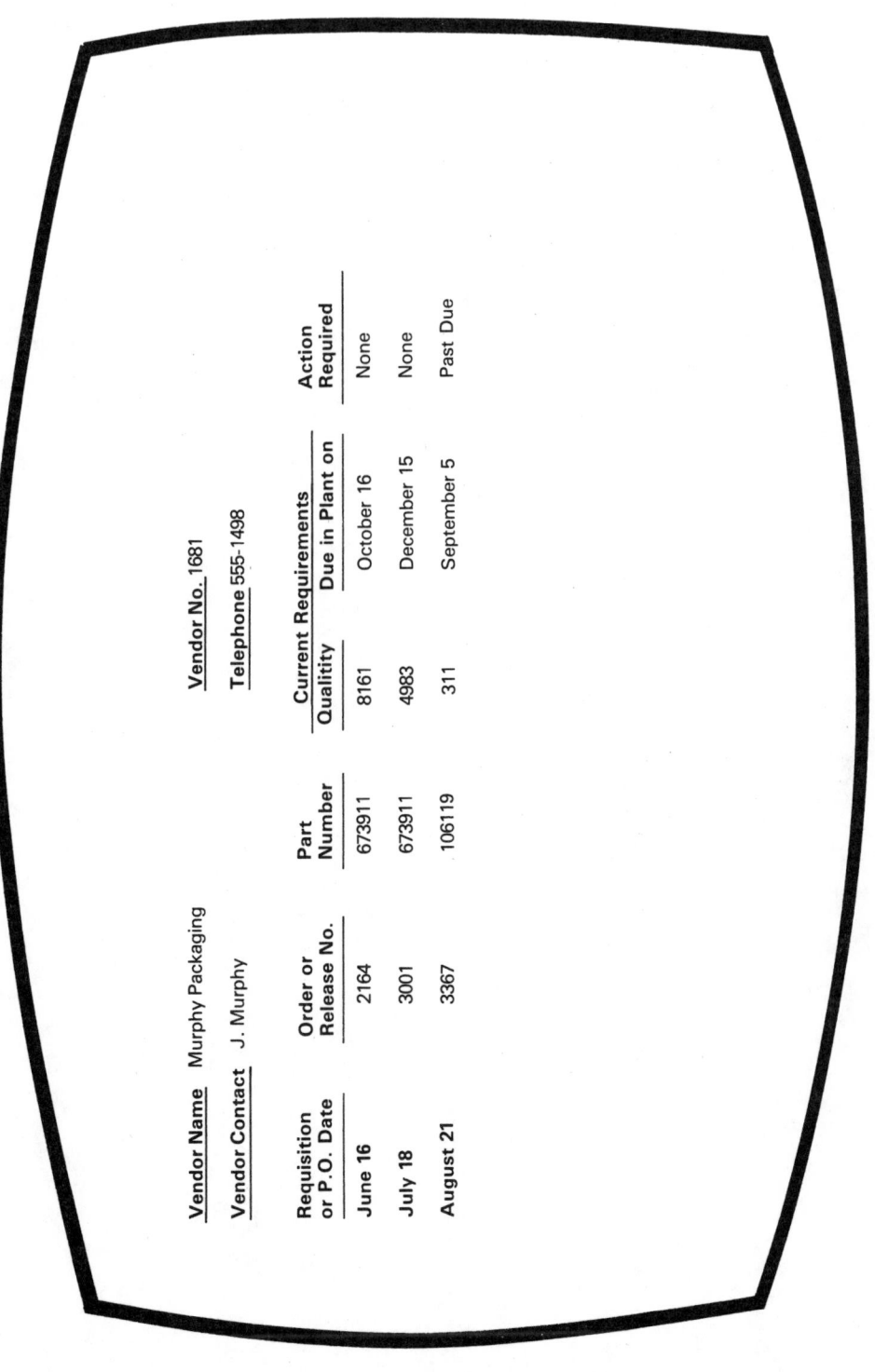

Vendor Name Murphy Packaging

Vendor Contact J. Murphy

Vendor No. 1681

Telephone 555-1498

| Requisition or P.O. Date | Order or Release No. | Part Number | Current Requirements | | Action Required |
			Quality	Due in Plant on	
June 16	2164	673911	8161	October 16	None
July 18	3001	673911	4983	December 15	None
August 21	3367	106119	311	September 5	Past Due

FIGURE 11–11: Last-Minute Requirements Report Screen

Distribution Requirements Planning:
Storeroom, Warehouse, and Distribution Control

12

CHAPTER HIGHLIGHTS

This chapter is about Distribution Requirements Planning (DRP), a combination of storeroom, warehouse, and distribution controls. You will learn some of the most desirable characteristics of DRP and eight benefits that it can help you achieve. In addition, you will find

- a nine-step program for analyzing storage areas and using space more efficiently
- a baker's dozen of time-phased storeroom improvements
- what to plan for in a successfully controlled warehouse
- eight steps involved in initiating a DRP system

As manufacturing and materials systems become more complex, new terminology is introduced that often tends to confuse the issue. An example of this is Distribution Requirements Planning (DRP), which, in reality, is a combination of

- Storeroom control, which involves raw material and finished components, usually located in smaller areas—all vital for work-in process production.
- Warehouse control, which includes the storage of finished goods, usually in larger areas, and necessary for quick service to the customer.
- Distribution control, which involves moving material to and from several warehouses at proper cost coordination.

TEN FUNCTIONS OF DISTRIBUTION REQUIREMENTS PLANNING (DRP)

The concept of DRP includes the ten functions listed below.

1. Receiving
2. Inbound inspection
3. Dispatching to storage
4. Placing in storage
5. Storage
6. Order picking
7. Order accumulation for shipping
8. Dispatching for shipping
9. Shipping
10. Cycle counting and validation

Effective DRP has the characteristics of a controlled environment, though not necessarily locked areas, since a two-bin control procedure for expense items can be used. Other important elements include:

1. Clean, well-organized storage areas with the various items carefully labeled.

2. Items placed in the storage area by considering the frequency of requisitions—high use items up front, low demand in the back.

3. Location of items well planned, either by a fixed storage placement using the part number as a location number or by a random method with a procedure to find the correct location easily.

4. Access to storeroom and items restricted to those persons well familiar with various storage rules and security regulations.

5. Transactions carefully documented, through either a manual or CRT system.

6. Staffing established considering the variability of demand—both peaks and valleys.

7. Cycle counting items, selecting ones to check based on frequency of transactions, ABC classification, and impact of a stock-out on the inventory system.

8. Lists of items to be pulled from stock prepared in the same sequence as items are stored in the area to help reduce excess traveling. Refer to Figure 12–1 for a computer-prepared picking slip.

Once successfully established, DRP achieves these benefits:

- Forecast accuracy helps store items more effectively.
- Labor bottlenecks are reduced by variable crew size.
- Packages permit a weight/strength trade-off.
- Movement of materials is smoothed out.
- Distances traveled are cut by better layout.
- Utilization of cubic space is improved.
- Amount of packages handled is increased.
- Performance reporting is against set targets.

Customer	Order No.		Ship To	Via
Hlavin Corp.	3746		Cleve. Hts. Ohio	UPS

Part No.	Description	U/M	Quantity	Store Location	Issue Amount
0401	Hood-Steel	ea.	1	B16	
0911	Grill-Aluminum	ea.	1	B23	
7614	Wheel-Back	ea.	2	C07	
0113	Drive Shaft	ea.	1	D17	
1149	Headlights	pr.	2	E04	

FIGURE 12–1: Computer-Prepared Picking Slip

CHOOSING BETWEEN FIXED AND RANDOM STORAGE LOCATIONS

A "fixed" location for an item means that each part will always have the same permanent address, while a "random" location means a part will be in one or more storage places that can be changed over time. The fixed method requires a bigger storeroom (usually 20 percent larger) for a given number of items, while the random setup uses smaller storage area for the same number of parts. A fixed location procedure often (but not always) uses the part numbers as a location "address" by placing the items in part number sequence. The random procedure necessitates one or more variable location addresses (in lieu of the part number) for each item in the storeroom.

Sometimes a blend of both methods can be used. For example, it may be desirable to store certain items close to the front door, such as the "A" and "B" inventory class parts, frequently requested items, or all small parts, using a random location. Then place the "C" and "D" slower moving items using a fixed location in the back part of the room.

Using a Numbering Scheme for a Fixed Location

For service organization and smaller manufacturing companies, a combination of the commodity code number and a unique sequential number can serve the dual function of grouping like items together as a fixed storage location address.

1. A basic five-position item number can be used.
2. A typical number is "14671." The first two numbers (14) indicate the commodity group (special envelopes). Refer to Figure 12–2 for list of these code numbers. The last three numbers (671) are a unique sequence within the group. You might wish to refer to Chapter 2 for a discussion of Commodity Codes.
3. The entire number is also the bin or pallet location in the storeroom, since items are placed in the item number sequence.

ANALYZING THE STORAGE AREA: A NINE-STEP PROGRAM FOR MORE EFFICIENT USE OF SPACE

Considerable space is wasted in many storerooms. A nine-step program should be used to identify unused areas and practices that hinder the efficiency of the warehousing operations. A work plan should be developed to provide a

Commodity Group	Commodity Number	Specific Commodity
Autos & Trucks	01	Gas & Oil
	02	Rentals & Leases
	03	Purchased Vehicles
	04	Miscellaneous
Computer	07	Continuous Paper
	08	Custom Forms
	09	Envelopes
	10	Hardware Equipment
	11	Software
	12	Stock Paper
Envelopes	15	Standardized
	14	Special
	16	Miscellaneous
Food Service	20	Dishes & Silverware
	21	Non-perishable Foods
	22	Paper Supplies
	23	Perishable Foods
Forms	25	Flat Forms Stock
	26	Governmental
	27	Graphic Design
	28	Multi-copy Forms Stock
	29	Non-Stock
Furniture	30	Personal
	31	Standardized
Marketing	33	Brochures
	34	Promotion Materials
Office Equipment	37	Calculators
	38	Copy Machines
	39	Dictation Machines
	40	Photocopying
	41	Security
	42	Service/Maintenance
	43	Typewriters
	44	Used Equipment
	45	Word Processing
	46	Miscellaneous

FIGURE 12–2: Service Industry Commodity Codes

Commodity Group	Commodity Number	Specific Commodity
Office Supplies	50	Binders & Folders
	51	Paper
	52	Pens, Pencils, etc.
	53	Ribbons
	54	Rubber Stamps
	55	Staplers & Staples
	56	Miscellaneous
Paper	60	Calling Cards
	61	Checks
	62	Special Paper
	63	Standard Paper
Special Services	65	Mail
	66	Telecommunications
	67	Temporary Help
	68	Travel
	69	Transportation
Stationery	70	Personal
	71	Special
	72	Standardization
Supplies	75	Cleaning
	76	Landscaping
	77	Lighting
	78	Maintenance
	79	MRO
	80	Miscellaneous
Warehouse	85	Bins & Racks
	86	Cartons & Containers
	87	Miscellaneous

FIGURE 12–2: Service Industry Commodity Codes (cont'd)

method for employees to become familiar with the physical facilities and limitations of the storeroom, the demands placed on the storeroom, as well as the practices and policies in effect to satisfy those demands. Specifically, complete the following tasks:

1. Analyze the warehouse facility to document all physical characteristics. Determine the quantity and effective capacity of storage containers cur-

rently in use. Draft a detail layout of the warehouse noting all movable and immovable objects, showing the picking sequence. (Refer to Figure 12–3.)

2. Observe the storeroom employees stocking and **pulling** goods; critically analyze their needs for material handling equipment and storage systems, based on how they used the equipment presently available.

3. Interview the storeroom supervisors to determine their problem areas and suggestions for improvement.

4. Study the Receiving/Shipping Department as related to inventory control, purchasing, and storeroom practices.

5. Review the receiving/shipping dock procedures to identify hindrances to effective handling of receipts.

6. Ascertain the practices and policies of the storeroom in general, including access, security, supervision, paperwork and maintenance.

7. Compute current storage space requirements from inventory data compiled.

8. Project space requirements three to five years into the future based upon the company's estimated growth rate.

9. Prepare layouts of the storeroom and dock area to define recommendations for these areas.

When this study is completed, make a summary of recommendations including cost estimates, responsibilities, and target dates using the format in Figure 12–4.

HOW TO PLAN SPACE REQUIREMENTS

Once the item commodities and sequential identification numbers have been established, the next phase is to determine how much space will be required to store the maximum expected quantity of material. Ten steps are necessary:

1. Count the quantity of an item on hand (as of a specific date).

2. Estimate the number of bins or pallets (or a fraction of a bin or pallet) required to store the quantity identified in step 1. This is done using a stock density chart shown in Figure 12–5. The bin (and/or pallet) space density is expressed as an approximate percentage.

3. Determine the maximum expected quantity by adding the normal reorder quantity to the safety stock.

4. Calculate the maximum space requirement by a simple ratio calculation. For example, if no. 2 pencils have 180 packages on hand using .60 (60

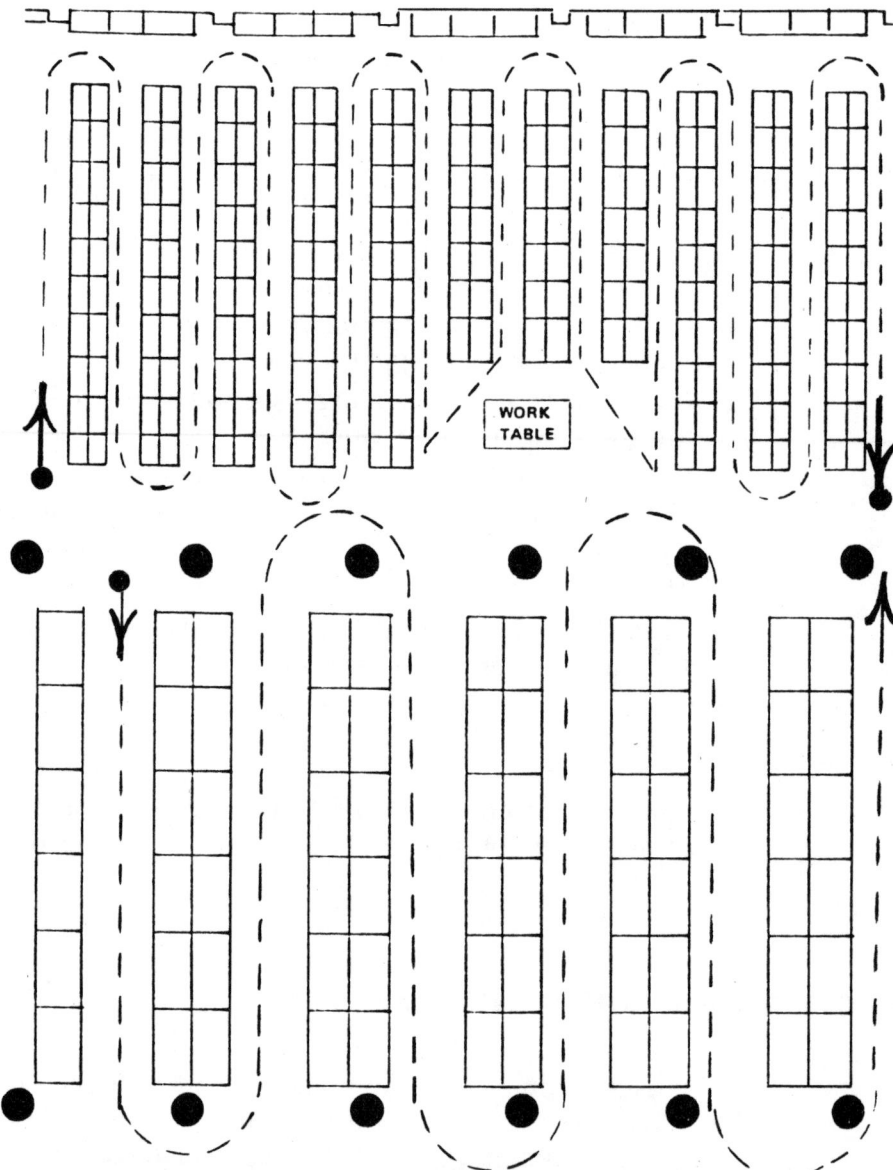

FIGURE 12–3: Warehouse Layout for Continuous Picking

percent expressed as a decimal) of one bin, and the maximum expected quantity is 450 packages, then

$$\frac{450}{180} = 2.5 \times .60 = 1.50$$

which is one full bin plus half of a second bin.

Sequence Number	Category	Recommendation	Costs to Implement			Responsible Individual	Target Dates		Status as of __/__/__
			In-house	Out of Pocket	Total		Start	Finish	
1.	Warehouse Structure	Move overhead lights from above bins to aisles to permit increase of bin height and visibility							
2.	Storeroom Procedures	Store high volume forms near front.							
3.	Storeroom Procedures	Provide an office area for supervisors							
4.	Receiving/ Shipping	Set aside staging area for stock items							
5.	Material Handling	Purchase high reach lift truck							

FIGURE 12–4: Warehouse Improvement Report Typical Section

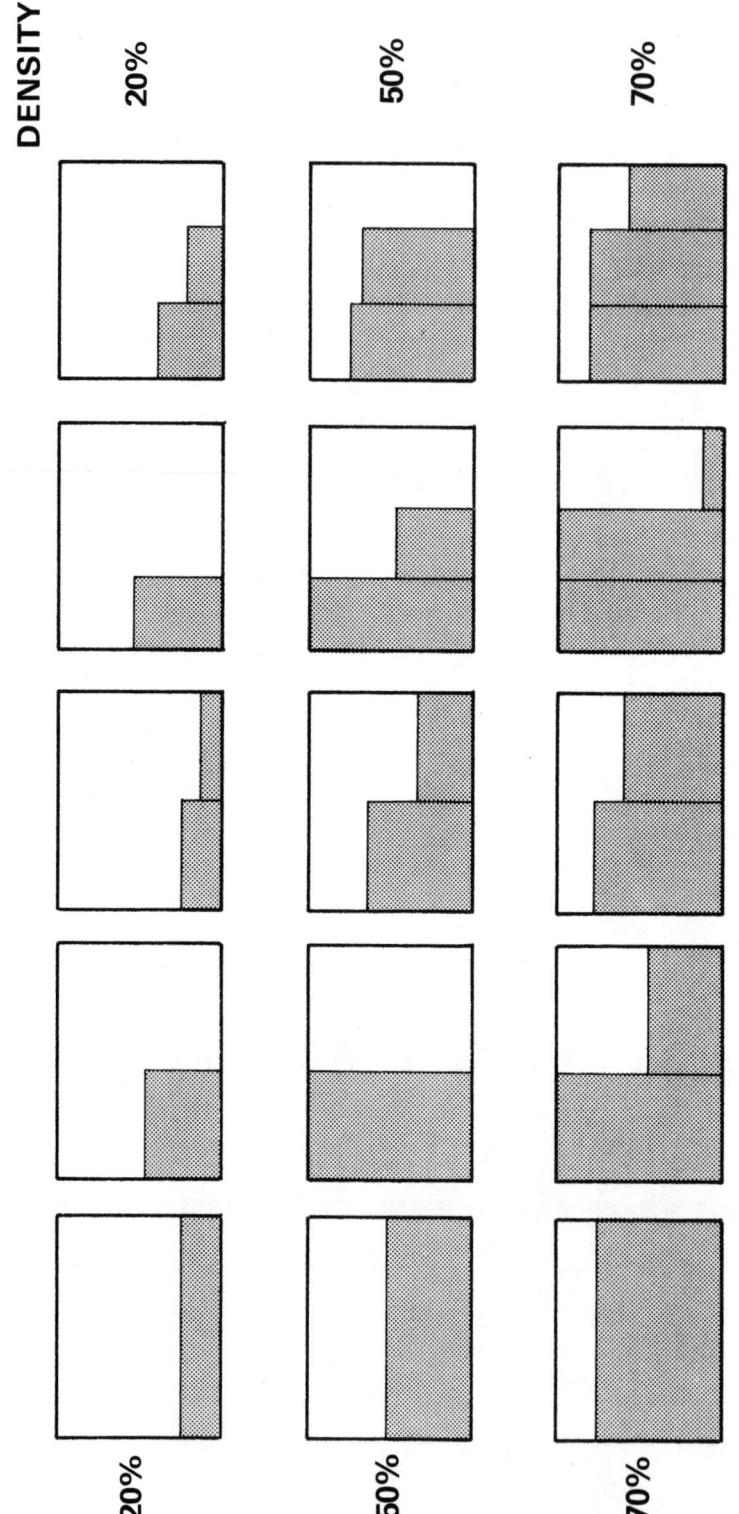

DENSITY

FIGURE 12–5: Bin and Rack Stock Density Chart

256

5. Add all the bins necessary to contain the maximum expected space requirement for all items. The Space Calculation Worksheet shown in Figure 12–6 can be used in this step.

6. Count the number of bins available in the existing stockroom.

7. Subtract the number of bins required (step 5) from the number of bin spaces available (step 6) to determine if there is any surplus or shortage of bins. If there are no extra bins, then additional bins must be added, including enough for future expansion.

8. Divide the number of extra bins by the number of commodity group numbers to obtain what is called the "skip interval" of subsequent expansion purposes. For example, if you use the 35 commodity groups and have 525 extra bins, the skip interval is 15 (525 ÷ 35 = 15).

9. Lay out the storeroom again, placing items in bins in a sequence beginning with item number 01001. When all of group "01" have been placed in the bins, skip 15 bins for future expansion, and then start placing group "02" in the bins.

10. Perform the same tasks in steps 7 through 9 for pallets.

Item Description or Form Number	Balance on Hand as of 1/18/XX	Unit of Measure	Actual Space Used			Maximum Quantity Possible (a)	Max. Space Reqd.		
			Bin	Rack	Pallet		Bin	Rack	Pallet
Form No. B801	40	each	50%	—	—	40	.50(1)		
No. 2 Pencils	186	package	—	30%	—	410		.66(2)	
Computer Paper	396	cartons	—	—	75%	1400			.26(3)

Actual Calculations

(1) $\dfrac{40}{40} = 1 \times .50 = .50$

(2) $\dfrac{410}{186} = 2.2 \times .30 = .66$

(3) $\dfrac{1400}{396} = 3.5 \times .75 = .263$

Note:

(a) Maximum quantity is Recorder Quantity (EOQ) plus safety stock.

FIGURE 12–6: Space Calculation Worksheet

A BAKER'S DOZEN OF TIME-PHASED STOREROOM IMPROVEMENTS

As with any improvement program, numerous revisions can be made with increased efficiency, so here's a baker's dozen, sequenced from easy to do to quite difficult, for consideration by your company:

1. Set up a stocking plan that places the most active parts in the middle section of a rack or cabinet. Figure 12–7 illustrates this method.

2. Prewrap items in standard measures such as a dozen bearings, a gross of wires, and ten brackets. Also, receive from vendors standard quantity cartons in well-marked packages (then issue in standard sizes too!).

3. As an alternate method, set up a random locator system using the computer if space is limited.[1] The storeroom can have the same locating system as a small city using "streets," "house numbers," "floor numbers," and "apartment number." Each location address is a six digit alphanumeric code. An example is

$$\underline{Y}\ \underline{C}\ \underline{03}\ \underline{B}\ \underline{2}$$

The first alpha character is the city; in this example "Y" is the parts storeroom. The second alpha character is the street or aisle (some actually call them streets and they run between a set of racks or bins). The third and fourth numeric characters comprise the house number. Odd num-

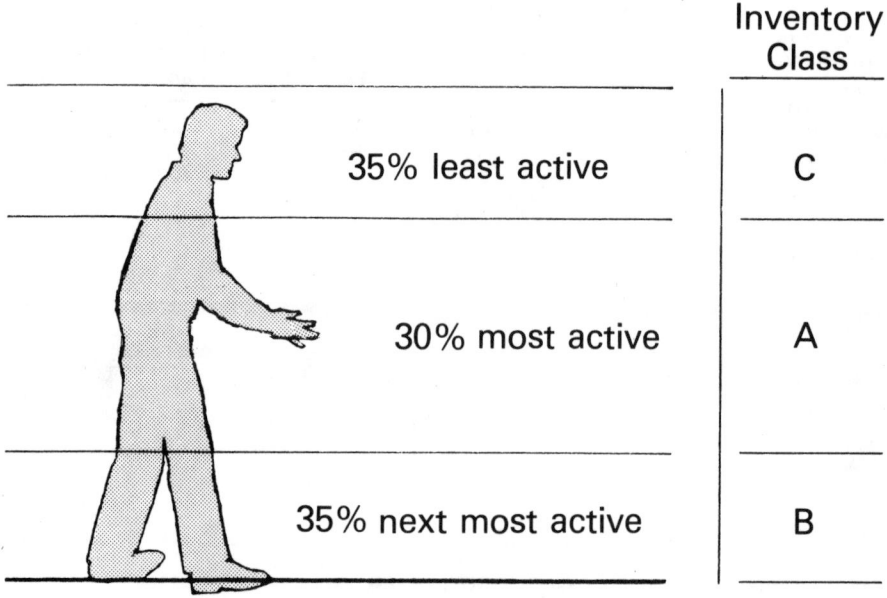

	Inventory Class
35% least active	C
30% most active	A
35% next most active	B

FIGURE 12–7: Bin or Rack Stocking Method

bers are on the left side of the street and even numbers are on the right. In the example, "03" is the second rack opening on the left-hand side of "C" street. The fifth character (alpha) is the floor and the sixth (numeric) is the apartment number. In the example, "B" is the second rack cross-member from the floor, and "2" is the second apartment on floor "B."

The middle three locators in this address (<u>C</u> <u>03</u> <u>B</u>) are the three-dimensional coordinates within the storeroom. This allows for simple sorting of withdrawals for efficient parts picking. For example, one sort on the street column separates lift truck requirements due to aisle width. A second sort on the house address column allows for complete picking of the aisle in one pass. In the case of a small part, a quick glance at the floor column tells that the stock attendant can reach the part without a lift truck. ("A" and "B" are within six feet of the floor, while "C" goes from six to nine feet and "D" goes from nine to twelve feet.)

4. Prepare alternate stock location tags, printed in an unusual color, for use in overstock situations (no inventory stocking plan is perfect).

5. Program your computer to check for obvious errors, such as to reject an inventory transaction for 976,871 pieces when the previous high was 91,000.

6. Purchase adjustable shelves that slide on floor rollers for smaller parts which can save space.

7. Communicate unfilled order requirements from the warehouse, via CRT, to other company warehouses for better customer service and use of inventory. Figure 12–8 is a multiple warehouse inventory information CRT screen.

8. Move picked items to takeaway conveyers whenever possible to minimize walking.

9. Install "carousel" type racks, which lessen square footage space requirements but increase cubic usage.

10. Reduce handling of material by limiting staging of orders.

11. Use all open space at the top of the room by installing taller racks.

12. Institute electronic picking racks which, through readout units on the shelves, eliminate picking lists.

13. Install shelves for small parts that are actually electronic scales wired to a controller that makes continuous weight count readings. Any addition or removal of parts changes the weight count and a computer inventory update is immediately made.

All these techniques can jointly or individually increase the efficiency and effectiveness of the warehousing function. This leads to the ultimate . . . an automated storage and retrieval system.

WAREHOUSES INVENTRY STATUS REPORT

As of 03/03/xx

Part No.	Description	Cleve	Atlanta	Dallas	Total Qty
0911	Grill-Aluminum	0	0	48	48
0398	Wheel, Front	163	62	0	225
7614	Wheel, Back	11	67	184	262
1092	Battery	0	0	4	4

FIGURE 12–8: Multiple Warehouse CRT Screen

SUCCESSFUL WAREHOUSING:
WHAT TO PLAN FOR

Today, the ultimate is a "high-bay" computer controlled warehouse where finished goods are stored for distribution to the ultimate customer. In planning such a storage environment, you should consider such statistics as the

- number of line items received and issued per day
- range in number of orders issued each day
- number of trucks (and railroad cars) loaded and unloaded each day
- number of pallets (and cartons) handled per day
- frequency of emergency customer orders
- amount of downtime incurred by material handling equipment
- quantity of material handled per work hour

A typical manufacturing company stores inventory in areas that comprise 30 percent of its total space, with warehousing costs constituting about 7 percent of the sales dollar. Good warehouses are successful due to reduced item handling, smooth material flow, standardized packages, and productivity targets. Since the cheapest space is the area closest to the ceiling, a high bay warehouse makes use of this space. This concept makes use of

- Special lift trucks, a cross between conventional lift trucks and automatic storage–retrieval systems (called ASRS).
- Automatic storage and retrieval systems ranging from manually controlled stacker cranes to fully automated systems, some of which reach to 40 feet.
- Driverless horizontal movement loading and unloading systems, controlled by wire guided or electronic devices, whose travel routes can be easily modified.
- Item-picking methods that bring the part to the picker, then takeaway conveyers move the items to shipping docks.[2]

EIGHT STEPS FOR USING A PRODUCTIVE
DRP SYSTEM

A DRP system is necessary when a company produces finished products and then places this material in two or more warehouses, awaiting customer orders for shipment from these stocking locations. In effect, DRP is an extension of the MRP system inputting the distribution network requirements into the master schedule. DRP monitors the finished goods inventory while MRP watches raw material and work-in-process.

Figure 12–9 illustrates a DRP system as compared to the conventional MRP system. The actual steps to follow are:

1. Obtain a forecast projection of the customer needs for your product.
2. Determine the actual on-hand stock balance.
3. Determine if any finished goods inventory is "in transit."
4. Subtract actual and in-transit amounts from forecast needs to get net requirements.
5. See how long the stock will last until you reach safety stock or stock-out position.
6. Using the data (in step 5), subtract the lead time necessary to replenish the inventory at the warehouse to arrive at the factory completion (shipping to warehouse) date.
7. Repeat each step for each warehouse in the distribution system.
8. Use data from step 6 input as input to the master schedule.

The horizon for these steps should be at least the total cumulative product lead time including raw materials, or 12 months, whichever is greater.

How to Determine Distribution Strategy

It is difficult to determine manually the optimum locations of manufacturing plants and warehouses, the proper inventory levels, and transportation considerations. This is accomplished through the utilization of a computerized Distribution Model. Figure 12–10 is a typical report, prepared by the LOGISTEK III Software Program.[3]

The general objective of this Distribution Model is to identify the manufacture/distribution network strategy that provides the company with the right combination of distribution service to market and lower total distribution cost. The model has the capability to develop the distribution network, which provides the lowest total of all relevant distribution costs. It has the capability also to consider the impact of level of service on market share and sales, quantitatively. This enables you to develop the interaction between cost and revenues as a function of distribution service, and solve for maximum contribution to profit.

The model handles complex national and international distribution evaluations considering all of the pertinent costs of distribution—multiple levels of manufacture, transportation, warehousing, inventory, and other relevant costs (such as taxes)—and determines the best combination of these that will satisfy

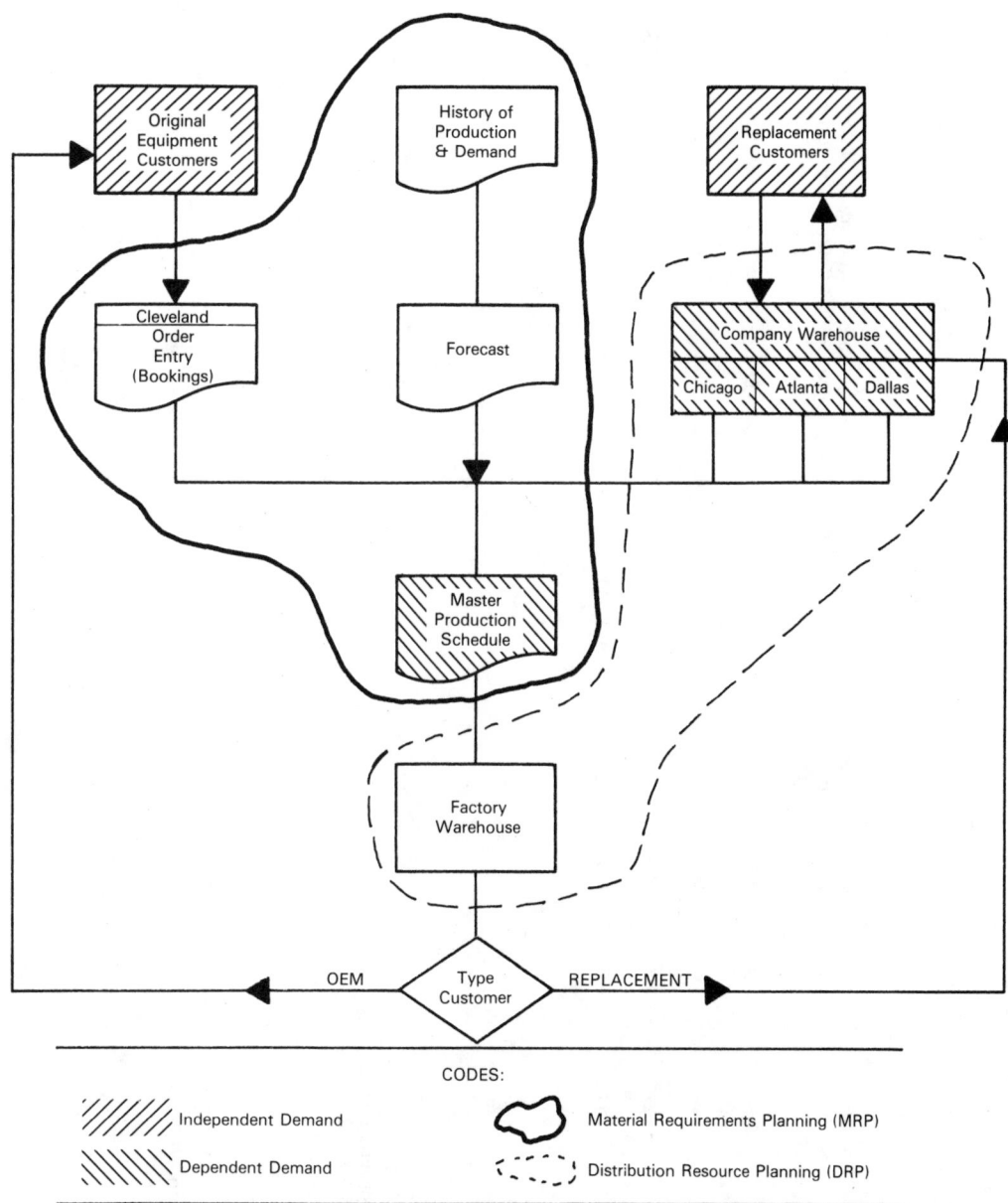

FIGURE 12–9: Comparison of MRP and DRP Demand

LOGISTEK III REPORT - R.G. CEPT Company (all data in 000, except D)

Data Date 3/3/xx   Run Date 3/4/xx

Warehouse Number and Location (A)	Yr. Ship. in Pounds (B)	Yr. Ship. in Cases (C)	No. Ship. to Cust. (D)	Shipments in Cu. Ft. (E)	Net Sales by Loc. (F)	Inbound Frt. Csts. (G)	Total Mfg. Cost (H)	Alloc. Plt. Ware. Cst. (I)	Field Ware-house Cst. (J)	Inventory Csts. (K)	Out Frt. Cst./Cust. (L)	Tot Mfg. & Log. Cst. (M)
01 Cleveland Plant	19,311	966	2,544	772	$9,464	$157	$6,909	$373	$68	$411	$454	$8,372
02 Plastatron Division	7,598	380	1,001	304	3,746	62	2,735	148	27	162	179	3,313
03 Chicago Warehse.	2,216	111	292	89	1,062	18	775	42	8	48	52	943
04 Atlanta Warehse.	323	19	63	15	316	3	231	12	2	5	8	261
05 Dallas Warehse.	2,210	108	271	86	1,084	18	791	40	7	48	52	956
Totals	31,658	1,584	4,171	1,266	$15,672	$258	$11,441	$615	$112	$674	$745	$13,845

SUMMARIES AND ANALYSIS: For each location and total

Total Manufacturing and Logistics Costs;
Add columns G, H, I, J, K and L = M

Logistics Costs as a percent of manufacturing costs;
Add columns G, I, J, K and L, then divide by H

Contributions of one location to all logistics;
Any specific location number in column B
divided by column B total

Gross Profit contribution of each location;
Subtract column M from column F

(B)	(C)	(D)
Yearly Shipments in Pounds	Yearly Shipments in Cases	No. Shipments to Customers
(E)	(F)	(G)
Shipments in Cubic Feet	Net Sales by Location	Inpound Freight Costs
(H)	(I)	(J)
Total Manuf-acturing Cost	Allocated Plant Warehouse Costs	Field Ware-house Costs
(K)	(L)	(M)
Inventory Carrying Costs	Outbound Freight Costs to Customers	Total Manufacturing and Logistics Costs

FIGURE 12–10: LOGISTEK III Cost Analysis Report

market requirements at the lowest total of all of these costs. The components of the network identified include:

- Where each of the various product lines is best manufactured (this may include the number and location of manufacturing plants).
- Number and location of warehouses to best serve markets at the lowest total of all of these costs.
- Transportation linkages between manufacturing plants and warehouses and between warehouses and customer markets.
- Whether consolidation and pool shipping should be used, over what general shipment route, and where a full truck load should be broken down into individual shipments.
- What products should be stocked at each location and what levels of inventory of each product line should be carried.
- Other distribution functions important in individual applications

In applying the model, the user has the option of solving for the lowest total cost network of all of these components, or incorporating the impact that varying service levels have on market share and sales in each of the individual markets and by market channel. If proposed service levels are especially good in specific markets, and if prior evaluation has indicated that good service impacts sales positively, revenues may be indicated to increase, thereby offsetting any added service cost involved and increasing profit contribution.
The model handles multiple echelons as well, dealing, for example, in two or more levels of manufacture (raw materials, to subassemblies, to final assembly) and multiple levels of warehousing, for example, the master-satellite concept.

Most importantly, this program is flexible in that specific cost functions and service requirements and special management constraints can be factored into the model in designing the national logistical strategy.

ONE LAST DRP SUGGESTION

Many DRP systems develop inaccurate record balances by not returning unneeded material to the warehouse. Therefore, use the form in Figure 12–11 to help resolve this problem.

```
┌─────────────────────────────────────────────┐
│                                   No. 61974   │
│                                               │
│            RETURN THIS MATERIAL               │
│                 TO STORES                     │
│                                               │
│   THESE  PARTS  ARE  NOT  CURRENTLY           │
│   REQUIRED AT THIS LOCATION.  PLEASE          │
│   PUT   IN   A   CONTAINER,   COUNT   THE     │
│   NUMBER OF PARTS, FILL IN THE BLOCKS         │
│   BELOW  AND  SEND  PIECES  TO  STORES        │
│   BUILDING.                                   │
│                                               │
│   ──────────────────────────────────────     │
│   AUTHORIZED                                  │
│        BY                                     │
│      (NAME)                                   │
│   PART NUMBER          │  NUMBER OF PIECES     │
│                        │                       │
│   ──────────────────────────────────────     │
│                                               │
│          NOTE TO STORES PERSONNEL:            │
│                                               │
│   THIS FORM WILL SERVE AS A RETURN TO         │
│   STORES MATERIAL CREDIT. FORWARD IT          │
│   TO PRODUCTION CONTROL AFTER PLAC-           │
│   ING PARTS IN STORES LOCATION.               │
│                                               │
│   ────────────┬──────────────────────────     │
│    BIN NO.    │                                │
└───────────────┴───────────────────────────────┘
```

FIGURE 12–11: Return to Stores Tag

CHAPTER REFERENCES

1. R. B. Brooks, "Develop Stockroom Accuracy Create a Parts Bank," *APICS Conference Proceedings*, American Production and Inventory Control Society, Falls Church, VA, 1977.

2. Reprinted by permission of the Harvard Business Review. "Making Warehousing More Efficient" by Kenneth B. Ackerman and Bernard J. La Londe (March/April 1980). © 1980 by the President and Fellows of Harvard College; all rights reserved.

3. "LOGISTEK III Distribution Model." Software Program, Harvey N. Shycon, Ernst & Whinney, Washington, DC, 1985.

How to Control Inventory Management in Special Industries

13

CHAPTER HIGHLIGHTS

Good inventory control is good inventory control, regardless of the industry. However, a number of industries do have special inventory control needs. This chapter presents the best ways to handle these unique material environments.

Six major inventory environments are given as the classifications for all industries. Then, three of these—and their main commodity groups—are examined in detail: financial service industries, retail inventory, and health-care management.

Also included is a section on when to use material requirements planning (MRP) for special industries, namely, hospitals and restaurants.

Let us begin with a perspective of several industries, listing their products or services as well as their primary inventory control system—Reorder Point (ROP) or Material Requirements Planning (MRP).

Industry	Typical Products	Primary Inventory System
Product industries		
Job shop	Machine tools	MRP
Flow manufacturing	Television receivers	MRP
Project manufacturing	Ship building	MRP
Process industries		
Job shop	Pharmaceuticals	MRP
Flow manufacturing	Coal	ROP
Project manufacturing	Chemicals	MRP
Service industries	Banks	ROP
Subcontract services	Plating	ROP
Health-care institutions	Hospitals	ROP
Government contracts	Aerospace	MRP
Capital equipment repair	Turret lathe	ROP
Maintenance, repair, and operating	Facility operations	ROP
Retail	Clothing store	ROP

SIX MAJOR INVENTORY ENVIRONMENTS

All of the industries listed previously can, for inventory management purposes, be classified in six major inventory environments. These environments include:

1. *Simple manufacturing*—usually with sales below $10 million and/or a single level bill of material product.

2. *Complex manufacturing*—with sales usually in excess of $10 million and several levels in the bill of material.

3. *Service industries*—financial institutions, government agencies, and educational organizations.

4. *Retail stores*—requiring material to meet ever-changing consumer demands and distribution requirements.

5. *Health-care institutions*—hospitals, nursing homes, and so forth, with their special patient care supply needs.

6. *Process industries*—such as an oil refinery or a coal company that consists of a continuous operation.

Figure 13–1 indicates the major commodity groups for each of these six inventory environments.

Inventory Commodity Categories	Simple Mfg.	Complex Mfg.	Service Industries	Health-Care Industries	Process Industries	Retail Stores
Raw Materials	(✓)	✓			✓	
Purchased Components	✓	✓			(✓)	
Finished Components	✓	✓			(✓)	
Work-in-Process		✓			(✓)	
Finished Goods	✓	✓			✓	✓
Operating Supplies		✓	✓	✓	✓	
Maintenance Stores		✓	✓	✓	✓	
Office Supplies		✓	✓	✓	✓	✓
Forms, Envelopes & Paper		✓	✓	✓	✓	✓
Printshop Supplies			✓	✓		
Capital Equipment	✓	✓	✓		✓	(✓)
Tools & Dies		✓	✓		✓	
Books				✓		
Food Supplies				✓		
Medical Supplies				✓		
Pharmaceuticals				✓		
Operating Room Supplies				✓		

Codes:

✓ for most companies
(✓) optional inventory catagory

FIGURE 13–1: Commodity Groups for the Six Inventory Environments

269

FINANCIAL SERVICE INDUSTRIES

Bank inventory control runs in two extremes: money (one has to control the stuff) and service items such as forms, envelopes, pencils, and floor polish. While money is well controlled, service items also need considerable attention.

Two analyses provide perspective to the bank service environment challenge: the line item cost and the total value of the requisition. In this typical example, 62 percent of the requisition values are less than $50, and 67 percent of the line item quantity is worth less than $10. Thus, the bank inventory system must be capable of accounting for numerous small transactions.

	VALUE OF REQUISITIONS	
	Total Value	Line Items
Less than $10.00	34%	67%
$10.00–$24.99	16 ⎫ 62%	17
$25.00–$49.99	12 ⎭	7
$50.00–$99.99	11	4
$100.00–$249.99	12	4
$250.00–$999.99	11	1
Greater than $999.99	4	0
TOTAL	100%	100%

For detailed service industry inventory, commodity codes provide a method to establish a simple priority system: (1) critical items such as checks, (2) required items represented by passbooks, and (3) convenience items such as staplers. Figure 12–2 in Chapter 12 lists these commodity groups.

A policy should be developed that considers "stock in" (the available inventory on hand) percentage, which should be varied by type of items. This policy should study the stock usage trend (anticipated changes in demand), seasonal stock (such as year-end statements) and buffer stock for random fluctuations (reruns of a computer report).

The Supply Catalog: Primary Control Document

A primary control document in service industries is the supply catalog, which lists stock item number, description, and especially the unit of issue. (Figure 13–2 is a typical computer-prepared catalog page.) The typical introduction below explains the methods to use this catalog.

Commodity Group Number	Title	Item Number	Description of Item	Form No. (Optional)	Type Item Stock	Type Item Numbered Nonstock	Packaged Method & Qty.	Unit of Issue
10	Envelopes	10061	Manila plain (9½ x 12½)	—	x	—	Box of 100	Box

FIGURE 13–2: Supply Catalog Page Example

A. Introduction

1. This catalog has been developed to explain the inventory control system. The proper use of the catalog will mean savings in time and effort for your department.

2. Samples of the stock requisitions and stock credit forms have been attached to your manual. They have been color-coded for your convenience.

3. Requisitions are to be made on a dual use stock/nonstock requisition form and the return-to-stock credit form to return unneeded material. Inventory management will accept items for credit only if the stock item is still active in inventory. All credits must be approved by the inventory manager.

4. When ordering nonstock forms, use the same requisition and send it to Forms Control with the actual document, if appropriate.

5. All stock requisitions and stock credits must be prepared on the new forms.

6. It is the responsibility of each department to fill out its stock requisition and credit forms properly. Be sure to order supplies at least 30 days before inventory on hand is depleted. Inventory management, which processes requisitions and credits, reserves the right to return poorly prepared documents.

B. Multipurpose Requisition

Figure 13–3 illustrates this dual use form, which should be used for either stock items (after having referenced the supply catalog for ordering information) or nonstock items, in which case, the requisition directly goes to Purchasing. However, in the event of a stock-out, one copy of the requisition serves as a back order notice while the original is sent to Purchasing as a requisition.

C. Guidelines

Fill in each requisition using these guidelines:

1. *Requisition date:*	Date of order.
2. *Charge to:*	Responsibility center or department to be charged.
3. *Deliver to:*	Department and person receiving goods, the building and floor.
4. *Quantity Requested:*	Be certain to use exact quantity.
5. *Unit of Issue:*	Refer to unit of issue column in supply catalog for correct information.

NO. 31617

DATE _____

( ) Stock ( ) Nonstock - Forms Control
( ) Nonstock - Purchasing

Responsibility
Center No._____

Requested By: _____ Approved By:_____
Vice President (over $1000)

Approved By_____ Approved By:_____
Sr. Vice President (over $5000)

Charge to				Deliver to		
Quantity Requested	Quantity Issued	Unit of Issue	Stock or Form Number	Description (in detail)	Unit Price	Total Price

Date _____ Filled by _____ Remarks _____

Vendor Name and Address	TAXABLE☐ EXEMPT☐	OUR PURCHASE ORDER NUMBER
_____	Vendor No. _____	
_____	Confirming To:_____ Date_____	
_____	Terms and FOB_____ Payment Disc. _____	
_____	Conditions Other _____	
	Buyer Authorization: _____	
	(Must be signed to be valid)	

Vendor Please Note: Unless you provide us written expressed exception to the contents of this order, we will assume you agree and will pay your invoice accordingly.

FIGURE 13–3: Service Industry Requisition and Purchase Order

6. *Stock Number:*　　　Five-digit number of item being
　　　　　　　　　　　　ordered.

7. *Description:*　　　　Refer to supply catalog. Enter
　　　　　　　　　　　　exact description of stock item as
　　　　　　　　　　　　found in catalog. If nonstock,
　　　　　　　　　　　　describe as specifically as
　　　　　　　　　　　　possible.

Snap out and retain the file copy. Send balance of set to Inventory Management for stock items or Forms Control for nonstock items. For stock credit, use same guidelines as for the stock requisition.

Stock Status Report

Figure 13–4 is a typical service industry Stock Status Report. This document not only indicates the quantity balance-on-hand but also year to date usage and months' supply on hand information.

THE RETAIL INVENTORY ENVIRONMENT

Challenges for the consumer-oriented retail sales environment usually fall into two general categories; the first is a requirement of having "so many" of a group of items on hand to sell to the customer; inexpensive rings are a good example of this inventory. The second is where a specific item is necessary, such as a 1983 Ford engine bearing in an auto parts supply store.

Groups of Like Items Control

This control system was developed based on an analysis of the sales of giftshop items during an eighteen-month period. An "ABC" inventory classification analysis was performed to determine what type of items had specific demands.[1]

　　Numerous retail businesses have a wide range of customer requirements in that both expensive and inexpensive items have variable demands. The information regarding the quantity on hand by specific item does not always have to be exact. It is more important, for example, to have a variety of rings in a certain price class (twenty rings ranging in price from $10 to $20) than it is to have five silver rings with stones at $15.50 each, ten silver rings without stones worth $12.00 each, five rings each with a turquoise stone at $18.95, and so forth, available for sale.

　　Usually two-thirds of the sales dollars in a year's time come from items that have a unit dollar value greater than $10. Yet these items represented only 10 percent of the 30,000 plus pieces in the storeroom. Therefore, control

Report No.:: RGCO14
Report Name: Stock Status
Report Frequency: Week Ending Friday

Page: 34
Run Date: 03/05/XX
Information Date: 03/01/XX

Catalog No.	Description	u/m	Com. Code	Average Cost	Lead Time	Quantity on Hand	Value on Hand	Avg. Mo. Usage	Months' Supply on Hand	On Order
10061	Envelopes, Manila	Box of 100	10	$15.50	1 Week	337	$5223.50	97	3.5	0

FIGURE 13–4: Service Industry Stock Status Report

should be established over these two-thirds of the items (called the "A" and "B" classification) on a periodic basis but not to keep as close a track of the more inexpensive "C" class items (worth less than $10).

The system is initiated by taking a physical inventory of all control items; in this case, those whose sales value at retail was worth more than $10. The Retail Physical Inventory Worksheet (Figure 13–5) is utilized for this inventory keyed to the store layout. Once the initial quantities on hand are obtained, they are posted to the inventory control record as the starting control quantity.

The Retail Inventory Control
Part Number Code

A five-character inventory code is used. The five positions in the item code number indicate the commodity group, the specific type of item, the retail

Location _____ Counted by _____ Sheet____ of ____

INVENTORY NO.	DESCRIPTION VENDOR PUBLISHER	QUANTITY	RETAIL PRICE	EXTENSION	CLASS

FIGURE 13–5: Retail Inventory Worksheet

dollar value range, the time period when it was purchased, and the name of the supplier. This system allows for up to 100 specific classifications in ten general groupings. The groupings (in this example) include containers, scientific, Indian jewelry, and geology shop, and are listed in Figure 13–6. The system has a fair amount of flexibility and includes a provision for seasonal and other miscellaneous requirements, since details regarding the value of the item, date purchased, and even supplier identification are available.

Five Steps to Determine Code

1. Select one of the ten commodity groups.
2. Locate the number that indicates each item within groups.
3. Locate the number that indicates price range.
4. Locate the letter that indicates the quarter and year in which the item is received.
5. Select supplier alphabetical desegregation.

Example: An Indian necklace that costs $28.00 and was received in May, 1987, from Trader Tim, would have as an inventory number—445NH.

40—Indian goods commodity group
44—Indian goods, necklace
 5—cost range $25.00 to $49.99
 N—received in second quarter, 1987
 H—supplier is Trader Tim

Inventory Control Tags

Three tags are used in this control system. A tear-apart, two-section tag is used for the great majority of the items. This tag lists the control code number for inventory control and the specific price for sales information. There is room for style as well as size on the tags, which are generally available from local office supply houses. For inventory control purposes, all that is needed is the five-character identification number. When the item is sold, the bottom half of the tag is torn off and stapled to the bag containing the merchandise or taped to the larger merchandise as an identification receipt for the customer. The other half is sent to the office for subsequent posting to the computerized inventory control report or to a manually posted control book.

A smaller tag is used for little items such as rings. No receipts for these items are given to the customer though an identification slip can be given to indicate that it is a legitimate sale. The third (largest) tag is used for books that cannot have a tag stapled to them. In any event, one of the three "tags" for all control items (that is, those worth more than $10) must be sent to the inventory office for subsequent posting.

SECTION A & B

00 Containers	20 Art Works	50 Eskimo Crafts	70 Books
00 Miscellaneous	20 Miscellaneous	50 Miscellaneous	70 Miscellaneous
01 Ceramic & China	21 Foreign	51 Carvings	71 Records
02 Glass	22 Alva	52 Wall Hangings	72
03 Metal	23 Glass	53 Masks	73
04 Wood	24 Ceramic	54 Jewelry	74
05 Birdfeeders	25 Wood (decoys)	55	75
06 Windchimes	26 Hangings	56	76
07 Bookends	27 Paintings	57	77
08 Birdhouses	28 Metal	58	78
09 Baskets	29	59	79

10 Scientific	30 Regular Jewery	60 Geology Shop	80 Paper Goods
10 Miscellaneous	30 Miscellaneous	60 Miscellaneous	80 Miscellaneous
11 Binoculars	31 Rings	61 Geodes	81 Prints
12 Barometers & Thermometers	32 Earrings	62 Slabs	82 Posters
13 Scopes	33 Bracelets	63 Rocks	83 Totes
14	34 Necklaces	64 Fossils	84 Greeting Cards
15	35 Pins	65 Petrified Wood	85 Postcards
16	36	66 Bookends & Desk Sets	86 Stationery
17	37 Alva	67 Rock Polishers	87
18	38 Buckles	68 Clocks	88
19	39 Mens	69	89

40 Indian Goods	90 Seasonal & Other
40 Miscellaneous	90 Miscellaneous
41 Rings	91 Toys
42 Earrings	92 Easter
43 Bracelets & Watchbands	93 Christmas
44 Necklaces	94 Clothing
45 Pins	95 Floral
46 Rugs	96 Mens
47 Sand Paintings	97 Lamps
48 Belts	98
49 Mens	99 Consignment

SECTION C: VALUE OF ITEM

0-	$0.01 - $ 4.99
1-	5.00 - 9.99
2-	10.00 - 14.99
3-	15.00 - 19.99
4-	20.00 - 24.99
5-	25.00 - 49.99
6-	50.00 - 74.99
7-	75.00 - 99.99
8-	100.00 - 499.99
9-	500.00 - up

SECTION D: DATA PURCHASED

CODE	DATE
A	1981
B	1982
C	1983
D	1984
E	1985 - First Quarter
F	1985 - Second Quarter
G	1985 - Third Quarter
H	1985 - Fourth Quarter
I	1986 - First Quarter
J	1986 - Second Quarter
K	1986 - Third Quarter
L	1986 - Fourth Quarter
M	1987 - First Quarter
N	1987 - Second Quarter
O	1987 - Third Quarter
P	1987 - Fourth Quarter
Q	1988 - First Quarter
R	1988 - Second Quarter

SECTION E: SUPPLIER

CODE	SUPPLIER
A	Buckley Jewelers
B	Patrick's Silversmiths
C	R.G. Cept Traders
D	Brown-Bow
E	Reservation Indian Arts
F	Robert J. Brown
G	Indian Traders
H	Trader Tim
I	Edwards
J	Jack's Stores
K	Mr. Christopher
L	Indian Traders
M	Mang Mag
N	Betsey's Boutique
O	Gold Traders
P	Timberjack

FIGURE 13–6: Retail Commodity Coding Method

Inventory Control Record:
Primary Control Document
for Posting Information

The inventory report sheet is the control document used (Figure 13–7). In a manual procedure, there is one sheet for each of the control groups maintained, which means a maximum of 100 records for the entire system if all codes were used as shown in Figure 13–6.

The commodity name and its control groups, such as Indian Goods–Necklaces, are placed on the blank form. The first step is posting the initial physical inventory count. All subsequent receipts of materials (plus) and/or sales of materials (minus) are posted to this record. After the system has been used for some time, the average monthly usage and the latest physical inventory quantity can be calculated. Then the balance on hand for the manual system is calculated on a periodic basis, usually weekly. In a computerized

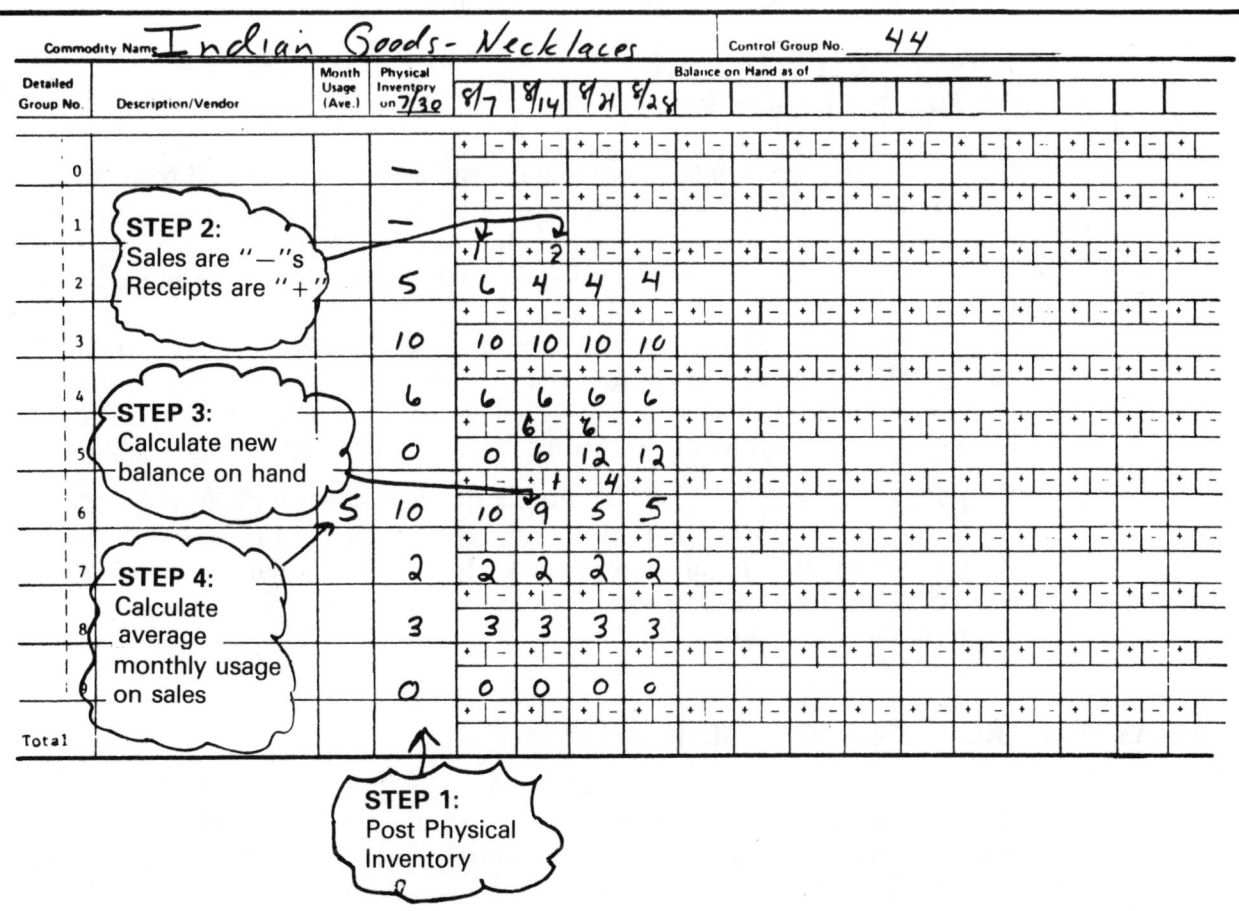

FIGURE 13–7: Retail Inventory Control Record

system, the posting should be done daily. (It should be kept in mind that items worth less than $10 or even a lower control point can be used if desired. For example, "C" items that range from $5 to $10 could be coded "1," and those that sell for less than $5 could be coded "0.")

After a period of time, at least three months, the average monthly sales are calculated from the "minuses" entered on each form for each line item. The average monthly sales are posted in the appropriate column as shown and are used in monitoring decisions. In this example, if there was an average monthly sale of 5 and a physical inventory on hand of 15; then, in effect, there are three months' supply of this item. The converse, of course, could also be true. Sales could jump up to 15 a month and, with 15 items on hand, there would be only a one-month inventory.

Any reordering decisions by items should be made using the most recent physical inventory and the figures for average monthly usage, namely, sales. Although this explanation has concentrated on a manual control, with the availability of smaller computers, an on-line, real-time control report similar to the manual worksheet can be implemented.

Using the Control Record for Statistical Analysis

Certain statistics for management's analytical use can be obtained from studying the information posted to the control book. For example, inventory can be analyzed by date purchased. You might learn that 52 percent of the material has been on hand for more than one year (received prior to the period code of a year ago).

It is also possible to investigate the sales versus inventory investment by date purchased, and by doing so learn that 43 percent of the sales were from inventory on hand more than one year. This analysis indicates some slow-moving inventory on hand and action is necessary to reduce this problem.

Suggestion: As a general rule of thumb, maintain a month's supply of those items that can be quickly reordered and a maximum of three months' supply for those items that require more time. However, seasonal items can be an exception. In this case, you might submit a single order for an amount sufficient to last the eight-week Christmas season.

HEALTH-CARE INVENTORY MANAGEMENT

Hospitals must serve very special persons—their patients—while at the same time containing costs and adhering to a myriad of regulations. As with many service organizations, inventory management, purchasing, and internal distribution are so closely related that a materials management organization is a natural.

Organize Items into Groupings

Any effort to establish management control over the hospital's inventory must begin with an analysis of the current state of affairs, preparing a schedule like that below. All inventory items are placed in one of three general groupings—stock items required by multiple using units, stock items for only one using unit, and nonstock items. The following information is typical of a 200-bed hospital.

USUAL INVENTORY TURNOVER	VALUE OF INVENTORY	CATEGORY OF ITEMS	ITEMS
		Stock Items—Multiple Using Unit	
3.1 Times	$ 35,000	—Miscellaneous	1,000
2.3 Times	7,000	—Forms	800
		Stock Items—One Specific Using Unit	
3.5 Times	60,000	Operating Room	300
4.8 Times	50,000	Pharmacy	2,500
3.7 Times	15,000	Dietary	1,000
		Nonstock Items	
1.8 Times	18,000	Multiple Using Units	2,000
5.2 Times	15,000	One Specific Using Unit	1,000
3.7 Times	$200,000	TOTAL	8,600

Target Investments by Commodity Group

Once this schedule is prepared, the investment target by commodity groups should be determined. This investment is similar to the information contained in Figure 13–8. This summary, by hospital commodity/storage location groups, shows the inventory investment per bed, group investment target, actual investment, the recent annual issues, and finally the group turnover.

Determine Deliveries Based on Importance to Patients

The next step is to ascertain how goods are delivered to the using units—that is, those who need the material. There is no one correct way to distribute items. Usually two or more methods should be used, selecting from

1. Cart exchange
2. On-site replenishment

Inventory Commodity Group	Investment Per Bed	Target Investment (A)	12/31 Actual Investment	Actual to Target Variance	Annual Issues	Turn-over
Dietary	$40	$8,000	$6,716	$1,284	$194,764	29.0
General Stores	195	39,000	59,148	(20,148)	360,803	6.1
Housekeeping	25	5,000	4,917	83	40,319	8.2
Laboratory	30	6,000	3,844	2,156	25,755	6.7
Laundry	20	4,000	3,319	681	12,280	3.7
Maintenance	25	5,000	7,698	(2,698)	29,483	3.8
Medical/Surgical	190	38,000	49,335	(11,335)	310,810	6.3
Office Supplies	30	6,000	11,625	(5,625)	75,563	6.5
Operating Room	130	26,000	56,369	(30,369)	174,744	3.1
Pharmacy	240	48,000	88,966	(40,966)	338,071	3.8
Printed Forms	15	3,000	8,484	(5,484)	80,598	9.5
Radiology	70	14,000	35,163	(21,163)	239,108	6.8
Sterile Processing	90	18,000	16,596	1,404	81,320	4.9
TOTAL	**$1,100**	**$220,000**	**$352,180**	**($132,180)**	**1,963,618**	**5.6**

(A) Calculated based on the average census of 200 beds
   (Inventory investment per bed X 200 beds).

FIGURE 13–8: Hospital Inventory Investment Targets and Analysis

3. 31-day traveling requisition
4. Case cart
5. Blanket purchase order
6. User stock special order
7. Combination requisition/purchase order
8. Emergency requisition
9. Urgent telephone requests

For successful inventory investment in health care, the items controlled should receive more—or less—attention based on their importance to serving the patient. This is accomplished by using an extension of the ABC stratification system (refer to Chapter 5) and classifying each item by using an inventory "Decision Tree" style coding chart as shown in Figure 13–9.

RESPONSE AND CODES

SEQUENCE	QUESTION	IF ONLY ONE, USE THIS COLUMN			IF MORE THAN ONE, USE THIS COLUMN
		IF YES, USE THIS COLUMN		IF NO, USE THIS COLUMN	
		IF YES, USE THIS COLUMN	IF NO, USE THIS COLUMN		
1	HOW MANY DEPARTMENTS USE THIS ITEM?				
2	IS THERE STORAGE SPACE IN THE DEPARTMENT?				
3	DOES DEPARTMENT WISH MATERIAL MANAGEMENT TO CHECK STOCK AND REORDER?				
4	IF ISSUES ARE FIVE OR MORE IN THREE MONTHS, EOQ IS GREATER THAN ONE, AND ANNUAL DOLLAR ISSUES ARE:				
	$5,000 OR GREATER	A F	A I	A L	A
	$ 500 TO $4,999	B G	B J	B M	B
	$ 499 OR LESS	C H	C K	C N	C
5	IF PRESENTLY STOCKED ITEM HAS NO ISSUES IN PAST THREE MONTHS:	↑	↑	↑	D
6	IS THIS AN EMERGENCY ITEM?	↑	↑	↑	E
7	ALL OTHER ITEMS ARE NON-STOCK.	↑	↑	↑	X

PROCEDURE TO USE:

ASK EACH QUESTION IN SEQUENCE. AT THE FIRST "YES" ANSWER THE LETTER IS THE PROPER INVENTORY CODE.

FIGURE 13–9: Hospital Inventory Coding "Decision Tree"

Establish a Standardization Committee

The next task requires considerable work and consists of establishing a workable "Standardization Committee." Since inventory investment in hospitals (and most other industries) increases in direct relationship to the number of items, a successful way to control inventory is through such a committee; comprised of representative membership from the Medical Staff, Nursing, Biomedical Engineering, Materials Management, and Accounting departments. This committee should be guided by

- Administration policy statement
- Definitive procedure
- Advisory personnel
- Minimized variety of items
- Evaluation process checklist

WHEN TO USE MATERIAL REQUIREMENTS PLANNING FOR SPECIAL INDUSTRIES

MRP in Hospitals: A Five-Step Procedure

In this last section, let's take a look at the future, the use of the more complicated Material Requirements Planning (MRP) in hospital inventory management. Several years ago, it occurred that the inventory control technique called MRP could be applied in hospital materials management systems. One operation was selected—a simple appendectomy—and a test of the concept was made. A bill of material was developed by merging the surgeon preference items, sterile processing supplies, disposable materials, patient charge items, and general use materials into a two-level indented document. The history of appendectomies at the hospital was obtained and a forecast was prepared from the data. The more recent Surgery Schedule was studied and an Appendectomy Forecast projected by week for the next six months was developed. This was used as the "master schedule"; by multiplying the number of operations each week times bill of material quantities, the "gross requirements" were determined.

The next step was to obtain the present amount of inventory on hand for each of the items. By subtracting this amount from the gross requirements, the "net requirements" for each item were determined. The data was given to vendors (who were then told to deliver needed supplies on Blanket Purchase Order Releases) and to Sterile Processing (who made a production plan). This initial study, of course, considered each item as "independent demand" in that no other relationships—such as gauze, which is used in most operations—was considered.

Once established, MRP in hospitals follows this five-step procedure:

1. Input: Operating room (O.R.) schedule for next month
2. Reference: O.R. case cart "bill of material" list by procedure
3. Output: Specific item quantity needs
4. Comparison: Quantity needs to actual amounts in storeroom
5. Action: Order items required but not in storeroom

MRP in Restaurants: Eight Requirements

MRP also has applications in Food Service (hospital cafeterias) or even a large restaurant. The following criteria are required by this type of MRP system:[2]

1. A master production schedule exists. This basically is the menu and the forecasted usage of the raw materials.
2. All inventory items are uniquely identified. This means that all items (such as fries, hamburgers, and buns) are identified and there is no ambiguity in their names.
3. A bill of material exists. This is basically the same thing as a recipe. It tells what goes into the product.
4. Inventory records containing data on the status of items in inventory exist. This tells how many are in stock as well as how many are on order of every inventory item (i.e., buns, fries, hamburgers).
5. Integrity of file data exists. This means that if the records say that there are five items in inventory, there really are five items in inventory.
6. Individual item lead times are known. This indicates that the time from placing the order to the time of receipt of the order is known.
7. Every item goes into and out of stock. This means that no item can be consumed before it has been recorded in the inventory records.
8. Here is an example of a Food Service ABC Analysis:

Class	Number of Items	Dollar Value	Food
(Ā)	10%	60%	Hamburger Milk Bread Hotdogs
B	20%	20%	Ice Cream Fish Chips Lettuce
C	70%	20%	Spinach Liver Beets Prunes

Other Optional MRP System Uses

Another optional use of MRP systems is for tooling that can either include the tooling requirements in the bill of material or develop an independent tool structure file and then a bill of tool file.[3]

Advantages of controlling tools by MRP include enforcement of all the normal disciplines associated with an MRP net parts type of system, including

- Accurate tool inventory
- Tool consumption report
- Tool cost reporting
- Accurate and timely tool ordering
- Realistic scheduling of requirements within the tool crib and a basis to plan the facilities' needs and investment in tooling required to support a master schedule
- Accurate engineering change data coordinated in the tool master

CHAPTER REFERENCES

1. R. L. Janson, "Inventory Control Techniques for a Retail Sales Environment," *Production and Inventory Management*, American Production and Inventory Control Society, Falls Church, VA, First Quarter 1979.
2. Jeffrey Jones, "The Use of Material Requirements Planning (MRP) in a Food Service Installation," *Production and Inventory Management*, American Production and Inventory Control Society, Second Quarter 1979.
3. S. Galligan and M. Mokris, "Integrating Tool Control into a Standard Manufacturing System," *Production and Inventory Management*, American Production and Inventory Control Society, Falls Church, VA, 1981.

Measuring Results of Inventory Management

14

CHAPTER HIGHLIGHTS

This chapter focuses on the major documents and reports that are used to measure results in inventory management. Nine key document categories are listed and explained in detail.

Also included is a step-by-step procedure for do-it-yourself report designing.

KEY MANAGEMENT DOCUMENTS TO USE IN CONTROLLING AND MEASURING INVENTORY RESULTS

There are nine categories of inventory management CRT screens, documents, and reports, which can be utilized in various inventory environments:

1. Sufficient daily CRT displayed "action" reports provide, on an exception basis, up-to-the-minute inventory information for operating decisions.

2. "Status" reports, using up-to-date variable information, are produced periodically showing all or part of a data file.

3. Computer generated "working" documents, such as tags and forms, are necessary to administer the inventory procedures.

4. Historical "reference" reports, on a regular or as-needed basis, provide detail fixed information from which to make analysis and then control decisions.

5. Inventory "System Maintenance, Conversion, and Control" reports are used to measure accuracy and timeliness of data, highlighting areas where improvement is necessary.

6. "Analysis and exception" lists, using special information sorts, are usually received on a request basis and produced in a batch mode.

7. An "Inventory and Purchasing Budget," by monitoring monthly recent incoming customer orders, permits control of newly purchased material, in order to keep inventory turnover at the desired level.

8. "Simulation Reports" utilizing inventory and related data are used to project cause and effect statistical relationships.

9. A monthly "Key Indicator Report" provides, in easily read statistical and graph format, trend indicators for inventory system management.

All of these categories are summarized in Figure 14–1. The major documents and reports are explained in the following section.

INVENTORY "ACTION" REPORTS FOR UP-TO-THE-MINUTE INFORMATION

The purpose of Inventory Action Reports, which are displayed on terminals (or paper) using up-to-the-minute information, is to alert inventory controllers of basic daily inventory data for operating decisions. Another reason is notification when a specific item's forecast, customer requirements, and/or balance on hand exceed certain preestablished control limits. Figure 14–2 is an

Group No.	Type Reports	Typical Examples
1	ACTION REPORTS - one item or very exception oriented, worksheets or CRT response and/or Hard Copy (Printed) Turnaround. Data up to date.	• Items Requiring Ordering Review • Shipping Priority List • Past Due List
2	STATUS REPORTS - "variable" up to date, some file data supressed, periodically produced.	• Open Customer Orders • Inventory allocation & balances • MRP Worksheet
3	COMPUTER PRODUCED TAGS & FORMS- needed to work the inventory procedures, occassionally manual input	• Bar Code Bin Labels • Packing Slips • Requisitions
4	HISTORICAL REFERENCE LISTS - usually "fixed" data, periodically, batch produced.	• Inventory Master • Bills of Material • Shipments by Part number
5	SYSTEM DATA MAINTENANCE, TRAINING, CONVERSION & CONTROL - needed to establish and maintain files	• Master file revisions • Transaction Edit List • System Report "Menu" Listing • System CRT Familiarization Training
6	ANALYSIS & EXCEPTION LISTS - special sorts on request of historical reference lists.	• Inventory Turnover by Part • Customer orders held for Credit • ABC analysis
7	INVENTORY TARGETS & BUDGET- periodic information for monitoring purposes	• Inventory Levels • Inventory & Purchasing Level Revisions
8	SIMULATION REPORTS - using inventory and related data to project possible statistics	• Inventory Investment Profitability • Cost Revisions Impact • EOQ vs. Service Levels
9	PERFORMANCE MEASURES- statistical and graphics.	• Key Indicator Report • Productivity Measures

FIGURE 14–1: Inventory Management Standard Documents and Reports

inquiry style CRT display that lists, by category, items whose statistics are "outside" these preset limits. Other typical reports in this category include:

- MRP planning worksheet report
- Daily dispatch priority report
- Recommended buy report
- Reschedule notices due to customer order changes
- Master schedule action report
- Past due vendor orders

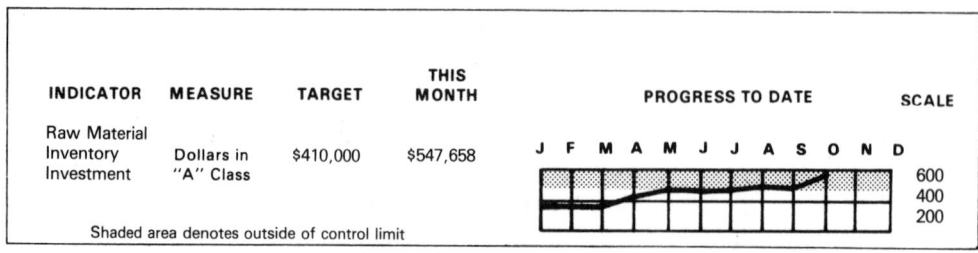

FIGURE 14–2: Statistics Outside Control Limits

INVENTORY "STATUS" REPORTS TELL YOU WHERE YOU ARE

The major example of an inventory management "status" report is the inventory list that details various up-to-date information such as the balance on hand. (Refer to Figure 14–3.)

The substantial variety of status type reports include:

- Manufactured part open order status report
- Open purchase order status report
- Subcontracted/outside processing lot control list
- Customer order backlog balances due by product line
- Finished parts in shipping on customer hold

INVENTORY STATUS REORDER REPORT						
Commodity Group	Part Number	Description	Unit Measure	Unit Cost	Last Useage Date	Last Order Date
On Order	Balance On Hand	Allocated	Available	Order Point	EOQ	Safety Stock	Vendor or Manufactured

FIGURE 14–3: Inventory Status Reorder Report Contents

COMPUTER-PRODUCED TAGS AND FORMS

This third group includes computer generated working documents necessary to administer the inventory procedures. These forms and tags have a turn-around nature to them. A good example is the Daily Cycle Count Report which contains a list of those parts the computer has selected for cycle count quantity validation. This report contains a provision, on the right column, for the cycle counter to record the current quantity at the storage location(s).

Other documents in this category include Inventory Movement Tickets, Bar Code Bin Identification labels, annual Physical Inventory List, computer produced Inventory Ledger Cards, and Shipping labels. Sometimes manually produced documents, such as a requisition, are utilized in this category.

INVENTORY "REFERENCE" REPORTS FOR HISTORICAL AND FORECAST PROJECTIONS

This fourth category includes the batch processed, printed reference reports, replete with both historical and forecast projections allowing inventory personnel to augment information obtained from CRT status inquiry. The primary reference is the Inventory Master Report, depicted in Figure 14–4. Other such reference reports are

- Material Locator Listing
- Aged Inventory List
- Part Group Summary
- Bill of Material Listing
- Manufacturing routings
- ABC usage dollar distribution
- Vendor purchased parts quantity price breaks

INVENTORY MASTER REPORT				
Part Number	Description	Unit of Measure	Inventory Class	Store Location
Lead Time	Mfg. or Pur.	Reorder Point	Safety Stock	Reorder Quantity	Actual Cost
On Hand	On Order	Reserved	Usage Last Year	Issues YTD	Std. Cost

FIGURE 14–4: Inventory Master Record Contents

INVENTORY SYSTEM CONTROL REPORT FOR HIGHLIGHTING ERRORS

This fifth category of inventory reports consists of batch processed, printed computer reports. The purpose of this group is to alert the Inventory Personnel whenever errors begin to creep into the system. Some of these errors are the results of information input inaccuracies. Other times the errors are determined as part of the cycle counting procedure. Included in this group are training and familiarization reports to help personnel use the computerized inventory system.

- Inventory management computer system "menus"
- CRT training familiarization screen
- Forecast last revision date control
- Inventory, B/M, and routing transaction accuracy report
- Transaction inputs rejected
- Inventory item master file changes list

ANALYSIS AND EXCEPTION INFORMATION FOR SPECIAL INFORMATION SORTS

The sixth category is the Analysis and Exception Lists; two special reports are

- *Inventory Analysis Report.* This shows the number of months inventory coverage (supply on hand) and highlights items with excess inventory coverage caused by change in customer demands or poor inventory practices. Opportunities for inventory reductions, disposition of obsolete inventory, and more effective use of warehouse facilities are some advantages that could be derived by the effective use of this management report (Figure 14–5).
- *Inventory by Type Product.* This shows summary purchase amounts by type of commodity, such as computer stock paper, custom computer paper, forms, and various office supply categories. This report should be used to monitor expense against budget by category and for budget projections.

Other reports in this category can include:

- Production overruns; excess versus factory order schedule
- Months' supply on hand; highest down to 6 months on hand
- Cycle count error analysis summary by storage location
- Excess stock by vendor
- Stockout percentages by part; highest to 5 percent level

INVENTORY ANALYSIS REPORT						
Commodity Group	Part Number	Description	Annual Usage	Average Turnover	EOQ/Lot Size	ABC Class
Minimum	Maximum	Average Monthly Usage		Average Inventory Dollar Level	YTD Receipts	YTD Issues/Usage
YTD Adjustments: Gross	Net	Primary Customer Contract		Telephone Number	Month Supply on Hand	

FIGURE 14–5: Inventory Analysis Report

- Physical inventory net and absolute error variances
- Missing inventory tag list

INVENTORY AND PURCHASING BUDGET FOR CONTROL OF NEW PURCHASES

For successful control of inventory investment, a seventh report group is useful. This one requires close information input coordination from the Sales Order Entry Department (with information about current level of customer orders), the Inventory Control Department (with information about current level of inventory balances on hand) and the Purchasing Department (with information about current open purchase commitments). All of this information is used in the "Inventory and Purchasing Budget."

How to Create an Inventory and Purchasing Budget: Two Target Areas

In an inventory control system, various techniques are used to determine what actual order quantity should be given to the vendor (and the Manufacturing Department as well) to meet the customer requirements. These order quantity calculations can be judgmental using an estimated reorder quantity, or statistical with a calculated economic order quantity. It is common, as a result of the reorder quantity determination, to buy more items than actually are needed in the specific future. Many times, buying more than the next period's requirements is a correct economic decision for an individual item, but the cumulative impact may result in excessive amounts of inventory. Therefore, what is required is a control at the intermediate commodity group inventory levels as well as the total inventory dollar investment.

The "Inventory and Purchasing Budget" procedure addresses these needs. To establish such a practice, management initially determines two targets—an inventory balance on hand target and an open purchase order commitment target. This determination is based on historical usage information, desired safety stock, forecast of future requirements, vendor price break quantities, and/or guidance from various individuals.

Once a determination is made regarding the targets, an "Inventory and Purchasing Budget" is created. This budget is like a department expense budget, except it concerns dollars in inventory and dollars on open purchase orders. The budget is organized by department and/or commodity group categories such as steel, copper, resins, packaging, office supplies, tooling, and so forth. (Although this example explains the purchasing orders control, it is possible to also include manufacturing orders.)

Code Number	Group Description	Last Year Usage	This Year Forecast
10	Injection Resins	$1,062,000	$1,176,000
20	Blow Molding Resins	513,000	587,000
30	Colorants	141,000	149,000
40	Inserts	88,000	94,000
50	Packaging	114,000	129,000
60	Equipment	293,000	217,000
70	Tooling	124,000	148,000
80	Office Supplies	92,000	104,000
90	Outside Services	61,000	72,000
100	Miscellaneous	102,000	110,000
	TOTAL	$2,590,000	$2,786,000

FIGURE 14–6: Commodity Groups' Purchases for Plastatron Division

Ten Steps for Calculating Targets and Establishing the Budget

The actual steps to calculate the targets and establish the budget are:

1. Assign to each inventory item a commodity group name and code number, preparing a list similar to Figure 14–6. This example utilizes data from the R.G. CEPT Plastatron Division.

2. Obtain last year's purchases or actual inventory usage for each group, as well as this year's forecast (also see Figure 14–6).

3. Establish an "inventory standard target" for each commodity group. This target can be calculated quickly by dividing the annual usage by the turnover desired. For example, if a company wishes to turn its colorants (code number 30 on Figure 14–6) four times this year, divide $149,000 (this year's forecast) by four to obtain the three months' target amount of $37,250. (For a more elaborate calculation see the procedure described in Chapter 10.) This figure, as well as the others that will be developed, should be posted to the "Inventory and Purchasing Budget Calculation Worksheet" shown in Figure 14–7.

Code No.	Commodity Group	Inv. Std. Target	Curr. Mo. Purchase Req.	Open Pur. Target Mo.	Total Purchases	Dollar Budget	Act. Inv. On Hand ($)	Open Pur. Ord. ($)	Total Dollars	Diff. of Bud. vs. Act. Status
30	Colorants	$37,250	$12,417	1.25	15,521	$52,771	$19,300	$24,600	$45,700	$7,071
──STEP 1&2──▶		STEP 3	STEP 4	STEP 5	STEP 6	STEP 7	──────▶	STEP 8 ──▶		STEP 9

FIGURE 14–7: Inventory and Purchasing Budget Calculation Worksheet

4. Determine, as of a given date, "current month purchase requirements" for each commodity group. This can be done using one-twelfth of the last year's purchases (or historical usage) or of the forecast of requirements for this year, using the information also in Figure 14–6. For the colorants, this would be $149,000 divided by 12 or $12,417.

5. Set a target in terms of "open purchase target months" requirements for each commodity group. This target usually is the overall vendor average lead time. Figure 14–7 shows a 1.25 month target.

6. Multiply the "current month purchase requirements" (step 4) times the number of "open purchase target months" (from step 5) to get "total purchases" target in dollars.

7. Add dollars in step 3 and in step 6 to get the "dollar budget" for each commodity group.

8. Determine, by commodity, the present "actual inventory on hand (dollars)" and the value of "open purchase orders (dollars)." Add these two amounts to obtain "total dollars." In Figure 14–7, the inventory value of $19,300 plus open purchases of $26,400 totaled $45,700.

9. Subtract the "total dollars" (step 8) from the "dollar budget" (step 7). Any positive difference is the dollar amount, which can be committed on new purchase orders or blanket order releases. In Figure 14–7, the total dollar of $45,700, subtracted from the budget of $52,771, leaving a $7,071 difference. Since the "total dollars" is less than the "dollar budget" (a positive balance), then additional purchase commitments can be placed.

10. Review, whenever there is a significant change in customer incoming orders, the "inventory standard target" (step 3) and the "current month purchase requirements" (step 4), and repeat steps 5 through 9. At a minimum, the budget should be recalculated annually.

Interpreting the Ten Steps

The value of the "inventory and purchasing budget" is that it is very responsive to short-range changes in customer order mix as well as any seasonal changes. Suppose that, when recalculating in step 9, you learn that customer needs have decreased. The "inventory standard target" has become $12,000 and the "current month purchase requirements" is $10,500 a month for these supplies. Then the "dollar budget" becomes $25,125 ($12,000 inventory standard plus $13,125 open purchases). When this $25,125 revised budget (step 7) is compared with the actual status of $45,700 (step 8), $20,575 worth of colorants on "open purchase orders" must be canceled.

How to Simulate Various
Inventory Conditions

Since the inventory investment is a substantial company asset, the proper or incorrect use of this investment can have a far reaching impact on company profitability. It is possible to simulate or project these "cause and effect" relationships. A good example is the Inventory Investment Profitability Report, which by using certain assumptions in a fairly simple model, can help guide company executives in making inventory management decisions. Figure 10–3 is this report for the R.G. CEPT Company; you will note the influence of (1) the three years sales growth on inventory requirements, and (2) three different stock item service levels as represented by varying safety stock levels.

Other possible inventory related simulations could include:

- Projected inventory value for next 12 months based on forecast
- Quarterly financial projection
- Inventory commitments by quarter for next three years
- Forecasted turnover report
- Possible EOQs at various sales levels

PERFORMANCE MEASURES:
KEY INVENTORY REPORT OF STATISTICAL
INDICATORS

Key indicators (the ninth and last report group) are a means by which a company can measure their inventory investment with special emphasis on return on this asset called inventory.[1] These indicators use details comparing to standards by type of industry. The effect of items such as obsolete/slow-moving inventory and inaccurate inventory records, all of which impact company profits as well as measurement of productivity, can be covered. You should calculate your own company's inventory indicators through use of the worksheet approach using Figure 14–8. There are nine headings that are used in the key indicator report. These are (1) the indicator number, (2) the actual indicator, (3) the measure that is being used, (4) a target, (5) the performance during the month just completed, (6) a graph of the progress to date for the year, and, at the far right, (7) a scale which accompanies the graph plus space to show (8) last year's and (9) the current year-to-date statistics.

Report Number ____________ Department ____________ Prepared By ____________

	Indicator	Measure	Target	This Month	Progress to Date Months												Scale	Last Year	YTD
					J	F	M	A	M	J	J	A	S	O	N	D			
1																			
2																			
3																			
4																			
5																			
6																			
7																			
8																			
9																			

FIGURE 14–8: Key Indicator Worksheet

Indicators: A Management-by-Objective Approach

These indicators show, by trends, the possibility of problems developing within the inventory management system. Indicators do not solve a problem, but rather call attention to the possibility or even the probability of a serious trend developing. The basic concept is a management by objective approach wherein the manager selects his or her indicators, chooses the targets, collects the statistical data, and then personally analyzes the performance results.

It is not necessary to be exact for either setting the target or collecting the monthly measure. A general idea of the statistical target measure is often adequate. For instance, if a company processes hundreds of inventory requisitions a day, then at the end of each day, after the requisitions have been processed, the number of requisitions should be counted and recorded. It is even permissible to measure the height of a pile of requisitions in inches and record the daily average as "inches." The important indicator, in all of these, is the slope of the graph going upward or downward as suggested by the target.

Popular Indicators Used in Inventory Management

The nine indicators used commonly in inventory management are shown in Figure 14–9. However, this reporting method is quite flexible and can serve many needs. For instance, you might wish to use more creative inventory investment indicators such as

1. Forecast of customer needs—50 percent of anticipated customer orders
2. Raw material and component parts availability—90 percent of master schedule
3. Record accuracy—95 percent within 6 percent of actual
4. Months' supply—No more than 19 percent of items can have more than a 12 month's supply on hand
5. Turnover achieved—more than competitor's 4.6 times

Many chief executives do not understand the inventory problems and because of this lack of understanding fail to give adequate recognition or sufficient support. If you communicate good and bad points, both department and senior management will gain understanding and support. Once developed, the inventory control indicators join other companion measures being forwarded to the vice-president and then the president. This reporting chain of command pyramid is depicted in Figure 14–10. Note at the intermediate level the vice-president is sent the 18 most important indicators and the president

DEPARTMENT AND INDICATOR	MEASURE	TARGET	CURRENT MONTH	PROGRESS TO DATE	SCALE
INVENTORY CONTROL					
1. TURNOVER	INVESTMENT TO COST OF SALES	8X	3.1X		8 6 3
2. STOCKOUTS	OF COMPONENT PARTS	8%	15%		15 10 5
3. STEEL	SUPPLY ON HAND (DAYS)	30	48		60 40 20
4. RECORD ACCURACY	CYCLE COUNT TO PERPETUAL BOOK	95%	67%		100 80 60
5. INVESTMENT	ACTUAL TO TARGET	1:1	1.7:1.0		2:0 1:5 1:0
6. SLOW MOVING	MORE THAN 1 YEAR SUPPLY	8%	19%		30 15 5
7. STORAGE SPACE	OPEN BINS IN WAREHOUSE	0.2:1.0	0.4:1.0		1.00 0.50 0.00
8. PHYSICAL INVENTORY	ABSOLUTE ERROR	10%	22%		30 20 0
9. PURCHASED COMPONENTS	BACKORDERED PARTS	39	96		120 70 20

FIGURE 14—9: Nine Inventory Statistical Indicators

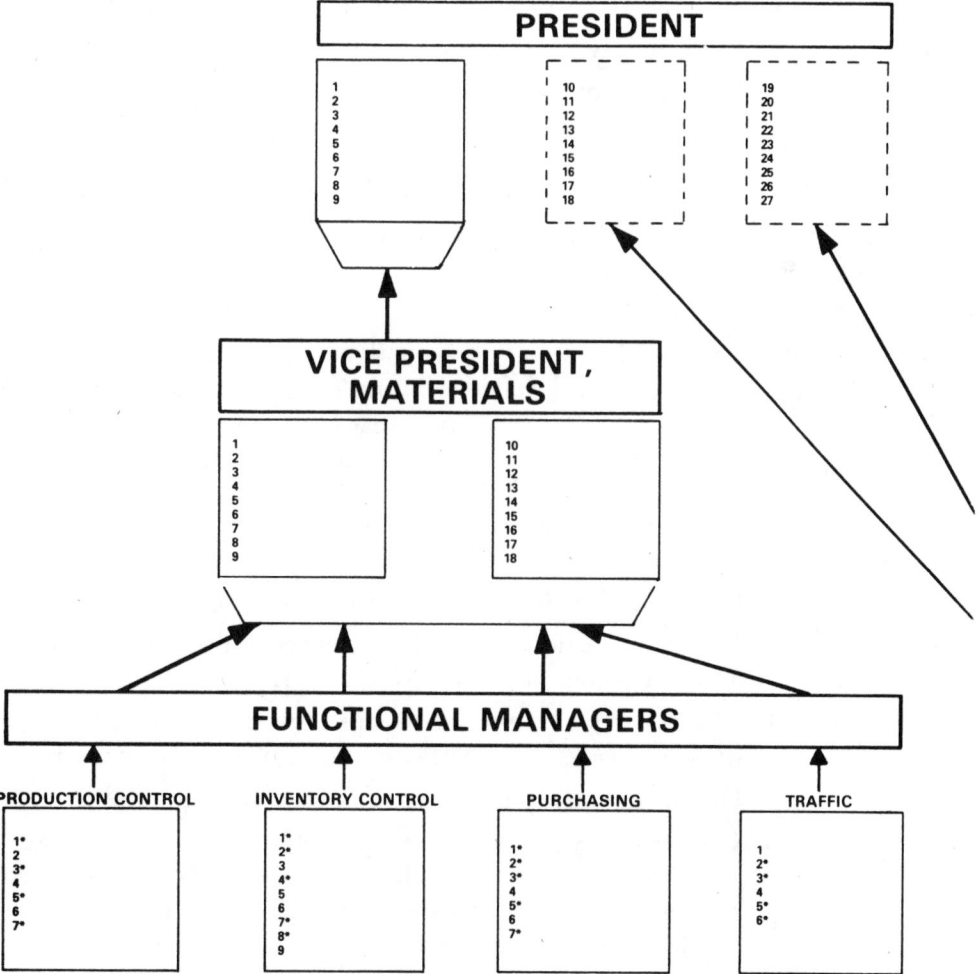

* Denotes a report forwarded up to next and final management levels

FIGURE 14–10: Key Indicator Pyramid Reporting Relationship

a maximum of 27 measures. These more important indicators are jointly selected by the department manager and his or her immediate superior.

In addition to the indicators suggested in Figure 14–9, other possible statistical inventory and related measures are

- Nonproductive inventory; parts with no demands in last year
- Average line item and quantity picked by storeroom employees
- Company versus industry (SIC) inventory/shipments ratio
- Open orders by gross profit margin

- Number of inventory system improvements installed
- Projected average weeks-supply-on-hand
- Frequency of item picked errors in warehouse
- Overtime percentage to normal hours by stockroom

DO-IT-YOURSELF REPORT DESIGNING: A SIX-STEP PROCEDURE

It is possible that some of these document and report configurations do not meet your information needs. Should this be the case, then, using the inventory management data base, along with a software package, design your own report format. To achieve a special report format you need to follow this procedure:

1. Collect two or more documents or reports that contain the information "fields" you wish.
2. Obtain a pair of sharp and preferably long-blade scissors.
3. Cut apart sections from the gathered reports that you wish to include in a new, combined information report.
4. Lay out on a white piece of paper these sections in a left to right sequence of headings as you want them to appear in the new report.
5. Check that your computer data base contains the data you wish.
6. Request the systems analysis person to write the program that will create your report. Be sure to tell the frequency you wish to receive the report as well as the report's distribution within the company. This last step would not be necessary if you have a computer report generator.

CHAPTER REFERENCE

1. Reprinted by permission of the *Harvard Business Review*, by Robert L. Janson, "Graphic Indicators of Operations," November–December 1980, Copyright © 1980 by the President and Fellows of Harvard College; all rights reserved.

How to Plan
and Initiate an
Inventory Management
Computer System

15

CHAPTER HIGHLIGHTS

This chapter begins with how to plan for an inventory computer system, then shows you how to put your ideas into action.

The widening range of hardware computer systems now available are discussed, as are computer system objectives and control characteristics.

Nineteen steps in planning, qualifying, and acquiring a computer system are also given. Not all of the steps may be necessary for your needs, and you are encouraged to modify the steps as needed.

The various types of data bases and tips for evaluating software programs are offered.

Finally, you'll learn of twelve benefits that can be achieved by successfully installing a computerized inventory management system in your company.

In the old days, we used filing cabinets and an adding machine to produce what was called an inventory system. Today, we use an automated computing machine to produce an inventory system, and we call it a "computerized system." Why? Because computer system designers have emphasized the hardware, not the equally important software. The fact that so much of the information and calculations are hidden from the user adds to feelings of distrust.

In today's business environment, if you have more than 1,000 active parts in your inventory system, and your sales exceed $1 million annually, you should use a computer to help manage the investment in inventory. In this discussion, let us first review how to plan for a computerized inventory system, and see how to plan the implementation of the new system.

PLANNING AN INTEGRATED COMPUTERIZED SYSTEM: A FOUR-PHASE APPROACH

Ten years ago, the R.G. CEPT Company began a four-phased program to establish a fully integrated computerized system. These steps were to

1. Combine manual procedures with computer reports prepared by a service bureau.
2. Expand computer involvement by purchasing a central mainframe.
3. Install Cathode Ray Tubes tied to the mainframe using operator input with batch processing at night.
4. Establish a Distributed Processing Network linking the central mainframe to local mini-computers in the various plant, warehouse, and storage locations.

BLENDING MANUAL AND COMPUTERIZED PROCEDURES: BUILD IN FLEXIBILITY

During the design of a computerized system, it is important to build in maximum flexibility to anticipate probable future advances in equipment, methods, and company growth without regard to EDP hardware limitations. This flexibility should be limited only by the imagination and ingenuity of those participating in the system's design. The flexibility in design applies to the basic concepts of the system, which in turn determine the logic for programming the computer.

If one is not careful, it is at this point that a computer programmer or system designer may impose inflexible thinking, which may be based on a desire to achieve simplified or conventional programming. The inventory manager should not accept as gospel the explanation that technical computer restrictions will prevent ideas and specific needs from being designed into the system although sometimes these restrictions are indeed present. Check around, getting a second opinion from other qualified people.

As refinements are continually made in the company's EDP plan, however, it is inevitable that some portions must be dropped. This will be kept at a minimum if each department head has done a thorough job of planning before sending a representative to the company meetings which created the EDP plan. It is possible to design and develop a system for any department, but it must be tailored to the organization's needs, financial structure, and the business objectives of the department. While performing the change to automation, a bit of computer "Public Relations," as suggested by this comment, always helps: "This new inventory report takes the place of your old Kardex. The world hates change but progress comes only through change. Please help make this work."

FIVE MAIN HARDWARE COMPUTER SYSTEMS AVAILABLE

A widening range of hardware (the physical equipment used in data processing, such as the computer and its terminals) is now available. There are several different types of computer systems, as described below.

Batch System for Grouping Information

In a batch system, information is collected during the day and keypunched or otherwise processed, usually at night, in one group called a "batch" of information. Not only is the information processed at one time, but it is also put into the computer system in the same manner. Controls over the input are based on a batch number, using a total of selected data contained in each group.

On-Line System Linking a CRT Terminal to Main Computer

On-line systems utilize a CRT terminal linked to the main computer. Authorized personnel can call up a variety of information from the computer data bank. The data may have been batch-processed the previous night and therefore may be as current as 5:00 P.M. on the preceding day. In other instances, information—receiving reports, for example—could be as current as one hour ago. Up-to-the-moment calculations of inventory levels, however, are not available. Data can also be entered in the main computer through the terminals.

Real Time Program Allowing Ongoing Updates

A real time computer program also uses a CRT terminal. The information is entered on-line into the computer but is updated simultaneously. For example, open or incomplete customer orders will be updated based on the time the last shipping report was entered into the system, also through a CRT.

Special Terminals

Many special-purpose terminals are available. One model has an optical mark reader, a bar code printer, and an alphanumeric printer. It can be used for processing requisitions by reading optical marks and for translating marks into numbers and letters. It can also be used as a turnaround document terminal to validate the requisition or to supply additional data.

Computer-to-Computer "Conversation"

A computer terminal in an inventory department at one company can "converse" directly with a computer at the customer's Purchasing Department. The effect of these systems is to have a paperless ordering system.

DISTRIBUTED PROCESSING SYSTEM

A more recent development is the use of distributed processing systems. In these systems, a major computer processing unit is linked with smaller computers in other locations, such as warehouses. The local, smaller computer becomes an extension of the larger computer, which is called the "host." This system often gives the user greater control of data entry and document preparation. It relieves the host computer of some functions and tends to reduce total operating costs. Sometimes planning functions are done at the host computer while certain operating functions are done at the local computer.

COMPUTER SYSTEM OBJECTIVES AND CONTROL CHARACTERISTICS

Objectives

- To provide service that is cost justified and timely.
- To obtain user input on a scheduled basis.
- To develop appropriate systems so that management can make informed decisions on behalf of the company.
- To develop short- and long-range inventory plans compatible with a company's business and strategic plans.

Characteristics of Good Control

- Uses a common data base to avoid duplication of files.
- Consists of accurate documentation of procedures, applications, and programs.
- Permits periodic reviews and updates to the master files.
- Ensures control of input data and accuracy and completeness of output.
- Safeguards against intruders, fraud, fire, and so forth.
- Leaves an "audit trail" of data-base changes.

PLANNING AND IMPLEMENTING A COMPUTERIZED SYSTEM: A 19-STEP PROGRAM

Before moving to convert to or upgrade a computerized system, inventory management must clearly and completely define its objectives in taking the action. Once this is done, the basic steps in planning, justifying, obtaining, and implementing a computerized system are those listed below. However, you should modify these steps to suit the specific environment in which the company is working. All the steps shown may not be necessary, especially in a small company or when a minor system change is being made.

Before getting involved in the rather elaborate program, you should read some basic material on computers, visit trade exhibits, and have preliminary discussions with hardware and software sales representatives to get an idea of the current computers available. Many people also interview users of computers to find out what experiences and problems they have had with the various types of machines and software.

1. Analyze existing system

2. Define purpose of the system

3. Develop project team and steering committee

4. Obtain information for preliminary system design

5. Develop conceptual design

6. Prepare justification

7. Present proposal

8. Design necessary system

9. Develop detailed system specifications

10. Estimate price breakdown for vendor proposal

11. Send requests for quotations

12. Develop quotation evaluation system

13. Select two better suppliers

14. Select best supplier

15. Set up schedule

16. Work on installing system

17. Test computer output reports

18. Conduct computer system familiarization seminars

19. Perform postaudit

FIGURE 15–1: Planning and Implementing a Computer System

Here are the 19 steps as listed in Figure 15–1.

1. **Analyze the existing system.** Critically evaluate the existing system so that satisfactory procedures, forms, and reports, including those that are inadequate or missing, are identified. For each unsatisfactory item, a recommendation should be made concerning the system improvements necessary.

2. **Define the purpose of the system.** Determine the primary problems and the desired objectives of computerization. Be guided by the company objectives and policies—both overall and for inventory management.

3. **Develop a project team and a steering committee.** A project team comprised of inventory and systems personnel, perhaps assisted by others such as manufacturing specialists, should work as a group, headed by the inventory manager. A steering committee, consisting of higher-level executives within the company, should review the work of the project team, critique it and approve it, and authorize continuing efforts. Then a tentative work plan (see Figure 15–2) should be developed that includes priorities, schedules and work-force individual responsibilities.

4. **Obtain information for preliminary system design.** In this step, identify what kind of information will be required from the system, when it will be required, and what its unique characteristics are.

5. **Develop a conceptual design.** Set up a large flow chart of a generalized nature showing the inputs, reference documents, and outputs of the desired system. You might wish to refer to Figure 4–3 for an example.

6. **Prepare a justification.** List both qualitative and quantitative benefits expected from the investment, including all the elements of the total system. Prepare an example of a cost-benefit analysis that could be used initially to summarize the expected cost and return on the proposed system. Bear in mind that costs are often distributed in about three equal parts—programming, equipment, and operation.

7. **Present the proposal.** The entire project team should present the proposal to management represented by the steering committee, stressing the advantages of the system, the time required, and the expected benefits. Sometimes it is desirable to use visual aids in making the presentation.

8. **Design the necessary system.** The desired system design should expand on the conceptual flow chart developed in step 5. It should, of course, be cost justified, as previously described.

9. **Develop detailed system specifications.** List the characteristics and explain the technical details of the desired system. These specifications should be prepared with the use of common sense. They should not be

restricted to those in any particular package available, nor should they exclude certain desirable features because they might cost too much. Remember to include data-base requirements.

10. **Establish an estimated price breakdown for the vendor proposal.** Detail costs of the subcategories of computer equipment, such as hardware and peripheral equipment. Estimate the software required for the computer program. A computer department programmer should also make a cost estimate for an internal company designed system. Then the trade-off can be studied. Figure 15–3 is a cost analysis worksheet you can follow for information and contents.

11. **Send requests for quotations.** Send a well-prepared request for quotation to at least four software and/or hardware vendors, carefully describing the various items required in the system. Then discuss proposals separately with individual suppliers who respond.

12. **Develop a quotation evaluation system.** Using formal documents or large spreadsheets, list the various information furnished by the hardware and software vendors to create a comparative matrix evaluation system. Study closely the software system user documentation; an outline is suggested in Figure 15–4.

13. **Select the two better suppliers.** Looking at not just the lowest priced, but the least-overall-cost computer system, invite the two vendors with the better quotes to separate meetings to discuss in depth the details of their quotations. In carrying out this step, keep in mind that the price on the request for quotation is not necessarily the vendor's final price. It is advisable to see installed systems at other locations. To accomplish this, follow up with the vendor's references to obtain other user experiences with the system.

14. **Select the best supplier.** Negotiate the final specifications, price, terms, and conditions.

15. **Set up a schedule.** Begin the implementation phase with a revised design and implementation schedule. Communicate broadly to management the plan and the rationale for it. Conduct a series of training sessions to brief inventory personnel and others about the planned revisions.

16. **Work on installing the system.** During installation pay particular attention to hardware equipment and the software programming instructions. Perform necessary customizing or tailoring of the programs. Remember to document the procedures as well as all subsequent software and procedural changes in a Standard Operating Procedure manual.

17. **Test the computer output reports.** Debug as necessary until the programs are accurate. Be certain that the users sign off their agreement on the final format. Make certain the software suppliers continue their assistance; do not accept the system until fully satisfied.

PROJECT TITLE _____ PROJECT NO. _____ CHAIRPERSON _____ REPORT DATE _____ PREPARED BY _____

Sequence Control No.	Task Description	Planned Accomplish-ment	Responsibility	Authorized Budget				Percent Complete (Est.)	Paid		Committments			Total Paid & Committee	Est. Additional Costs	Total Est. Cost
				Capital Equip.	Salaries	Expenses	Total		Invoices	Salaries	Hard-ware	Soft-ware	Other			
	(a)															(b)

(a) Includes significant steps including such things as management projects, systems projects

(b) Additional comments should be attached as necessary

FIGURE 15–2: Project Work Plan and Progress Report

18. **Conduct computer system familiarization seminars.** Since so many studies have shown training is essential for success, carefully plan these seminars. Keep the sessions interesting and well paced; explain all aspects.

19. **Perform a postaudit.** Check the accuracy of the original cost-benefit justification for the new system. Do this at the end of the first full year of use and again at the end of three years.

Project Description_____
_____Control   No._____
Submitted By_____Date_____
Approved By_____

		Areas of Costs	Typ. %	First Year	Second Year	Third Year
Cost of Project	Development	System Design	5%			
		Programming	3%			
		System Documentation	3%			
		Testing	5%			
		File Conversion	4%			
		Additional Personnel	3%			
		Training Users & Operators	5%			
		Implementation	6%			
		Subtotal	34%			
	Computer	Software Package	-			
		Base Price	10%			
		Modifications	3%			
		Enhancements	3%			
		Support	5%			
		Hardware	-			
		Equipment	20%			
		Installation	3%			
		Maintenance	2%			
		Facility Improvements	5%			
		Subtotal	51%			
		Operating Expense	15%			
		Total Project Cost	100%			
Benefits Expected		Inventory Carrying Cost Reduction				
		Purchased Cost Savings				
		Cost Avoidance				
		Supply Reduction				
		Payroll				
		Other (Specify)				
		Total Benefits Expected				

Return on Investment

$$\text{Return on Investment} = \frac{\text{Total Benefits Expected} _____}{\text{Total Project Cost} _____} = _____ \times 100 = _____ \%$$

FIGURE 15–3: Cost Analysis Worksheet

I. SYSTEM OVERVIEW

Introduction - a general description of the objective of the computer system, features and options.

Inputs - description of the method(s) of entering data into the sustem, mentioning the various transaction categories.

Reports - explanation of the various system outputs beginning with transaction edits to identify input errors, then describing the routine, exception and special request reports.

II. GENERAL INFORMATION

User Responsibilities -expresses the duties of user's regarding input data.

Completing Input Forms - describes how information is translated into computer format.

Field Notation - explains the name and purpose of each section on an input form.

Entry Rules - concerning proper rules for input coding so data will be accepted by the system.

FIGURE 15–4: System User Documentation Outline

III. PROCEDURES

Introduction - explaining the purpose of the "how to do it" regarding the system procedures.

Preconversion forms - those documents which help the user gathering correct data.

Conversion process - the steps and timing by which data is formally placed into the system.

IV. TRANSACTION INFORMATION

Introduction - general information regarding the transactions of the system.

Transaction - specific identification of each transaction, providing name, code, and brief description.

V. INPUT FORMAT

General - relating inputs with the procedures previously described.

Entries - describing the various forms which must be completed for the report outputs to be developed.

VI. REPORTS

Introduction - explanation of general report contents, either conversion, routine or on request type.

Report Description - description of each report's name, type, run frequency and contents.

FIGURE 15–4: System User Documentation Outline (cont'd)

DETERMINING WHAT YOU WANT TO ACCOMPLISH: INVENTORY SYSTEM INFORMATION REQUIREMENTS

An early step in making the transition to integrated computerized inventory management is to prepare a list of what you want the system to accomplish —called system information requirements. The following is a partial example of such a list. It can be prepared by studying the current manual and computerized forms and reports presently being used by the company. In fact, a quick way to describe the computerized system needs is to show the headings of existing reports—in "computerese" these are called "fields." Some typical requirements are

- Provide for the following lot sizing techniques:
    - —Economic order quantity
    - —Fixed quantity
    - —Period order quantity
- Identify items as slow moving, obsolete, or current.
- Accept the addition of any manual allocations.
- Calculate lead times based upon order quantity.
- Analyze the status of an item and, if certain selection criteria are not met, notify material control to cycle count the item.
- Analyze all parts according to predetermined classes of period usage value. Classes are defined in terms of percentage of the total usage value.
- Maintain historical transactions that allow the sourcing of inventory discrepancies such as
    - —Dates and quantities of last receipts
    - —Source of unscheduled issues
    - —Date of last physical inventory count to be traced
- Provide for control of component material issues to orders using manual issues.
- Interface with manufacturing and purchase order systems.
- Reschedule allocation record due dates with quantities if and when the parent supply order is rescheduled or has had its quantity changed.
- Provide for multiple inventory locations with balances on hand for each and in total.
- Calculate or specify order points based on
    - —manually preset order points
    - —computer-derived order points.
- Process "bar coding" information.
- Calculate safety stock where safety stock equals a constant times the mean absolute deviation (MAD) adjusted for lead time.
- Maintain year-to-date information on both receipts and issues of particular inventory items.
- Maintain transaction history files and audit trails for any input transactions that affect inventory adjustment levels. In addition, these audit trails must carry responsibility codes.
- Display current on-hand quantities by part number.

THREE DOCUMENTATION LEVELS
TO DEVELOP IN YOUR SYSTEM DESIGN

All of your work in establishing the new inventory system will be of little value unless adequate documentation is available. These three types—called levels —should be developed.

1. *Conceptual design*—a well-thought-out plan prepared by the users and data processing system designers and then approved by management. It provides a top level overview of the proposed system showing basic interrelationships and general procedural flow. The outputs of a conceptual design are written narratives accompanied by overview-style flow charts.

2. *General design*—a highly interactive description developed by the users and system designers based on approved assumptions in the conceptual design. This provides a second level of detail for each individual system, which further amplifies the processing within the system from a generalized viewpoint to assist in obtaining additional understanding. The outputs are written descriptions of each system's input and output reports.

3. *Detailed design*—a more mechanical step by the system programmer consisting of tested and debugged programs for final user and management sign off approval. It provides a third level of detail for each system, which clarifies the individual component subsystems by highlighting the essential transaction processing and their required data files. The outputs are detail lists of transactions, master files, operating procedures and process flows.

FOUR MAJOR TYPES OF DATA BASES

A data base is a collection of information processed by the computer. Creation of a uniform data base requires standardization of a number of elements. For the requisitioning cycle, for example, there should be standard ordering specifications, nomenclature, ordering units, units of measure, and commodity codes of all repetitively purchased materials and stores items.

Standardization of commodity data is essential in the cycle because the information is perpetuated in mechanical form for subsequent processing in other functions. Four major types of data base files are usually identified, as shown in the table on p. 317.

File Type	Purpose	Examples
Master file	Relatively permanent records containing standard descriptions, statistical, identificational, and historical information. Used as a source of reference and for retrieval.	Inventory file
Transaction file (also called "detail file")	Collection of records describing transactions by the organization. Developed as a result of processing the transactions and preparing transaction documents. Used to update a master file.	Customer order file
Report file	Records extracted from data in master or transaction files in order to prepare a report.	Report file for past due customer orders
Sort file	A working file of records to be sequenced. May be the original or a copy of the master file, transaction file, or report file.	Transaction file sorted by part number for inventory balance updating

A TERMINAL ON EVERY DESK?
THE CHOICES AND TRADE-OFFS

Whether to have a terminal on every desk is the question facing inventory managers who wish to use a CRT. Three choices are available:

DUMB TERMINALS	**SMART TERMINALS**	**INTELLIGENT TERMINALS**
simply provide a two-way communication link between the user and a computer	have a limited microprocessor, a small memory, and generally are not user programmable	include a powerful microprocessor, a larger memory, and are user programmable in a high level language
Computer Dependent	Partially Dependent	Stand-Alone

Then there is the question, does an employee really need his or her own CRT? These are the trade-offs:

Printed Report	*vs.*	*CRT Inquiry*
Multiple references		Few references
More paper files		Less paper files
Lower cost		Higher cost
Some delay		Instantaneous

No matter which CRT is selected, three methods are available to use the terminal in addition to the ability to obtain, or request, a hard copy report:

On-line inquiry, such as determining the customer order status.

On-line entry, when you want to revise order promise date.

Real time, so you can obtain the latest inventory requirement date.

HOW TO EVALUATE SOFTWARE PROGRAMS

Five important steps are necessary to make this most critical decision. At each step, certain less qualified software vendors are eliminated. At the first step, perhaps eight software houses might be in contention, two or three are at the third step, and the best vendor is selected in step five.

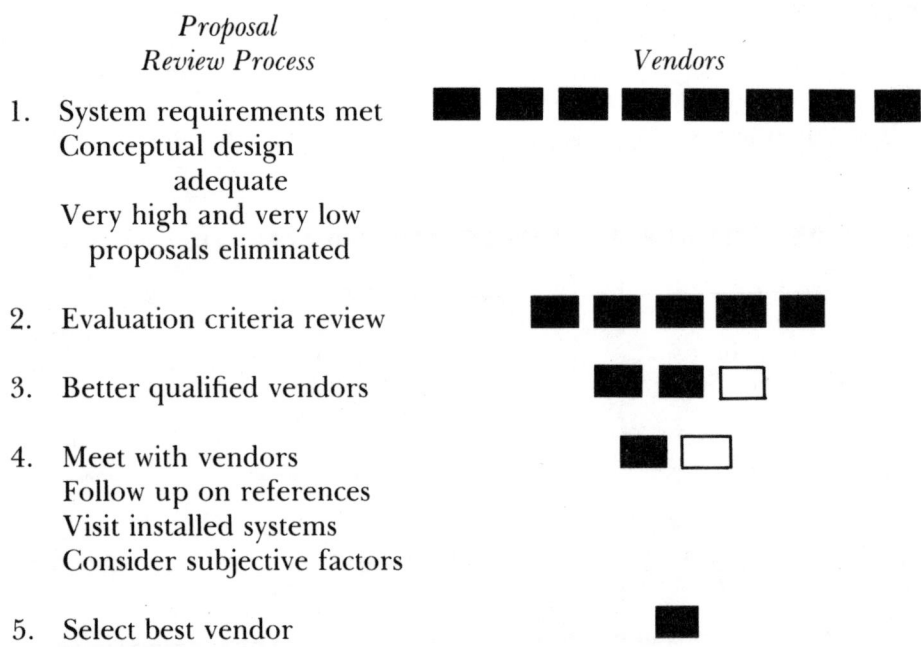

	Proposal Review Process	*Vendors*
1.	System requirements met Conceptual design adequate Very high and very low proposals eliminated	
2.	Evaluation criteria review	
3.	Better qualified vendors	
4.	Meet with vendors Follow up on references Visit installed systems Consider subjective factors	
5.	Select best vendor	

Step two is accomplished by providing the selection committee members with considerable prestudy material followed by a day-long discussion of the merits of the vendors not eliminated in step one. At the end of the discussions, each person "votes" by ranking the remaining possible vendors, using the following three criteria groups. These groups consider the various computer companys' experience, the ability to meet your system specifications, and your group's opinion of several important system elements.

I. Computer Company Experience

Software name	Report generator
License fee	Number of installations
Hardware required	Date of first installations
Number of terminals	Level of integration
Query facility	On-line and interactive
Installation timing	Number of installations

II. System Specifications (Partial List)

Inventory item by class codes	Inventory picking list
ABC analysis	Receiving notice
Inventory location	Inventory multiple storerooms
Lead times	Inventory shortage report
Reorder points	Physical inventory
Safety stock	Cycle counting
EOQ analysis	Inventory adjustments
Inventory status and tracking inquiry	Summary of inventory activity
Material availability projection	Item costing
Inventory valuation	Statistical measures

III. System Elements

Simplicity	Training
Documentation	Security
User friendliness	Stability
Programs	Vendor interest
Support (on and off site)	Performance
Standard system	Processing time

IV. Overall Evaluation

Computer company experience	System elements
System specifications	Total rating

12 BENEFITS OF A COMPUTERIZED INVENTORY MANAGEMENT SYSTEM

Companies that successfully install a computerized inventory management system find they achieve these 12 benefits:

1. reduction of inventory-related paper filing
2. easier implementation of coordinated inventory purchasing with large-scale blanket contracts with resultant savings
3. reduction in overall clerical and supervision time
4. sizable savings in inventory carrying costs
5. reduction in paper work
6. standardization of pertinent data and terminology; everyone uses the same data base
7. accessibility of data to all authorized personnel, controlled with built-in security checks
8. reduction in time required for all forms of input, retrieval, computation, and response
9. adaptability and fast response to changes in priorities, prices, and other variables of management
10. centralized management without loss of utility of personnel to any outlying departments
11. savings in equipment and floor space, principally through elimination of files
12. improved communications among all personnel in the company

SOME THOUGHTS ABOUT THE FUTURE FOR COMPUTERIZED INVENTORY MANAGEMENT

- Management terminals are an integral part of the system, accumulating information in a chain of command control that begins with the inventory controller, progresses to the inventory manager, and ends with the president.

- The computer-aided system still requires manual procedures, so carefully integrate the electronically prepared data with the pencil created information.

- Menus and Files show a display of variables, called parameters, and options that can be selected to complete a task using data analogous to file drawer contents or a set of inventory cards.

- Rarely will a finished computerized system give you more than 90 percent of what you desire. This is true whether you purchase software or design the system yourself. Freeze what you have and add the other 10 percent later, but only after you have received considerable return on your time and money investment.

- Implementation is difficult because people who do not understand a computerized system have a fear of touching the CRT buttons, and generally resist change . . . any change.

- There are several training types: "Conceptual," in how the new system will operate, "functional," concerning the software impact on each department, and "operational," regarding how to get there from here (including what to do when you make a mistake).

- The day of the keypunch operator will soon be over; in the future the user will do his or her own data input.

Always remember: If you install a computerized system and do not change your way of doing business—namely, becoming more productive—you have wasted your time and money. For any organization, the transition to a fully integrated computerized system can be traumatic. As Figure 15–5 illustrates,[1] several phases of confidence, emotion, and even frustration often occur when much work needs to be done.

CHAPTER REFERENCE

1. Developed based on suggestions from Richard L. Davis, Andrew W. Moock, and Timothy R. Corman.

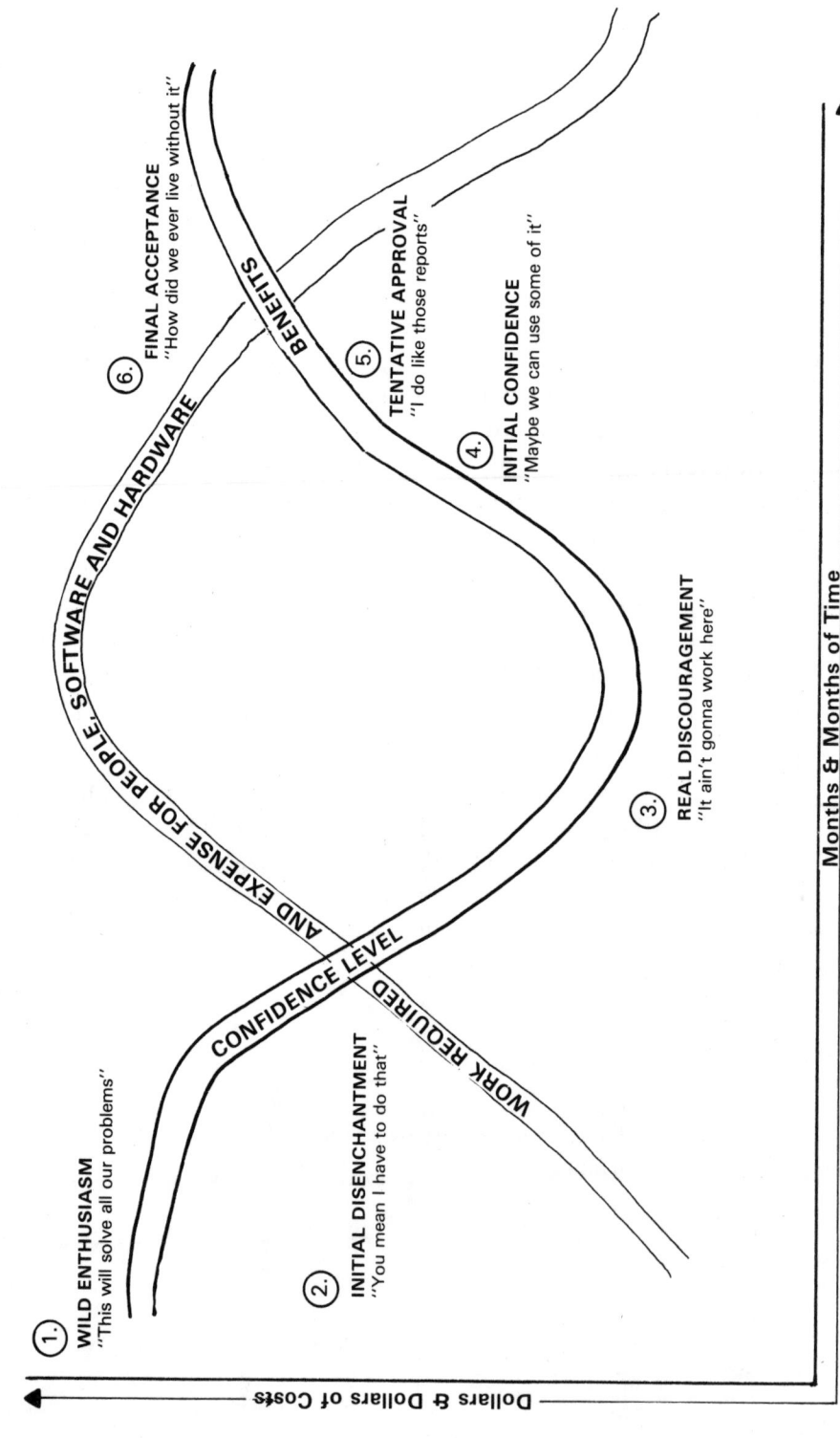

FIGURE 15-5: Computer System Expectations, Frustrations, and Results

322

Appendices

Appendix A

LIST OF DOCUMENTS AND FIGURES

Title	Number	Use Category		
		Mandatory	Helpful	Optional
30 Years of Prime Interest Rates	1-1			X
Assets of Manufacturing Companies	1–2		X	
Correct versus Wrong Reordering Decisions	1-3		X	
Effects of Carrying Costs on Profits	1-4		X	
Inventory Turnover—U.S. versus Japan	1-5		X	
Normal Versus Potential Company Profits	1-6	X		
Company Resource Planning and Control Conceptual Flow Chart	1-7			X
Inventory Management Policy Contents	1-8	X		
Five Inventory Organizations	1-9		X	
Inventory Data Base Browser	1-10		X	
Inventory Improvement Action Program	1-11		X	
Cost Versus Executive Efforts	1-12		X	
Inventory Control Computerized Item Master Record Screens	2-1	X		
Various Specifications Costs	2-2		X	
Commodity Codes	2-3	X		
Lead Time Analysis Screen	2-4		X	
CEPTmobile Cumulative Lead Time Example	2-5			X
Increase in Carrying Costs Due to Service Levels	2-6			X
EOQ Selection Matrix	2-7	X		
CRT Requisition	2-8	X		
Computerized Standard Cost Report	3-1		X	
Standard Cost Roll Up	3-2		X	
Elements in Cost Estimate	3-3			X
Carrying Cost Calculation	3-4	X		
Calculating Ordering Cost for EOQ Calculations	3-5		X	

Title	Number	Use Category		
		Mandatory	Helpful	Optional
Comparison of LIFO and FIFO Profits	3-6			X
LIFO Versus Inventory Reduction Trade-Off	3-7			X
Twenty Major Measures of Inventory Management	4-1	X		
Plant Walking Tour Guide	4-2			X
Inventory Management Cycle	4-3		X	
Inventory Turnover Calculation Method	4-4	X		
Scatter Diagram of Component Parts by ABC Class	4-5	X		
Inventory Management Improvement Program	4-6		X	
Characteristics of Inventory System in Five Companies	4-7		X	
Types of Inventory Control Techniques	5-1	X		
ROP and MRP Relationship	5-2		X	
MRP Narrative Flow Chart	5-3			X
Net MRP "Bucket" Report	5-4			X
Net MRP "Vertical" Report	5-4			X
Gross Manufacturing Resource Planning (MRP II) Systems	5-5			X
Net Manufacturing Resource Planning (MRP II) Systems	5-6			X
Changing an Indented Bill to Single Level Bill	5-7			X
Gross Material Requirements Planning Worksheet	5-8			X
ABC Classification Report	5-9		X	
Shortcut ABC Determination	5-10	X		
Inventory Management/MRP II System Selection "Decision Tree"	5-11		X	
Forecast Coordinator Position Description	6-1	X		
Product Life Cycle	6-2			X
Forecast Error Analysis	6-3	X		
Comparison of Forecasting Techniques	6-4		X	
Cost of Forecasting Versus Accuracy	6-5		X	
Item and Class Profiles	6-6		X	
Comparison of Three Forecast Techniques	6-7			X
Combination of Forecasts	6-8		X	
Information Sequence for a Qualitative Review of a Statistical Forecast	6-9	X		
Forecast History Report and Worksheet	6-10		X	
Combination Master Schedule and Forecast	6-11	X		
Physical Inventory Organization	7-1	X		
Pre-Physical Inventory Planning Report	7-2		X	

Title	Number	Use Category		
		Mandatory	*Helpful*	*Optional*
Electronic and Voice Character Recognition	7-3			X
Cycle Count Detail and Analysis Report	7-4		X	
Computer Numbered Inventory List	7-5		X	
Brief Inventory Instruction Booklet	7-6	X		
Physical Inventory Data Collection Worksheet	7-7	X		
Computer Produced Bill of Material	8-1	X		
Six Standard Bill of Material Formats	8-2		X	
Computer Produced Where Used Report	8-3		X	
Manufacturing Routing	8-4		X	
Receiving Department Action Guide	8-5			X
Kanban Formula	8-6			X
Universal Product Code	8-7		X	
Bar Code and Optical Character Recognition (OCR) Label	8-8			X
Inventory Management Document Control Center	8-9	X		
Inventory Responsibility by Position	9-1	X		
Employee Job Duty Worksheet	9-2			X
CRT Transaction File Requirements	9-3		X	
Inventory Seminar Outline	9-4	X		
Inventory Game CRT Screen	9-5			X
Inventory Game Results Calculation Form	9-6			X
Quick Calculation of Inventory Targets	10-1	X		
Inventory Statistics for Selected Industries	10-2			X
Inventory Computer Simulation	10-3		X	
Five Inventory Groups	10-4		X	
Inventory Targets for the R.G. CEPT Company	10-5		X	
Calculating Work-in-Process Investment	10-6			X
Inventory Target Worksheet	10-7	X		
Excess and Obsolete Inventory Procedure	10-8	X		
12-Step Inventory Reduction Program Story Board	10-9			X
Results of Three Inventory Reduction Programs	10-10			X
Analysis of Purchases	11-1		X	
Reductions Possible Under Just-in-Time	11-2			X
Vendor Capacity Planning Supplier Questionnaire	11-3		X	
Comparative Quotation Matrix	11-4	X		
Blanket Order Schedule and Release	11-5		X	
Vendor Capacity Planning Schedule	11-6			X
Subcontracting Vendor Tracking Screen	11-7			X
Combination Requisition and Purchase Order	11-8	X		
Discount Value Calculation Worksheet	11-9		X	
Rationale for Buying Decision	11-10	X		

Title	Number	Use Category		
		Mandatory	Helpful	Optional
Last-Minute Requirements Report Screen	11-11		X	
Computer Prepared Picking Slip	12-1			X
Service Industry Commodity Codes	12-2			X
Warehouse Layout for Continuous Picking	12-3		X	
Warehouse Improvement Report Typical Section	12-4			X
Bin and Rack Density Chart	12-5		X	
Space Calculation Worksheet	12-6		X	
Bin or Rack Stocking Method	12-7	X		
Multiple Warehouse CRT Screen	12-8			X
Comparison of MRP and DRP Demand	12-9			X
LOGISTEK III Cost Analysis Report	12-10			X
Return to Stores Tag	12-11		X	
Commodity Groups for the Six Inventory Environments	13-1			X
Supply Catalog Page Example	13-2	X		
Service Industry Requisition and Purchase Order	13-3	X		
Service Industry Stock Status Report	13-4		X	
Retail Inventory Worksheet	13-5			X
Retail Commodity Coding Method	13-6			X
Retail Inventory Control Record	13-7			X
Hospital Inventory Investment Targets and Analysis	13-8		X	
Hospital Inventory Coding "Decision Tree"	13-9			X
Inventory Management Standard Documents and Reports	14-1		X	
Statistics Outside Control Limits	14-2			X
Inventory Status Report Contents	14-3	X		
Inventory Master Record Contents	14-4	X		
Inventory Analysis Report	14-5		X	
Commodity Groups' Purchases for Plastatron Division	14-6		X	
Inventory and Purchasing Budget Calculation Worksheet	14-7			X
Key Indicator Worksheet	14-8	X		
Nine Inventory Statistical Indicators	14-9	X		
Key Indicator Pyramid Reporting Relationship	14-10	X		
Planning and Implementing a Computer System	15-1	X		
Project Work Plan and Progress Report	15-2	X		
Cost Analysis Worksheet	15-3	X		
System User Documentation Outline	15-4		X	
Computer System Expectations, Frustrations, and Results	15-5		X	

Appendix B

TYPICAL PHYSICAL INVENTORY INSTRUCTIONS

I. SCHEDULED DATES AND TIMES

The company physical inventory is taken once every year, usually at the end of June. There are three inventory categories: raw material, work-in-process, and finished goods.

Why take inventory?

The purpose of this inventory is to check the book accuracy of the raw material, parts, and assemblies against what is physically on hand, both in terms of quantity and the total dollar value.

Importance of a good job

Poor work cannot be tolerated during the inventory. Any abuse will result in an employee being sent home and a letter placed in his personnel file regarding the details.

Date and exact hours

Inventory will be conducted on Friday and Saturday, _____* and _____*. The hours on each day will begin at 7:00 A.M. and complete at 3:30 P.M.

Time of breaks and lunch

A coffee break will be held each morning from 9:00 A.M. to 9:20 A.M., lunch will be from 11:30 A.M. to noon, and an afternoon break will be conducted from 2:00 P.M. to 2:15 P.M. The cafeteria will be open to serve coffee and lunches. All inventory personnel, including salaried employees, must comply with the appointed times.

Overtime possibility

There is a distinct possibility work will be necessary on Sunday if the inventory is not completed by Saturday at 3:30 P.M. Individuals scheduled will be expected to work overtime.

*Fill in month and/or dates for your physical inventory.

II. ASSIGNMENTS BY SPECIFIC AREAS

There will be one individual with overall responsibility for the control of the inventory, its procedures, and documents. This coordinator will be _____, and he (she) will be located at _____ during the course of the physical inventory. _____ can be reached on extension _____ for any kind of inventory problem or question. Do not hesitate to contact him (her).

The individuals in charge of specific types of inventories are listed below. During the course of the physical inventory only, these inventory supervisors and all their personnel report to the inventory coordinator. These supervisors are also responsible to ascertain that backup crews will be available during the inventory in case of difficulty in certain areas.

Raw material _____

Work-in-process _____

Finished goods—warehouse _____

Finished goods—plant _____

The inventory supervisors within each category will be responsible for their own areas. They are to select the people to take the inventory count and to have all items properly identified by part number and description prior to the inventory. The area map (which is attached as Exhibit ** to these instructions) will denote the specific areas of responsibility for each inventory supervisor.

Any material that production will not be using during the days prior to the inventory can be precounted, providing the area is sealed from activity.

Work assignments

The employee work assignments are as indicated in Exhibit ** to these inventory instructions. Each person is to work only in the area assigned and cannot be changed to another team without the permission of the inventory supervisor. When a person or team is finished counting they are to obtain instructions regarding the next area to work.

Specific duties

Each person involved in the inventory will have certain duties, as follows:

Inventory coordinator—has overall responsibility for the inventory and will be located in the inventory headquarters. Will inspect all areas prior to inventory to guarantee all preparations are completed. This position often is the Inventory Manager.

Tag controller—assigns prenumbered inventory tags to specific individuals and checks the tags back to ascertain all numbers issued are accounted for.

Area supervisor—responsible for the inventory in one of the major divisions of the plant.

Group leader—directs the work of a counting group, usually twelve teams.

**List exhibit number and attach your document to these instructions.

Counter—performs the actual counting and is responsible for the accurate quantity and description written on the tag.

Checker—recounts items on a sample selection basis and assures that the correct quantity, description, and so forth is placed on the inventory tag.

Internal auditor—acts to spot check the effectiveness of the inventory as a representative of the company.

Outside auditor—represents the accounting firm to determine that an effective inventory is taken.

III. MATERIALS TO BE INVENTORIED

All material within the plant is to be inventoried unless specific authorization has been obtained in advance. These specific exceptions to this policy must be marked with "Do Not Inventory" tags, which will be signed by the appropriate supervisor. If requested, Inventory Management will provide a list of items (by type) to be inventoried and not to be inventoried. The raw material inventory will be counted in all plants as will the work-in-process inventories. The finished goods will be inventoried both in the plants and the warehouses. The specific exceptions to this policy are:

Returnable containers

These containers, which are the property of our vendors, need not be counted.

Tooling

All perishable tooling does not have to be inventoried. The tool room is responsible to mark them with the special orange "Do Not Inventory" tag.

Material on consignment

Certain of our customers furnish us with the steel for their orders. This material is not to be counted.

IV. PREINVENTORY PREPARATIONS

The appropriate managers are to receive a copy of the inventory notification letter approximately 60 days in advance of the date of the inventory. _____ is responsible for sending out this letter, which allows the supervisors to start advance planning for the inventory within their departments.

Shop cleanup

The housekeeping of our plant must be in excellent shape for the inventory. General organizing of material should start two weeks in advance. Actual floor cleaning begins three days prior to the start. Material should be arranged in a neat and orderly fashion to ease the job of counting. Empty all trash containers prior to the start of inventory. After the start of inventory no containers will be permitted to be emptied until the physical inventory is completed.

Notification of shutdown

Purchasing Department is responsible to notify all vendors, freight carriers, and other company plants of the inventory shutdown 30 days prior to the inventory via a form letter.

The receipts of goods will cease at 4:00 P.M. on Tuesday, _____*, and will start again at 8:00 A.M. on Monday, _____*. The last shipment will be made Tuesday, _____*.

Rejected material

Inspection Department should be instructed to clear all items and material either to stores (accepted) or return to vendor area (rejected). Rejected material is not to be inventoried; it is to be returned to the vendor before inventory.

Scrap removal

We do not wish any scrap material, small sheet steel, or millings in the plant during the physical inventory. Manufacturing is responsible to get all scrap material sent to the various dealers prior to Tuesday, _____*, at 4:00 P.M. Scrap containers must be emptied prior to the start of inventory.

Material arrangement

All items which are to be inventoried should be arranged in an orderly fashion. Identical parts should be stored in the same location. Parts which are in different stages of completion must not be mixed together.

All material should be identified prior to the first day of the physical inventory.

Wherever possible, return all empty vendor containers to the appropriate vendor prior to the start of inventory.

V. GENERAL INSTRUCTIONS

During the course of the physical inventory the supervisors will be directly responsible for the adherence to these instructions by the employees within their jurisdiction. Prior to the date of the inventory, the supervisor should make sure, by conducting appropriate training sessions, that the employees are familiar with the inventory instructions. These meetings should stress the importance of legible, accurate writing on the tags during the course of the inventory.

Inventory headquarters

The physical inventory headquarters will be in the main floor Manufacturing Office, telephone extension _____.

Inventory priority

We have scheduled to begin all areas concurrently. However, in the event of problems, we will give priority to work-in-process first, raw material second, component parts third, and replacement parts last.

*Fill in month and/or dates for your physical inventory.

Master inventory list

An EDP list of the inventory balances as of 5:00 P.M. Tuesday, _____*, and the Kardex records for raw material will be available in the headquarters to check any unusual counts.

Inventory progress reports

At the completion of each half-day of counting, each area supervisor is to indicate the percent complete status of his (her) area on the form posted in his (her) area. (See Exhibit **.)

Time reporting by area

Time cards are to be completed by all inventory workers, salary and hourly, showing time spent by area numbers. We will use this information for the planning of next year's physical inventory.

Housekeeping

Special attention must be made to cleaning the area and maintaining its cleanliness during the inventory. All trash and papers must be placed in the containers provided.

Unidentified material tag

If a person is unable to determine the description or number of an item, he (she) is to put on the unidentified material tag (Exhibit **) and continue on to the next item. The group leader will obtain help necessary to determine the correct data. Special help can be obtained from the quality control inspection personnel if necessary.

Emergency receipts/shipments during inventory

Any items received during the inventory period, or which must be shipped for special reasons, must have the approval of the inventory coordinator prior to this action being permitted. These items shall be listed on a special list which will be turned in to the inventory headquarters to assist in the control of items.

Accidents

Report all accidents to your group leader or area supervisor and proceed directly to the dispensary where a nurse will be on duty.

Answers to questions

Questions should be directed to the group leader, area supervisor, and inventory headquarters, in this sequence.

VI. SPECIAL INSTRUCTIONS

The steps to be followed are:

    A. One person shall be the recorder, the other the counter. Each team may switch these jobs from time to time.

*Fill in month and/or dates for your physical inventory.

**List exhibit number and attach your document to these instructions.

B. Counters shall use the three part tags. These tags are numbered, as each tag must be accounted for later. Make sure all tags are returned, properly filled out, and initialed if voided. All three copies are to be left on the counted material.

Verification

Checkers must verify that tags are made out correctly and completely as well as checking counts. If a discrepancy is found, call the inventory counter who made the count for a review and resolve the information together. Tag changes can be made by drawing lines through original count and substituting correct count. Additional description or location information can also be written on tag at this time. If tag corrections are going to make tag illegible, mark "VOID" across tag in capital letters, write a new tag, and turn voided tags in with unused tags.

Releasing area

When checkers and auditors are satisfied that counts are correct and complete, inventory takers will detach top white and second (blue) tags from hard copy and place in numerical sequence with unused and voided tags (all three copies) turning in complete blocks of tags received.

Scales

Scales must be rotated between first and second floor for small items subject to scale count. If scales are not available when you get this type of item, put blank tag in bin as a reminder and go back to it when scales are available. Write "Scale Count" in notes section of tag on these items.

Special material counting procedure

Due to its type, steel plate and sheet will be counted as follows:

- Three people will be assigned to take the physical inventory.
- Two people will move and identify material and count; the other person will fill out the inventory tag.
- One tag will be used for all full sheets, the same size, in same locations. (Note: If two or more full sheets with different dimensions are located in the same place, one tag will be made for *each* full size.)
- One tag will be used for *each* partial sheet, and a small drawing of the sheet shape will be made on the tag.

Master routing or bill of material files

These files will be made available by industrial engineering in the inventory head-quarters, for use as required.

Scale use instructions and calibration

The instructions for calibration and use of weigh counting scales are to be posted on the scale. All crews are to be instructed how to use those scales.

Production

No production will be permitted without the written authority of the inventory co-ordinator.

Movement of material during inventory

No material can be moved from one area to another without the inventory coordinator's permission. No movement of material within an area can be done without authorization by the area supervisor.

Last-minute issues (requisitions)

No requisitions during inventory will be permitted without special permission of the inventory coordinator.

Emergency counting crews

Four special backup teams will be available in the headquarters office for any unusual manpower needs.

VII. INVENTORY LIST, TAG USE, AND CONTROL

The inventory tag control lists will be administered by the physical inventory headquarters by the inventory controllers specifically assigned to this task. All tag numbers must be accounted for prior to the release of a specific area. The inventory tags should be controlled using the inventory control lists shown in Exhibit **. These sheets will be used to account for the return of each tag as it is received from the counting area.

VIII. COUNTING AND TAG WRITING

The responsibility for the tag rests with the inventory supervisors and the counters. In inventorying the parts, like items may be combined on one tag if they are located in the same or adjacent area. If the same item is located in separate areas, two separate tags will be necessary.

Employees will not be permitted to take tags home. All unwritten tags must be turned in at the end of the day to the area supervisor.

Tag completion—Print clearly and do not erase (See Exhibit _____** for example.)

1. *Part number* of item inventoried.
2. *Quantity* of item inventoried, except on plate or sheet steel, where number of plates or sheets and dimensions will be recorded in description and converted to weights after the inventory.
3. *Circle* the type of unit counted as pieces, pounds, feet, and so forth.
4. Fill in exact *bin location* or, on items not in bins, describe location as precisely as possible.
5. Put *part name* in description or on raw material describe type of material, grade of material and complete dimensions. Use a separate tag for same material with different dimensions.
6. Fill in *clock number* of inventory taker.
7. Checkers will *initial* tags checked.

No inventory at location

Make out a zero quantity tag for items with an assigned location but no parts.

Multiple locations

When making tallies of the same item in more than one adjacent location, the calculations (list of figures) should be made on the back of the tag which can be easily checked later on.

Obsolete or slow-moving inventory

Any material thought to be obsolete or slow-moving items should have the "OSM" annotation written on the inventory tag in the block marked Special Remarks. Material that contains a previous year's inventory tag is a likely candidate for the "OSM" notation.

Rechecks

A follow-up system utilizing a list is to be used to assure that "requests for recheck" are actually accomplished on a timely basis.

IX. PROCESSING OF DOCUMENTS

The released tags are sent to the Inventory Control Department. The inventory counts for class A and B parts are to be compared to the EDP list or Kardex records. When comparing the amounts, if there is a significant difference, a recount will be taken. If adjustments are made, the amounts of these adjustments are to be sent to the Accounting Department, if the tags have already been cleared.

Inventory Control is to post the total amount counted for all class items (A, B, and C) within four workdays after the completion of the inventory. The second copy of the tag is to be used to obtain this total count. No receipt or issue transactions are to be done until this actual inventory count posting is completed.

Distribution of the three tag copies is as follows:

> White (original) goes to Accounting
>
> Blue goes to Inventory Control
>
> Buff (hard) remains with the material

X. CLEAN-UP, REPORT, AND PLANNING FOR NEXT YEAR

As each area is cleared up by the inventory coordinator, it is to be swept clean. All materials, cartons, and so forth have to be removed. The last copy of the inventory tag is to remain with the material.

Upon the completion of the inventory, the inventory coordinator and his (her) staff are responsible to summarize the inventory and to prepare a memorandum to _____regarding these results. This inventory report should detail what problems existed in the course of the physical inventory and provide recommendations to alleviate these difficulties in the subsequent year.

This information should be reviewed six months prior to the next inventory when planning should begin again.

Appendix C

SUGGESTED READING

Aljian, George W. and Paul V. Farrell. *Aljian's Purchasing Handbook*. New York: McGraw-Hill Book Company, 1982.

Ammer, D. S. *Materials Management and Purchasing*. Homewood, Ill.: Richard D. Irwin, Inc., 1980.

Chambers, J. C., Mullick, S. K. and Smith, D. D. *An Executive's Guide to Forecasting*. New York: John Wiley & Sons, 1974.

Dudick, Thomas S. *Dudick on Manufacturing Cost Controls*. Englewood Cliffs, NJ: Prentice-Hall, Inc., 1985.

Greene, James H. *Production and Inventory Control Handbook*. New York: McGraw-Hill Book Company, 1970.

Hall, Robert W. *Zero Inventories*. Englewood Cliffs, NJ: Prentice-Hall, Inc., 1984.

Janson, Robert L. *Purchasing Agent's Desk Book*. Cleveland: Ernst & Whinney, 1980.

Juran, J. M. and others. *Quality Control Handbook*. New York: McGraw-Hill Book Company, 1979.

Kotler, Philip. *Marketing Management: Analysis, Planning & Control*. Englewood Cliffs, NJ: Prentice-Hall, Inc., 1980.

Orlicky, Joseph. *Material Requirements Planning*. New York: McGraw-Hill, 1975.

Plossl, W. G. *Manufacturing Control: The Last Frontier for Profits*. Englewood Cliffs, NJ: Prentice-Hall, Inc., 1974.

Schonberger, R. J. *Japanese Manufacturing Techniques*. The Free Press, New York, 1981.

Sloma, Richard S. *How to Measure Managerial Performances*. New York: Macmillan Publishing Company, Inc., 1980.

Western Electric Company. *Statistical Quality Control Handbook*. Charlotte, NC: Delmar Printing Company, 1983.

Wight, Oliver W. *MRP II: Unlocking America's Productivity Potential*. Williston, Vermont, Oliver Wight Limited Publications, Inc., 1981.

Index